Personal Finance

Publisher's Note

The editors of FC&A have taken careful measures to ensure the accuracy and usefulness of the information in this book. While every attempt was made to assure accuracy, some Web sites, addresses, telephone numbers, and other information may have changed since printing.

This book is intended for general information only. It does not constitute medical, legal, or financial advice or practice. We cannot guarantee the safety or effectiveness of any treatment or advice mentioned. Readers are urged to consult with their personal financial advisers, lawyers, and health care professionals.

The publisher and editors disclaim all liability (including any injuries, damages, or losses) resulting from the use of the information in this book.

And my God will meet all your needs according to his glorious riches in Christ Jesus.

- Philippians 4:19

Contents

Your money
Secrets to keeping more of what you earn

Banking
Mastering the ins and outs of borrowing and lending

Contents

Banking (*continued*)

Consumer credit
Take charge of spending to end debt forever

Home and auto
Savvy strategies for paying less and saving more

Contents

Property insurance
Smart ways to protect your possessions from disaster

Personal insurance
Getting the most coverage for the least expense

Contents

Real estate
Expert choices for buying, renting, and selling

Investments
Keys to building a successful portfolio

Taxes
Easy ways to soften Uncle Sam's sting

Retirement
Living the good life in your golden years

Contents

Retirement *(continued)*

Estate planning
Wise safeguards for your family and finances

Financial freedom — the key to happiness

Annual income twenty pounds, annual expenditure nineteen nineteen and six, result happiness. Annual income twenty pounds, annual expenditure twenty pounds ought and six, result misery.

— Charles Dickens, *David Copperfield*

As Dickens points out, there's a thin line between happiness and misery. Having a firm grasp of your finances can make all the difference.

This book provides the path to financial freedom. Now, that doesn't necessarily mean a life of fabulous wealth and luxury. But it does mean being free of debt and living comfortably within your means — which is priceless.

You'll get tips from experts on tax and investment strategies, real estate, insurance, and estate planning. You'll also learn how to plan for and enjoy your retirement.

But, perhaps most important, you'll discover how to set and stick to a budget. This is the foundation of any successful approach to personal finance.

Without a plan, it's easy to find yourself behind the eight ball. Mortgages, car payments, student loans, and credit card bills gang up on you in a hurry. Things can spiral out of control, leaving your finances, nerves, and even your marriage in tatters.

The temptation of instant gratification — in the form of countless credit card offers — makes living a simple, financially disciplined life very challenging.

But just because you can buy on credit doesn't mean you should. Resist the urge to overindulge. Stick to your budget, pay your bills and debts, save for bigger purchases, and continue to put aside funds for retirement. You'll be rewarded with less stress and more money.

And remember — in this world, it's not every man for himself. Consider using some of your surplus to help others. Whether you tithe to your church, donate to charities, or just help a friend or stranger in need, you're making a very important investment in mankind.

Regular giving not only helps the recipient, it also benefits you, the giver. Rather than being distracted by all the new trinkets and geegaws you can buy, you stay focused on what's really important in life — other people.

Giving also serves as an effective reminder to be grateful for what you already have. And it makes you feel good. Now that's making the most of your money.

Your money

Secrets to keeping more of what you earn

7 easy ways to spend less money

Don't give in to the cultural temptation to buy more and more things you don't need! You can cut back on unnecessary spending when you take these steps.

Stick to a weekly plan. Every Sunday, plan how much you'll spend that week. Withdraw precisely that amount of cash and stash your credit cards and ATM card at home all week.

Make a list. Before every shopping trip, make a list of what you'll buy and decide how much to spend — including sales tax. Take that amount of cash with you but leave your credit cards at home. This will help you buy only what's on your shopping list.

If you find something that you — or your children — simply must buy, put it on layaway. If you don't need it, you're less likely to take the time and trouble to go back for it.

Don't fall for "tricks." Retailers make less money when you spend less, so they tempt you with enticing ads and sales. Even with little or no discount, retailers can boost sales with prices ending in 9 or with "Sale" signs that don't say how much you save. Guard against pricing tricks like these and fight back with a little planning.

Shop only when you need to, advises Cynthia Yates, author of *Living Well on One Income*. Spend less time in stores and you'll have less time to be tempted to buy. Be wise about when you shop, too. "The best time to shop is when you are alone, unhurried, and well fed," says Yates. "Stress and hurry don't allow for thoughtful purchases."

Compare prices. Try comparison shopping to find out where you're paying too much. Grab a notebook and start writing down what types of items sell for less at different stores. For best results, start with things you buy often.

Check newspaper circulars for prices. Many stores will match competitors' advertised prices so take those circulars with you when you shop.

Use it or lose it. Buy economy sizes or buy in bulk to save money, but only when you'll use what you buy. "If you need one can of anchovies for a special recipe, spring for the grocery store price instead of buying a half-dozen shrink-wrapped at the warehouse store," says Yates.

Put your goals to work

Make your goals easy to measure and create a plan to reach them. Take Jane, for example. She set a goal to pay cash for the coat she needed for next winter. Every weekday, she dropped two quarters in an envelope instead of buying a soft drink for 50 cents at work.

At the end of each month, she deposited the resulting $10 in her savings account. After three months, she had $31.20, including interest. In 12 months, Jane saved enough to pay the $120 price, plus sales tax.

And avoid spending more when you can use up what you have. "I believe with all of my heart that most of us could feed our family for weeks with what we have in the cupboard," Yates says. "Using things up is my all-time favorite principle in life."

Advertise. Find a bulletin board in your community — at a church or grocery store, perhaps — where you can put your name, phone number, and a list of things you need.

Swap before you shop. Invite interested friends to participate in a swap meet where everyone can exchange items they no longer use for things they need.

Simple steps to a budget that works

"A budget is you telling your money what to do," says Dave Ramsey, best-selling author and nationally syndicated radio host of *The Dave Ramsey Show*. "You have to make your money behave, and a written plan is the whip and chair for the money tamer."

You can tame your money, too, even if you've failed at budgeting before. Follow Ramsey's tips for creating a budget you can live with.

Stock up on willpower. Think about what you want your money to do for you. Setting goals may seem silly at first, but it can help in a surprising way. "Your goals provide a driving force," Ramsey explains. "They get you fired up, and getting fired up is super important in taking control of your money."

Recruit an ally. If you're married, remember that two heads can be better than one. "Do not bring the budget down from on high and present it to your spouse as the law of the land," Ramsey says. "Work on the budget together, compromise, and come to an agreement."

Give progress a chance. Do you plan to design a permanent budget once and stick to it exactly every month? You probably need to be more flexible.

"Don't try to have the perfect budget for the perfect month because we never have those," Ramsey says. "Doing a budget is not a one-time deal. You must set up a budget every month."

Assign every dollar. Keep this goal in mind every time you work on your budget. "Spend every dollar on paper before the month begins," Ramsey says. "Give every dollar of your income a name." That means every dollar should be assigned to a spending or saving category. "Look at your monthly income and match it up with the month's savings, bills, and debts until you give every income dollar an outgo name," Ramsey advises. (See sample budget on next few pages.)

Monthly budget planner and tracker

Step 1 — Determine your gross income

- List all your sources of income and estimate the gross dollar amount (no deductions or withholdings) expected in the next 12-month period for each source. Be conservative and include only amounts you are certain to receive.

- Total all items for your gross income, and divide by 12 to determine your monthly gross income.

Step 1 – Monthly Budget Planner and Tracker		
Example: Annual gross income of $49,430.00	Example: Monthly gross income	Your monthly gross income
INCOME		
Monthly income before taxes	$4,119.17	
Investment income (stock, bonds, checking accounts, rental properties, royalties, etc.)	$0.00	
Other _____	$0.00	
Monthly Gross Income TOTAL	$4,119.17	

Step 2 — Deduct your taxes and charitable giving

- Using previous data from similar income-earning years, estimate the typical percentage for the categories listed on the Monthly Budget Planner and Tracker chart.

- Total the percentages.

- Multiply the percentage by the monthly gross income total. (Example: 10 percent of $4,119.17 would be .10 X 4119.17 = 411.92).

- Total all dollar amounts of deductions and withholdings.

Step 2 – Monthly Budget Planner and Tracker					
Deductions from Gross Income	Dollar amount example	Estimated % example	Actual amount	Actual % *	Difference in $
TITHE or CHARITABLE GIVING	$411.92	10.0%			
TAXES					
Federal tax	$617.88	15.0%			
State tax	$205.96	5.0%			
FICA and Local tax	$247.15	6.0%			
Other withholdings	$0.00	0.0%			
Medicare withholding	$0.00	0.0%			
Insurance or benefits	$32.95	0.8%			
Company retirement	$205.96	5.0%			
SAVINGS (planned)	$247.15	6.0%			
Total deductions per month	$1,968.97	47.8%			
* Actual Percentage is calculated by: (Actual amount ÷ Total gross income) X 100					

Step 3 — Estimate your expenses (See the following page)

- Estimate the typical monthly expense for the categories listed, adding any "other" expenses under Miscellaneous. Use receipts or records from recent years as guidelines. (See examples under "Actual Expense")

- Figure out what percentage that amount is of your net monthly income. (Example for Utilities: 279.52 4 2150.20 = .13 or 13 percent)

- Use information in the "Try not to exceed this %" column to identify any unusually high expenses. (Do not allocate more than 98% of your net monthly income for

Your money

Step 3 – Monthly Budget Planner and Tracker

**Net monthly income for living expenses	$2,150.20	Try not to exceed this %	Actual expense	Actual expense %	Difference in $
HOUSING	$752.57	35.0%	$784.82	36.5%	-$32.25
mortgage or rent	$591.31	27.5%	$645.06	30.0%	-$53.75
property taxes	$107.51	5.0%	$86.01	4.0%	$21.50
housing repairs	$21.50	1.0%	$21.50	1.0%	$0.00
insurance	$32.25	1.5%	$32.25	1.5%	$0.00
UTILITIES	$236.51	11.0%	$279.52	13.0%	-$43.01
electricity	$86.01	4.0%	$107.51	5.0%	-$21.50
gas	$21.50	1.0%	$43.00	2.0%	-$21.50
sewer and water	$21.50	1.0%	$32.25	1.5%	-$10.75
cable	$43.00	2.0%	$32.25	1.5%	$10.75
telephone	$43.00	2.0%	$64.51	3.0%	-$21.50
internet	$21.50	1.0%	$0.00	0.0%	$21.50
TRANSPORTATION	$344.03	16.0%	$483.79	22.5%	-$139.76
monthly car payments	$193.52	9.0%	$236.52	11.0%	-$43.00
gas, oil	$43.00	2.0%	$53.76	2.5%	-$10.75
car repairs	$21.50	1.0%	$32.25	1.5%	-$10.75
insurance	$64.51	3.0%	$129.01	6.0%	-$64.51
parking/public transp.	$21.50	1.0%	$32.25	1.5%	-$10.75
DEBT PAYMENTS	$86.01	4.0%	$322.53	15.0%	-$236.52
credit cards	$64.51	3.0%	$215.02	10.0%	-$150.51
loans	$21.50	1.0%	$107.51	5.0%	-$86.01
FOOD	$258.02	12.0%	$279.53	13.0%	-$21.51
at home	$215.02	10.0%	$215.02	10.0%	$0.00
outside home	$43.00	2.0%	$64.51	3.0%	-$21.50
PERSONAL INS.	$64.50	3.0%	$64.50	3.0%	$0.00
life insurance	$21.50	1.0%	$21.50	1.0%	$0.00
health insurance	$43.00	2.0%	$43.00	2.0%	$0.00
MEDICAL/HEALTH	$129.01	6.0%	$129.01	6.0%	$0.00
Doctor, dentist, etc.	$86.01	4.0%	$107.51	5.0%	-$21.50
Prescriptions	$43.00	2.0%	$21.50	1.0%	$21.50
MISCELLANEOUS	$236.51	11.0%	$247.28	11.5%	-$10.77
Gifts given	$43.00	2.0%	$64.51	3.0%	-$21.50
Bank charges	$21.50	1.0%	$10.75	0.5%	$10.75
Education	$0.00	0.0%	$0.00	0.0%	$0.00
Clothing/accessories	$107.51	5.0%	$107.51	5.0%	$0.00
Entertainment	$43.00	2.0%	$64.51	3.0%	-$21.50
Other _____	$21.50	1.0%	$0.00	0.0%	$21.50
TOTAL	$2,107.16	98.0%	$2,590.98	120.5%	-$483.82

** *Total gross income - total deductions*

Step 4 — Track your progress

- Record actual withholdings and expenses. Calculate actual percentages.

- Subtract the actual expense from the budgeted expense to see if it's negative or positive. A negative dollar amount in the "Difference in $" column means your spending has exceeded your planned or budgeted amount. Adjust spending. A positive dollar amount means you have additional income that can be added to savings.

- Track actual expenses for several months. Look for categories with entries that consistently exceed or fall short of planned amounts, and make adjustments to your plan.

Make a comeback. It's the end of month one and you've just discovered that you overspent somehow. Don't assume you have failed. "Your spending and your budget won't match up the first month," says Ramsey. "But that's okay. Look at receipts and bills and make adjustments to next month's budget. No one ever budgets enough for groceries on their first try."

Smart way to manage your money

You are the best manager of your own assets. Learn how to take charge of your own money and stop supporting lenders and retailers with cash that should be supporting you and your loved ones. Take your cue from Judy Lawrence's book, *The Budget Kit*.

It's a workbook chock-full of pages to record expenses, income, debt, and other financial transactions as well as worksheets to help you with the nuts and bolts of setting up a budget. Be respectful of your money and you will reap the benefits. Smart money managing can make you rich.

Here are some of the principles behind Lawrence's strategy.

Set goals for your gold. Decide what specific financial goals you want to reach, Lawrence advises. Think about long-term goals like retirement. Also decide what to achieve in the next few years, what to accomplish this year, and what you can do in the next month.

Write these all down, rank them by importance, and assign due dates. Next, estimate how much you must save to meet each goal. Figure how much to put aside each week to reach your total savings goal and then write down specifically how you'll make that happen.

Brace for Murphy's law. Open an extra account at a bank or credit union to store money for emergencies like car repair or a layoff. Lawrence says to accumulate about three months' worth of take-home pay.

End monthly mistakes. Lawrence says a monthly budget sheet coordinates your monthly bills and expenses with your take-home

---

Watch over your money with a mouse

With the right software and access to the Internet, you can:

- manage your checking account
- monitor your savings accounts
- receive and pay bills
- create a budget
- plan for retirement
- keep tax records and file with the IRS
- analyze and trade stocks
- track your investment portfolio

Consider software like Microsoft's Money or Intuit's Quicken. Before you choose, read recent product reviews to help you find out which one is best for your needs.

---

pay. But there's probably no such thing as an average month, so outline each month individually. Be sure to include planned savings — treat these like required expenses.

Track credit purchases. Are you a spendthrift? It's time to cut back. To decrease rampant spending, try this. Every time you use a credit card, write down the date, what you bought, and the amount charged. If you use several cards, keep separate sheets or columns for each. You'll see at a glance how much money you waste.

Plan a fiscal year. Lawrence strongly recommends laying out a yearly budget of planned expenses that aren't part of your regular monthly bills — things like new glasses or contacts, firewood, insurance premiums, vacations, or annual club fees. Review a previous year's spending and estimate what costs are likely to be this year.

Decide where you might cut back, then total the remainder and divide by 12. Now you can see how much to put aside monthly for these expenses.

Work together. Make budgeting a family affair, says Lawrence. By sharing the information, you also share the burden.

Turn clutter piles into useful files

A bright future awaits you when you clear up all the "financial clutter" in your life. Try these tips to help you get started.

Choose your weapons. Either file folders or software can help organize your financial records, suggests Carolyn Riticher, president of The Georgia Society of Certified Public Accountants and a stockholder with the Atlanta accounting firm, Windham Brannon.

"I like having the file folders with the names on them," Riticher says. "You might want to have general operating-my-house categories, like your utility bills," she points out. "Then you can set up others that are income tax related." Riticher suggests creating a group of annual files specifically for this year's records.

The other thing a lot of people don't do is keep a permanent file, Riticher says. These permanent files hold the types of financial records you'll keep for years to come. For example, you might put this year's W-2 in one of your annual files, but your previous W-2s may live in a file labeled "Permanent – W2."

Pick categories. How many file folders do you need, and what should you label each one? To get sample lists of category labels, search the Internet or get some basic ideas for free from the IRS. For general information on which records to keep for tax purposes, read the short IRS Publication 552 *Recordkeeping for Individuals*. Download it from *www.irs.gov* or order a hard copy by calling 800-TAX-FORM or 800-829-3676.

Attack the clutter. Once you choose the categories you need, label your folders and start filling them. Even if you use software to manage your money, remember to keep hard copies of any documents you might need to explain or prove items on a tax return, just in case the IRS happens to ask.

Save records to save money

Be sure to retain these records long enough, advises Carolyn Riticher, CPA. They could save you money, trouble – or both.

- W-2 forms until social security benefits begin.
- Each year's 8606 and 5498 forms for IRAs. When distributions start, keep each 1099-R.
- Records of home improvements. Some could affect the taxes you'll pay when you sell.

Go digital. Consider whether computer software can help organize your records. Some of Riticher's clients use software that combines on-screen check writing with an option that files completed checks into categories. That may mean fewer papers to file.

Finish the job. Most folks organize their records so they can always find them. To prevent more permanent loss of financial records or other important documents, keep hard-to-replace documents or records in a safe deposit box at the bank or in a fireproof safe. Examples of these include birth certificates, property deeds, mutual fund certificates, and insurance documents. "You can always make a copy to keep at your house if you want that information available," says Riticher.

Also, make a list of your records and documents, including where they are stored. Keep one copy and give a duplicate to a trustworthy person you or your family can contact in case of emergency.

Finding a great financial planner

Many people claim to be financial planners, but you better check their credentials before you ask for advice. Try these ideas to help you cut through the hype and find a qualified financial advisor.

Decide what you need. Consider what you'd like a financial planner to help you do. For example, a financial planner may be able to help you with any of the following tasks.

- taking charge of income and expenses
- tax planning
- managing investments, including assets in a 401k plan
- determining insurance needs
- planning for retirement

- estate planning

- funding a college education

Start searching. Where can you find financial planners? Ellen Turf, chief executive officer of The National Association of Personal Financial Advisors (NAPFA), recommends checking *www.napfa.org*, the NAPFA Web site, for a list of qualified planners near you.

To help narrow the list, check the backgrounds of your top choices or interview them directly. To check backgrounds, you can verify qualifications or ask the financial planner for references — such as former clients — that you can interview. Before you interview a financial planner directly, ask whether he charges for interviews or initial consultations.

Check credentials. Ask about both college degrees and professional certifications. Turf specifically mentions CFP (Certified Financial Planner), CPA/PFS (Certified Public Accountant/Personal Financial Specialist), and ChFC (Chartered Financial Consultant).

Check financial advisor qualifications

Find out whether your financial advisor really did earn that CFP (Certified Financial Planner) or ChFC (Chartered Financial Consultant) certification. You'll sleep better at night once you know for sure.

Call 888-CFP-MARK (237-6275) to verify that your financial planner earned a CFP from the Certified Financial Planner Board. And to confirm that your Chartered Financial Consultant is certified by the American College, call 888-263-7265.

"Look at their experience," Turf adds. "How long have they been doing financial planning?"

Talk about fees. Find out how a financial planner expects to be compensated. Commission-only means the planner earns commissions on any financial products you buy based on his advice. Fee-only financial planners may charge a per-project or per-hour fee. Some financial planners are paid a mix of fee and commission. Others may charge some percentage of the dollar value of assets or the income they manage on your behalf.

"We believe there is significant conflict of interest if the advisor stands to gain financially from any recommendations you may follow," Turf says. "The conflict of interest can cost you, both your out-of-pocket expenses and the quality of advice you are receiving."

Be straightforward. The experts at NAPFA also advise you to ask these questions.

- Will you work with me or will I work with one of your associates?

- Have you ever been cited by a professional or regulatory governing body for disciplinary reasons?

- Are there financial incentives for you or your firm to recommend certain financial products?

- Do you take custody of my assets? Will you have access to my assets?

- Are you registered as an investment advisor with the SEC or any state?

NAPFA offers a brochure of questions like these to help you find a qualified financial planner and ferret out possible conflicts of interest. For the full list, go to *www.napfa.org*. (Click on *Consumers* and then click on *How to Choose a Financial Advisor*.) For a free copy of the brochure by mail, call 800-366-2732.

Take charge after a layoff

You've just learned you're about to be laid off. What now? Even before you start a new job hunt, you can take steps to shore up your financial concerns.

Grab a pen and some hope. Opportunities to safeguard your finances or seek new income may come hot on the heels of layoff news, advises Edie Milligan in her book, *Blindsided: Financial Advice for the Suddenly Unemployed*.

If your employer begins your exit paperwork and meetings immediately, you may learn about valuable resources in your severance package or outplacement benefits. So grab a pen and take thorough notes on everything your employer tells you during the exit process. "Make people repeat themselves," says Milligan. "Make them wait while you write. Get their phone numbers so you can call them later for clarification."

Ask questions. If you're part of a large layoff, your company probably won't negotiate on the terms of your severance package. But do ask about the package's details. For example, ask how and when you will be paid, get specifics on the outplacement services your employer plans to pay for, and find out which of your benefits will continue and at what cost.

If your employer has not purchased outplacement service for you, politely complain and request it. "They may not be aware of how helpful it can be and how important it is to you," says Milligan.

Once you get home, read all the paperwork you've received and write down questions to ask. Then arrange to meet with your human resources department to get the answers.

Take action. During the three days following a layoff, Milligan recommends you go to your outplacement meetings and follow the instructions you get there. If your severance pay equals less than six months of regular income, file for unemployment insurance within three days, too. Remember, this is insurance — not part of welfare or any need-based program — so don't hesitate to file.

You'll need your social security number, W-2 form, hire date, and approximate weekly wage. To find the nearest One Stop Center where you can file, call the American Workforce Network at 1-877-US2-JOBS.

Budget for change. Look for temporary ways to cut expenses or unnecessary spending. Make a budget or change your budget so your spending can match your changed income until you start working again.

Stay insured. You might keep your employer's group health coverage temporarily, thanks to COBRA (Consolidated Omnibus Budget Reconciliation Act). If your company says you qualify, you can stay insured for 18 months — and sometimes longer. Just be ready to pay up to 102 percent of the full premium and be sure to apply for COBRA within 60 days.

Analyze early retirement options. Should you take early retirement if you might work again? Consider these factors. If you don't take it, you may have no health insurance if you can't find another job. If you do take retirement but find a job, you'll likely pay

Claim 'lost' money

You could be legally owed money and not even know it. But don't pay anyone to check for you. Instead, find out for free at *www.naupa.org*. Click on *Owners* and then *Find Property*. You might discover a refund from an old utility company, money from an escrow account, or something much more exciting. To be sure you don't miss anything, search in each state where you or your family have lived.

extra taxes on your early retirement benefits. If you want to retire permanently, calculate how this will affect your average income over the long term before you decide.

Don't drain retirement funds. Unless you're retiring, try to avoid dipping into your retirement savings. "Whatever financial pain you are going through, it is not as bad as the pain you will feel during retirement when you are missing this money," says Milligan.

Tips for starting a home business

You're seriously thinking about starting a home business. To help make a winning decision, ask yourself a few questions.

How will I pay my bills? "You need to have some money saved in advance to help cover living expenses," says David Geller, chief executive officer of GV Financial Advisors in Atlanta. "Plan that your initial expenses will be higher than you thought they'd be and your initial income will be lower." Geller suggests you save enough money to cover living expenses for six months to a year.

What if my plans change? "I really would sit down with a financial planner and try to get an understanding of the long-term financial picture," says Geller. Consider how a worst-case scenario might affect you. For example, you could ask, "What happens if I go two years without earning income? If that occurred, how much longer would I have to work before I could retire? How would I still fund college for my children?" Find answers to questions like these before you start a business, Geller says.

Can I replace my employee benefits? Leaving your employer probably means leaving your benefits package, too. Think about how and when you'll save for retirement. If you get life insurance, health insurance, and disability insurance through your employer, consider how you might replace them — and any other lost benefits.

Here's one way. After giving notice, ask your employer if you qualify for COBRA (Consolidated Omnibus Budget Reconciliation Act).
If you do, you might keep your group health coverage for up to 18
months — but only if you apply within 60 days of leaving. You
may pay up to 102 percent of the full premium, but you'll have
coverage while you seek other options.

Can tax planning help? Home business owners can take tax deductions for part of their home insurance costs, repair costs, utility
costs, and more. Find out how to qualify for these home office
deductions before you start your business. Here are a few things
you'll need to do to meet the requirements.

- Choose a separate space in your home to be used solely by the
  business — and not for any family activities.

- Plan how you'll keep your business and home expenses separate and then set up record-keeping accordingly.

- Prove that the home is the main location for the business and
  that business activity frequently occurs there.

- Provide evidence that the venture operates as a profit-seeking
  trade or business.

Contact the Internal Revenue Service or an accountant for details
on how to qualify for the home office tax deduction.

How can I prevent crises? Ask these questions to help avoid law-
suits, fines, catastrophes, and related financial concerns.

- What liability insurance, business insurance, or other insurance do I need? Do I need to make changes to my
  homeowner's policy?

- What permits or licenses do I need to legally run a business
  from my home?

- Will starting this home business break any zoning laws or homeowner's association rules? Will my daily business operations

break any zoning ordinances, local laws, or homeowner's association rules?

For more great questions to ask and information on starting a business, visit the Small Business Administration at *www.sba.gov* and the Service Corps of Retired Executives at *www.score.org*.

How to report a scam

You didn't get what you paid for. You didn't get what you were promised. And you didn't get satisfaction when you asked the responsible party to resolve your complaint. Start battling back with these resources.

Federal Consumer Information Center. Seek help from local law enforcement and your state or local consumer protection agency. To find the consumer protection office in your state, county, or city, visit the Federal Consumer Information Center at *consumeraction.gov / state.shtml*.

If you suspect you're a victim of identity theft, see *Act fast to limit identity theft damage* in the Consumer credit chapter.

Securities and Exchange Commission. Report investing fraud to the Securities and Exchange Commission (SEC). File a complaint at *www.sec.gov / complaint.shtml*. Or, write a detailed letter describing your complaint, including contact information for you and any persons or businesses mentioned in your letter. Send it to SEC Complaint Center, 450 Fifth Street, NW, Washington, DC 20549-0213.

North American Securities Administrators Association. Complain to the agency that enforces securities regulations in your state. To find it, visit the North American Securities Administrators Association at *www.nasaa.org* and click on "Find a Regulator."

Federal Bureau of Investigation. Notify the Federal Bureau of Investigation (FBI) about fraudulent financial reporting or trading activity. Call the FBI financial fraud hotline at 888-622-0117.

Also, contact the FBI about scams using the Internet. Visit the Internet Fraud Complaint Center at *www.ifccfbi.gov*. Your complaint will be forwarded to the agency that can best investigate or prosecute the people involved.

National Fraud Information Center. If you've been scammed by telemarketers or Internet con artists, ask the National Fraud Information Center to help you file a complaint with the right federal agencies. Visit *www.fraud.org*, or write to P.O. Box 65868, Washington, DC 20035.

Federal Trade Commission. The Federal Trade Commission (FTC) handles fraud complaints about Internet auctions, investments, mail-order shopping, charity scams, and much more. Although the FTC can't resolve consumer problems, your report could help build a case against the company that did you wrong. Write to FTC Consumer Response Center, Washington, DC 20580. Or call 877-FTC-HELP (877-382-4357). You can also visit *www.ftc.gov*.

U.S. Postal Inspection Service. Notify the U.S. Postal Inspection Service of any fraud or scam that used the mail. Visit *www.usps.com / postalinspectors* and click on "Mail Fraud."

Billing fraud doesn't just happen in your phone bills. To find out how to spot and combat billing fraud in all kinds of bills, visit *www. consumerwatchdog.org* and check out the billing project pages.

6 sure tip-offs to telephone fraud

The FBI says 14,000 crooked telemarketers con as much as 40 billion dollars out of trusting people every year. Keep your head and keep your cash. Hang up if you hear lines like these.

- "You've won a fabulous prize!" If you haven't entered a contest, be suspicious.

- "You only have to pay taxes, shipping, and handling fees!" Real prizes shouldn't cost you anything.

- "You can't afford to miss this high-profit, no-risk offer!" Not likely. Every investment carries some risk. Discuss big investments with a trusted friend or financial advisor first.

- "It's a brand new offer and printed material isn't available yet." Or maybe they say, "There isn't time to mail information." Either way, beware. A legitimate organization will happily send you literature about their program. Con artists will find any excuse to avoid it.

- "You must act now!" Scammers may tell you "this offer is about to expire," or "there are only a few left." Nonsense. An offer should be just as good tomorrow — after you have checked them out with the Better Business Bureau — as it is today.

- "All we need is some personal information." They might ask for a credit card, calling card, bank account, or social security number to verify your identity or secure your prize. You should never have to give this information over the phone for identification, especially to someone who calls you unsolicited.

Fight back against fraudulent telemarketers. Over half the people targeted by telemarketing fraud are over 50. Don't let them take you for a ride just because of your age. Arm yourself before the phone rings again! Show these predators you're not easy pickings for a scam.

Double-check area codes. To call the Caribbean, for instance, you dial a country code that looks a lot like an area code in the United States. Dialing an 809 code, then the phone number, connects you to the Dominican Republic. The code 758 dials St. Lucia, while 664 reaches Montserrat. You could rack up serious international charges by calling these numbers.

Check area codes you don't recognize before you dial them. Ask the operator where the code would call, or visit the *Directory Assistance* link at *www.consumer.att.com* to look it up on the Internet.

> For more information on phone bill fraud, including consumer bulletins with tips and warnings, visit *www.fcc.gov/cgb*.

Scan your phone bill. Look it over each month for long distance charges you don't remember making. If you find any, contact both your local and long distance telephone companies to discuss the charges.

Zap the call. You can also try the Telezapper, a handy black box you connect to any phone. It answers all your calls with high-pitched tones that fool most telemarketer software into thinking your number is no longer in service. However, some telemarketers have gotten "smart" software that ignores the tones, so a few calls may still get through.

Join the "Do-Not-Call" list. Register your phone number for free with the Federal Trade Commission's national Do-Not-Call list. To join by phone, dial 888-382-1222 from the telephone you wish to register. Or join online at *www.DoNotCall.gov*. You will stay on this list for five years, but you can renew after this time. Your state may also run its own "do-not-call" list. Check with your state attorney general or consumer protection program.

If you think you've been the target of a phone scam, call the National Fraud Information Center at 800-876-7060, or visit their

Web site at *www.fraud.org*. They can help you file complaints with the Federal Trade Commission (FTC), Federal Bureau of Investigation (FBI), your state attorney general, and local consumer protection programs.

Hang up on phone bill errors

You get what you pay for but sometimes you pay even more. Fight back against errors and outright fraud in your phone bill.

Grill your bill. "Review your monthly telephone bills just as closely as you review your monthly credit card and bank statements," advises Rosemary Kimball, Director of Media Relations for the FCC's Consumer and Governmental Affairs Bureau.

Your telephone bill may include charges from several companies. For each charge listed, your bill must show what service was provided and which company supplied it.

Consumers could have lost at least $250,000 to phone fraud in 2003. Instead, that's how much the Federal Communications Commission (FCC) probably saved or refunded to consumers by enforcing anti-slamming laws.

"Slamming" means someone switched you to a new phone company without your permission. And that's not the only phone bill fraud. "Crammers" may slip bogus charges into your bill for services you never agreed to buy.

Ask questions. Know what to watch out for to help you avoid phony phone charges. Ask these questions as you check your telephone bills.

- Do I recognize the name of every company on my bill? What services did each company provide?

- Does the bill show charges for calls I never made or services I didn't authorize?

- Are the rates each company charged the same as the rates that company quoted to me?

But don't stop there. Remember these tips, too.

- If you don't recognize the service listed for any charge on your bill, contact the company that billed you for it. Before you pay the bill, ask them to explain the service.

- Keep a record of telephone services you agree to and use.

- Before signing up for a phone service, carefully read all the forms and advertising materials, including all fine print.

- Know what services you received for small charges. Crammers often try to sneak $2 or $3 charges into thousands of customer bills.

Fight back. If you've been crammed, contact both your local phone company and the company that billed the charge. Ask to have the wrongful charge removed.

"Slamming complaints go to the state public utilities commissions in states that have chosen to enforce our slamming rules themselves," Kimball explains. In other states, complain to the FCC.

To file complaints with the FCC, call 888-CALL-FCC (888-225-5322) or visit *www.fcc.gov / cgb / complaints.html*. "We take these complaints to the phone company and work with them to arrive at a solution that is agreeable to the consumer," says Kimball.

Don't get burned on extended warranties

Steer clear of extended warranties. They are often not worth the investment. In fact, car dealers make the most profit off these overpriced policies.

Sellers of extended warranties claim these policies will cover the cost of repair on your new purchase once its factory warranty expires. But before you fork over the dough, calculate how much value you will really get out of this extra insurance.

"You can find warranties on consumer products and services. It can be appliances, computers, or electronic equipment in your home," says Nancy Piggush, an assistant in the Michigan Attorney General's Consumer Protection office. "Some new products come with a manufacturers warranty, and I often question why someone would also buy what's called an extended warranty."

Consider replacing before fixing. In this modern era of fast-paced technology, products are more reliable and cheaper to replace. Many, like washing machines, will work for years before signs of wear slow them down. Count how many repairs you will have to make on the machine in a year to justify the extra expense before you pay for a service contract.

Depend on computer's guarantee. Most computers come with a one-year manufacturer's guarantee. Fortunately, problems with the hardware usually crop up within the first year of a machine's life. A service warranty may provide technical help while you set up your computer. But otherwise, service contracts can cost more than fixing or replacing your machine with a newer one, which you will do in a few years anyway.

Read the fine print. Most car dealers offer very limited extended warranties that cover repairs beyond the scope of the manufacturer's warranty. Read the small print carefully. "When a breakdown happens, you may go to the repair facility and find out the warrantor or the service contractor won't cover this claim because something in the fine print has excluded it," says Piggush. "In the contract, they call them exclusions, pre-conditions, limitations, and definitions."

Be leery of contracts that exclude normal wear and tear. A dealer can use this opt-out clause freely. "The contract is often so narrowly worded it restricts a great number of problems in used vehicles," warns Piggush. In this case, you are better off budgeting for unexpected repairs.

If you like the safety features of a warranty, check the contract for these additional deal breakers.

- Make sure the underwriter is a major insurer or you risk losing your coverage when a company unexpectedly goes under.

- Reserve your right to cancel. "Usually, contracts will carry a cancellation date," says Piggush. "You have 10 days to cancel."

- Check what maintenance schedule you will be required to keep to maintain the warranty. If you don't get routine work done regularly, you may void the contract.

- Check the reliability ratings on the product you intend to buy. If your model doesn't have a history of mechanical problems, you may be paying for maintenance you will never need.

- Don't buy it sight unseen. "If a service contractor or warrantor will not give you a contract to read beforehand, that should put you on notice," warns Piggush.

- Make sure the warranty covers service at a dealership or mechanic near you. It may cost you more to drive far to get covered repairs than it will to pay a mechanic up the road to fix the problem.

- Don't feel pressured to buy an extended warranty from the dealer. Shop around and buy a cheaper, better one closer to the date the manufacturer's guarantee ends.

Blow the whistle on phony sweepstakes

You've just won $10,000 ... a trip to Jamaica ... the Australian lottery! You may hear lines like these every day from telemarketers or discover these announcements in your mailbox. Just remember, if it sounds too good to be true, it probably is. You could lose your savings, your house, and your good credit by falling for phony sweepstakes.

Learn to tell a legitimate sweepstakes from a corrupt contest with this winning information.

Don't fall for false promises. The Federal Citizen Information Center (FCIC) says to be suspicious of phrases like these.

- "You have been specially selected ..."

- "You have won ..."

- "Yours, absolutely free! Take a look at our ..."

- "Your special claim number lets you join our sweepstakes ..."

- "All you pay is postage, handling, taxes ..."

Never pay a fee. Hang up if a caller says you've won but must pay fees to claim your prize. Free is free. According to Federal Trade Commission (FTC) rules, valid sweepstakes must tell you that you don't have to buy anything to enter or win a prize. Making you pay a fee is the telltale mark of a scam.

Watch for copycats. Scam companies may use names that sound like well-known sweepstakes and ask for a deposit or other fees. The Direct Marketing Association suggests calling the real sweepstakes company to verify the offer.

Never pay up front. Con artists may ask you to send a refundable deposit or money for taxes or fees. Don't do it. If you win a real sweepstakes, you pay taxes to the Internal Revenue Service (IRS), not the company awarding the prize. And if you send money overnight or by wire, the crooks could have your cash in hand before you realize you've been duped.

Protect personal information. Never give an unknown caller your social security, bank account, or credit card numbers — especially over the phone. The Federal Trade Commission says legitimate sweepstakes will not ask for this financial information.

Keep an eye on others. Loved ones are not immune to phony sweepstakes. You may need to help them watch out for sham contests, especially if they receive a lot of mail or ask about sending money overseas.

Contact the authorities. Report suspicious phone calls or mail offers to your state attorney general or office of consumer protection, as well as the Better Business Bureau in the sweepstake company's home state.

You should also notify the National Fraud Information Center at 800-876-7060 or online at *www.fraud.org*. To file a complaint with the Federal Trade Commission, call them toll-free at 877-FTC-HELP or visit them on the Internet at *www.ftc.gov*.

Beware of coupon con artists

Clipping coupons can save you money, but beware of coupon scams that can cost you money. Follow the advice of the Federal Trade Commission (FTC) to protect yourself.

Dodge coupon clipping scams. "Make hundreds per week — or even thousands — just by clipping coupons in the comfort of your home," claims the ad. The con artists demand you pay fees up front, but they say those fees will be nothing compared to the money you'll make.

"If it sounds too good to be true, it probably is not true," says Don D'Amato, Assistant Regional Director for the FTC Northeast Region. Scammers know their promises of easy money are false.

Bypass bogus booklets. The coupon certificate booklet scam can rob both consumers and investors. Here's how it works. Let's say Mary wants to start her own business. Lured by claims of big profits, she pays a scammer hundreds — or thousands — of dollars for booklets of coupon certificates. Supposedly, she'll recover her money when she re-sells the booklets to consumers.

"When you think about it, coupons are something you can just cut out of a newspaper for free," D'Amato says. So Mary faces a struggle to sell enough booklets to recover her initial costs — let alone make huge profits.

Now the other side of the story. Joe Consumer pays $50 for a booklet. Joe expects to use each certificate in the booklet to select and order coupons that have no expiration dates. To do that, he must also pay postage and an outrageous processing fee. Unfortunately, Joe doesn't know the coupons he orders could be expired or counterfeit. Even if the coupons are genuine and unexpired, Joe still paid for coupons that manufacturers provide for free.

Watch for warning signs. Avoid scams like these by learning their danger signals. "If someone guarantees big profits, high income, or amazing savings in a very short period of time, your antenna should go up immediately, and you should be suspicious," D'Amato says. Also be wary of these danger signs.

- heavy pressure to act right away

- claims that the opportunity is risk-free

- promises this is a can't-miss opportunity

Question and investigate. Before you put money in a work-at-home or investment program, ask these questions.

- How does the company's refund policy work?

- What is my total cost for the work-at-home program, including supplies, equipment, and membership fees. What will I get for my money?

- Who pays me and when do I get my first paycheck? Will I be paid a salary or work on commission?

"If it's a legitimate opportunity, they should be more than willing to answer these types of questions," D'Amato says. Nervous or impatient responses may mean trouble.

Also, check out the company with your local consumer protection agency or Better Business Bureau. Call the one in the company's home city, too. Ask if anyone has complained about the work-at-home program you're considering. Finally, be sure every promise you hear is put in writing. Check for all of them in the contract before you sign it.

Resolve consumer disputes effectively

Stop settling for excuses about terrible service and inferior products. Follow these steps from the Federal Trade Commission and other organizations.

Go to the seller. Start with the store where you bought the product, or the company that sold the service. If the first person you talk with is not helpful, ask to speak with the manager. Keep moving up the chain of command until you find someone who will help you.

Check whether your local newspaper, radio station, or television station has an action line for consumer complaints.

Consumer complaint letter

(Your address)
(Your city, state, and zip code)

(Date)

(Name of the contact person, if you have one)
(Their title)
(Company name)
Consumer Complaint Division (if you don't have a contact)
(Their street address)
(Their city, state, and zip code)

Dear (Contact Person):

On (date), I (bought, leased, rented, or had repaired) a (name of the product, with serial or model number, or service performed) at (location and other important transaction details).

Unfortunately, your product (or service) has not performed well (or the service was inadequate) because (state the problem).

To resolve the problem, I would appreciate (state the specific action you want – refund, credit, repair, exchange, etc.). Enclosed are copies of my records.

I look forward to your reply and a resolution to my problem, and will wait until (set a time limit) before seeking third-party assistance. Please contact me at the above address or by phone at (home or office number with area code).

Sincerely,

(Your name)

(Your account number, if applicable)

Enclosure(s): (List receipts, guarantees, warranties, canceled checks, contracts, model and serial numbers, and any other documents you are including.)

Can't get anywhere with the local retailer? Speak to someone in the consumer affairs department of the company's headquarters.

Notify the manufacturer. Complain to the company that made the product if you have a warranty or can't get the seller to cooperate. Get the manufacturer's name and a phone number for customer service from the label, warranty, or other paperwork you received with the item.

Whether you contact the seller or the manufacturer, have this information handy.

- the product's name and serial number

- date of the purchase

- the history of the problem and how you have tried to solve it

Stay calm when you call and be polite — but firm. Insist on a resolution to your problem.

File a written complaint. Still not satisfied? Write a complaint letter. Include all the facts of your case, and keep it clear, short, and sweet. Use the sample consumer complaint letter on the opposite page as a guide.

- Include your name, phone number, and address so the company can contact you, as well as the product's name and serial number.

- Explain the steps you have already taken to resolve the issue, and what you would like the company to do now.

Visit these Web sites for further advice.

National Consumers League
www.nclnet.org

Consumer Federation of America
www.consumerfed.org

Consumer Resource Handbook
www.pueblo.gsa.gov/crh

- Enclose copies — never originals — of sales receipts, work contracts, warranties, cancelled checks, repair orders, and any letters you and the company have sent each other.

- Send everything certified mail and request a return receipt. It costs a little more, but you'll have proof down the road that the company received your letter.

Call in the big guns. These agencies offer different types of assistance. They'll even fight on your behalf. Contact them if your letter doesn't work, and explain the situation.

- your state attorney general

- the Better Business Bureau in the state where the seller or manufacturer is located

- your local consumer protection office

- the consumer action department of a local newspaper, television, or radio station

- the legal clinic at a local law school

Document everything. Finally, keep a log of all your dealings with the seller or manufacturer. Write down the names of everyone you speak with, the date and time, and what they told you. Make copies of all the letters or e-mails you and the company exchange, as well as any documents related to the complaint. You may need this information if you go to court. See the consumer complaint letter on page 30.

Never pay full price for major merchandise

Bargains are everywhere. You just have to ask for them. You may be surprised how many salespeople will drop a price or sweeten the deal to get your business. Herb Cohen, author of *Negotiate This! By*

Caring, But Not T-H-A-T Much, offers some tips to help you master the fine art of negotiation and get great deals on almost everything.

Don't be shy. In a culture of bar codes and price tags, it might seem strange to haggle over prices. But once you take the plunge, you may be surprised how many sales reps are willing to deal. A gentle inquiry like "Is that your best offer?" may drop the price at electronic stores, vegetable stands, reservations desks, and clothes boutiques.

Leave guilt at the door. Don't feel you're cheating a store of their profits by taking a discount. "No salesperson will ever sell you anything unless it's a profitable deal for him or her," Cohen says. "You don't have to feel sorry for them if you knocked $200 off the price."

Enlist some aid. Ask the salesperson for help. Play a little dumb, and your question will not elicit a negative response. Explain it in terms of need. You have a need — to buy the product. The

---

Treat yourself for less

If you're in the market for jewelry, fine china, crystal, estate silver, tableware, or giftware, you'll find better prices at Michael C. Fina. Call for a catalog or shop online at *www.michaelcfina.com* or 800-Buy-Fina (800-289-3462).

Get discounts on cruises from Vacations to Go at *www.vacationstogo.com* or 800-338-4962.

Find great buys on stereos, home theatres, and other electronics at Cambridge SoundWorks. Call for a catalog or shop online at *www.hifi.com* or 800-367-4434.

---

salesperson has a need — to make a profit. "What you don't want to do is see the other side as an adversary. See them as a partner in solving this problem," says Cohen.

See beyond the no. "Learn from your kids. All kids know how to negotiate," Cohen says. They aim high and don't stop asking if they get a 'no.' They simply find another level of authority to plead to. "Kids understand that 'no' is an opening bargaining position," Cohen says. "Whenever you ask somebody for something they didn't expect, they say 'no.' It's like a gut reaction. Kids persist. They persevere. They wear you down."

Ask the right person. The average sales clerk makes an hourly wage and doesn't usually have authority to dicker over prices. Ask to speak with a floor manager or a salesperson on commission. They are much more likely to make concessions to please a customer.

Know your stuff. Come prepared with price quotes from other companies or from the Internet. Know what your item cost the dealer and decide in advance what markup you are willing to give them.

Make a friend. "Always be a nice person," says Cohen. "Show interest in your salesperson, and they may cut you a deal. Never be rude, demanding, or petty when asking for a discount. Don't bad-talk the merchandise or try to bully the salesperson. Even if you get a discount, they will give it grudgingly.

Ask for add-ons. Sometimes the price won't come down, but the salesperson might add merchandise to sweeten the deal. If you buy a computer, ask for added software, or if you're booking a hotel room, request an upgrade or a late checkout. A dealer may increase the term of your warranty, or deliver a large item free of charge.

Walk away. "You have so much more power than the storekeeper. Why? You've got money," says Cohen. "Money talks. And it often says 'goodbye.' When you walk out of that store, they don't know if you'll ever come back." So if you can't get the discount you need, politely say you'll think about it and turn away. They may track you down with a better offer, or let you go. The key is not to want an item too much. Be patient and save your money for a better deal.

Where to shop for great deals

Leave the mall behind and you might be surprised how far you can stretch a dollar. Being on a fixed income doesn't mean you have to live a meager life. Try savvy shopping at consignment stores, flea markets, thrift stores, and yard sales. You'll get more bang for your buck.

Flee to flea markets. Flea markets bustle with vendors who sell new items, used goods, and even antiques. You may have to work a little to find the most thrilling discounts, but you could also find items you'll cherish for years to come.

"If you're shopping for bargains and treasures, you want to be there early. The good stuff goes out quick," says Jim Goodridge, author of books on buying and selling in flea markets.

For more bargain shopping tips like these, be sure to visit his Web site at *www.goodridgeguides.com*.

- Bring cash. Most vendors don't take checks and credit cards.

- Know what you would pay for the same item at a discount store. While flea markets may sell brand new items for less, some may not be bargains.

- Bring a tote bag to hold your purchases. Before you buy anything large, like furniture, be sure you have a way to get it home. Delivery service usually isn't available.

- Examine each item before you buy it. In most cases, you can't return the item for a refund.

Go sale-ing. Just like flea market shoppers, yard sale and garage sale buyers should be prepared to pay in cash and be savvy about prices. Keep these ideas in mind, too.

- Dress comfortably. Wear clothes that let you bend and stretch easily. Instead of a purse, keep money in a wallet in your pocket or in a pouch around your waist.

- Don't rush. You may miss the best treasures — often hidden among piles of stuff you don't want.

- Check items carefully for broken parts or stains that might not come out.

- Bargain for a lower price. The seller can say no, but chances are good your offer will be accepted.

Find the closeout area in your favorite discount department store, advises Rick Doble, online newsletter editor at *www.savvy-discounts.com.* "Closeout means an item is selling at a rock bottom price and probably isn't going to be stocked anymore," he says. So check the closeout section every time you visit the store.

Shop secondhand. Goods in thrift stores, consignment shops, and resale shops may be secondhand, but frequent shoppers can score spectacular deals. "It's amazing what you will find," says Rick Doble, editor of the online newsletter at *www.savvy-discounts.com.* His wife once bought a brand-name dress shirt for him at an unbelievable price — 25 cents.

Thrift shops, like the ones run by Goodwill and the Salvation Army, get their merchandise from donated goods. Because the proceeds go to charity, you can get a great deal and help a worthy cause at the same time.

The National Association of Resale and Thrift Shops (NARTS) suggests these tips for shopping in thrift, consignment, and resale stores.

- Inspect each item carefully for quality. Check how well it is made and the material it's made from.

- Explore a bunch of resale, consignment, and thrift shops to find which ones suit you best. Shops vary widely and merchandise does, too.

- Get to know the staff and find out if you can sign up for a mailing list to get sale notices, customer-only premiums, flyers, or newsletters.

- Find out the store's return policy before you buy.

To find resale, thrift, and consignment stores near you, check the phone book under categories like "Consignment," "Resale," "Thrift," and "Clothing Bought and Sold." Ask friends about their favorite shops, too.

For a list of NARTS member shops in your area, search in the shopping guide at *www.narts.org* or send $4 to NARTS, P.O. Box 80707, St. Clair Shores, MI 48080.

Buy big items at small prices

You can buy furniture or appliances for less than you might expect. Find out how from Rick Doble, editor of the online newsletter *Savvy Discounts* at *www.savvy-discounts.com*.

Seek out seasonal sales. Before you buy an appliance, find out its on-sale months. For example, sales on laundry appliances are most likely in March. Your best bets for sales on other major appliances are January, July, October, and November.

The best months to buy an air conditioner may be February and July. Air conditioners are more likely to go on sale during these two months.

Ditch an ancient fridge. When Doble replaces his 20-year-old refrigerator, the new fridge will help pay for itself. "I've looked at the statistics. I know that the new refrigerator is going to use about a quarter as much energy," he says. Those savings can really add up — especially if your fridge is nearly as old as Doble's. "Don't cry too many tears when your old refrigerator finally gives up the ghost," he says. "A new refrigerator is much more efficient."

Ask for a better deal. "If you buy more than one appliance, I would ask for a deal," advises Doble. "Once you settle on a price, ask for free delivery and free set up." You may not get them, but you have little to lose by trying.

Check price and value. Compare prices, but compare value, too. Although a national chain quoted Doble a cheaper price, the higher local store price included such extras as new unit delivery and both disposal and removal of the old unit.

Skip local furniture stores. Instead, order new furniture direct from companies in North Carolina furniture hubs like Hickory or High Point. Before you order, check the color, request a swatch of fabric, and check other features — such as finish, cloth, options, and upholstery — to be sure you get what you expect. Plan to put money down when you order, but plan to save, too. "From what I've found, you can get as much as 30 percent off," Doble says.

Shop garage sales. Consider buying informal furniture at garage sales. Before you buy, check the condition of the item carefully to make sure it's a good value.

Save on mattresses and more. "Mattresses are a whole world unto themselves," Doble says. Even comparing one mattress to another is tricky. Learn about mattress-shopping and more from Doble's *Savvy Discounts* book or get additional money-saving ideas at *www.savvy-discounts.com*.

Surf your way to extra savings

Your computer can be a powerful ally to help you save money. Find where the cheapest prices hide with sites like *www.mysimon.com*, *www.dealtime.com*, and *www.pricegrabber.com*.

Get useful product reviews from *www.amazon.com*, *www.productopia.com*, *www.epinions.com*, or *www.cnet.com*. You can even check out reviews of online shopping sites at *www.bizrate.com*.

For information about safe online shopping and avoiding online scams, check out the Federal Trade Commission's Web site dedicated to e-commerce and the Internet at *www.ftc.gov/bcp/menu-internet.htm*.

7 safety tips for online auctions

You're not ready to give up online auctions, but you don't want to be a scam victim either. Use these tips to protect yourself and leave scammers wallowing in bitter disappointment.

Inspect the site. Before you use any auction site, find out what the site's rules are. They may be similar to other sites you've tried — or completely different. Read up on the how-to's before you bid.

Also, check whether the site offers any protection for buyers. For example, is the page where you enter your credit card number secure — with the padlock emblem at the bottom? What happens if you have a dispute with the seller? Does the site offer free insurance or guarantees for items that are undelivered or different from what the seller claimed?

Investigate the seller. Some sites include seller feedback ratings so you can find out how satisfied most folks are with the merchandise from that particular individual. Get the seller's phone number and call to confirm that it's correct. This may also be a good chance to ask questions about the product before you bid.

If you're dealing with a company, check to see if any complaints have been filed with the Better Business Bureau at *www.bbbonline.org*.

Focus on the details. Be sure you know exactly what you're bidding on. Read the description carefully. Check whether a photograph is available and examine it closely. As with most shopping, the devil is in the details, so read the fine print closely. Check for words like "refurbished" that may give hints about the condition of the item.

Avoid overpaying. Before you bid, find out the market value of what you're trying to buy. Web sites such as *appraiseitnet.com* or *www.hiddenfortune.com* may help.

Set your ceiling. Set a top bid limit and stick to it. Just like with real-world auctions, it's easy to get carried away and bid more than an item is worth. Before you start bidding, decide how much you're willing to pay and don't go higher.

Protect yourself. If the site offers an escrow service, you're fairly well protected. An escrow service works as a middleman between the buyer and seller. When the service receives payment from the buyer, it notifies the sender to ship the item. When the buyer receives the item, the escrow service gives the money to the seller. This protects both parties. However, if you pay with a credit card, it's much easier to dispute the charges if a problem does occur.

Capture the moment. Save and print all information related to the transaction.

Get a great deal on a cell phone plan

Your wireless phone bill doesn't have to leave you penniless. Take steps to get the most value for the least cost.

Discover what works best. "Not all wireless carriers serve all areas equally well," says Joseph Bradshaw, General Manager at WirelessAdvisor.com. Find out which companies serve your area best. "Ask the people who live, work, and travel in the areas where you want to use your wireless phone," Bradshaw suggests.

If you are moving to a new area, Bradshaw recommends Internet discussion forums, like the ones available at *www.wirelessadvisor.com/forums*.

Count the minutes. To find the best plan for you, consider how you use your phone. "Look at your past bills and get a feel for how many minutes you use per month," says Bradshaw. Hunt for a plan with enough total minutes to cover your monthly usage — plus a few minutes extra just to be sure. Avoid using more minutes than your plan provides. "That's when things get expensive," Bradshaw says.

"Seek out plans with off-peak hours that are earlier in the evening and later in the morning," he adds. The more calls you can make during off-peak hours, the more money you'll save.

Compare prepaid to bucket costs. The per-minute cost is usually higher for prepaid plans than for "bucket of minutes" plans. If your total minutes-per-month is low enough to make a prepaid plan worthwhile, be sure to find out when your prepaid minutes expire.

Beware of traps. Whether you're just browsing available plans or ready to sign a contract, ask questions and watch out for these potential troublemakers.

- Federal, state, and local governments can all charge taxes that show up on wireless bills, but these may not appear in advertised rates. "Get a list of all the taxes and fees that will be added before you sign the contract," advises Bradshaw.

- Find out how many months or years the contract covers. "Only sign up for a one-year contract. Do not let them entice you into a two-year contract," says Bradshaw.

- Ask how long the trial period lasts. Canceling after the trial period has expired will cost you. "One of the most-asked questions we get at WirelessAdvisor.com is 'Do I have to pay the cancellation fee?' Yes! Unless you don't mind ruining your credit rating and not getting cell phone service again," says Bradshaw.

- No matter what the salesman says, the contents of the contract are what you're bound by. So read the contract carefully and keep a copy.

- "Don't pay for extras you don't need. These days, wireless companies want to sell you all the latest technologies," Bradshaw says. "If you don't need e-mail, Internet, picture phone capabilities, etc., be sure they have not been added into your plan."

The world of wireless is constantly changing and growing, so visit *www.wirelessadvisor.com* to learn more about choosing a cell phone plan. You can also point your browser to *www.fcc.gov/cgb* to read consumer fact sheets about cell phone plans.

Save dough at the supermarket

Cynthia Yates has a knack for saving. She has written four books on how to budget, including *1,001 Bright Ideas to Stretch Your Dollars*, and her latest, *Living Well on One Income*. In fact, her thrifty tips could trim your grocery bills by as much as $50 to $150 a month, without cutting back on food. Just follow these tricks of the trade.

- Learn prices so you know a good deal when it comes your way.

- Get to know your grocers. "Talk to produce managers, stocking clerks, butchers, and store managers," Yates says. Ask questions and you may find out about special deals.

- Check the shelf price tag. It usually lists the price per pound or ounce, which can help you compare the cost of similar products.

- Bend and squint to find the best deals. "The less expensive products," she says, "are usually on the lowest shelves."

- Buy items in bags rather than boxes if you have a choice. Bagged foods generally cost less.

- Consider going generic. "Generic or store brands are often just as good as the gourmet brands," Yates says. And they might be cheaper.

- Check the expiration date on dairy products and other perishable foods before you buy.

- Ask the store to break up bunches of produce so you can buy a smaller amount. There's no sense paying for more than you will eat.

- Weigh prepackaged foods, like fruits, vegetables, and meat. They sometimes hold more than their label claims. Yates says, "You may find a 5-pound pack of spuds weighing in at 6 pounds."

- "Shop seasonally," she advises. "Prices drop when markets have an abundance of certain foods." Holidays and back-to-school seasons, for instance, have their effect — for better or worse — on store prices.

- Steer clear of the gourmet aisle and processed food. "You can rip your own lettuce, or cut your own cheese, or season your own drumstick," Yates says.

- Skip the junk food. "Back off on the stuff that isn't good for you in the first place," she advises. An occasional treat is OK, but too much can drain your budget and your health.

- Don't give in to impulse buys while shopping.

- Avoid overbuying. "I believe everyone should have enough water and food stashed to get through a week or so, should an emergency come along," says Yates. But she discourages hoarding. One of her rules — buy only what you eat, and eat what you buy.

- Check the prices at checkout. "Mistakes happen," she warns. "Watch the register and check receipts." A checker may scan an item twice, or the sale price may not ring up.

- Don't live with inferior products. "Politely return," she says. "If you have purchased a product that has gone bad, or not held up within reason, take it back."

Grocers sometimes use tricks to sell you more food. "A lot of these things are carrots on a stick," Yates points out. "Don't be a donkey." Watch out for these four grocery store gimmicks.

- Placing staples, like milk, in the very back of the store forces you to walk past all the tempting aisles.

- Grouping items together encourages you to buy more than one product — like putting salsa next to the chips, or caramel dipping sauce by the apples.

- Setting items on the ends of aisles makes you think they are a special deal. But they may not offer the best price. "Sometimes," Yates says, "a walk down the aisle will find something less expensive."

- Giving away a free item with a minimum purchase, Yates says, only works in your favor if you had planned to spend that much money anyway.

Enjoy a thrifty night on the town

You can paint the town red without going into the red. Shel Horowitz, author of *The Penny-Pinching Hedonist* and owner of *www.frugalfun.com*, knows how to eat out on the cheap and save big on after-dinner entertainment. Sample a few of his ideas.

4 ways to look great at cut rates

- Get your hair cut, colored, styled, or permed at a beauty school.

- Avoid buying "dry clean only" clothes, if you can. If you can't, shop around for the best service and price.

- Don't buy an evening gown for that rare formal occasion. Rent or borrow one instead.

- Buy new clothes at off-season sales but also frequent thrift stores, consignment shops, and yard sales.

Know before you go. Read up ahead of time to fork over less cash for your dinner. For example, scan your newspaper and check radio station Web sites for coupons, discounted gift certificates, and advertisements for specials. Also find out which restaurants have early bird specials. If you're willing to eat between 4:30 and 6 p.m., you'll get more bang for your buck when dining out.

Master menu magic. Even if your favorite restaurant charges high prices, you can shrink your bill with a little clever ordering. Bypass that full meal or meaty main entree. Instead, order a meatless entree or an appetizer. If that's not enough, try two appetizers or several side orders. Drink water instead of alcoholic beverages, and you'll save even more.

Buy discount cards. For discounts at restaurants, you could buy a dining card or a booklet of restaurant coupons. But before you purchase either of these, find out which restaurants they cover. Only buy one that offers discounts at restaurants you already visit.

Be a food tourist. Some ethnic food restaurants give you a lot of food for the price. Restaurants that specialize in Chinese, Mexican, or Italian food can be good values.

Win your dinner. Does your favorite radio station run contests for restaurant gift certificates — or do you know of a station that does? Put that station's number on speed dial and start listening. You might win dinner for two, after-dinner entertainment, or both.

Ask to pay less. AARP discounts, senior citizen discounts, and student rates can crop up in all sorts of restaurants and entertainment venues. If you belong to one of these groups, ask whether a discount is available.

Usher in a good time. You can see top-name performers, great plays, musicals, and concerts for less than a penny. How? Volunteer to usher at these performances. You'll be asked to dress up and spend time leading people to their seats. You might have to arrive an hour early and stay an hour late. Yet, when the lights go down, you can enjoy the show.

Keep your fun cheap. "With just a little creativity, you can find all kinds of honest, fair, non-rip-off ways to get entertainment for little or no cost," Horowitz says. Check your local newspaper, Web sites, bulletin boards, and free publications for free cultural events and low-priced entertainment. Be sure to find out what's available at nearby colleges or universities, too.

Buy bargain theater tickets

You could get local theater tickets at a 25 to 50 percent discount if you live in a major city. In New York, take cash or traveler's checks to TKTS at Broadway and 47th. You can buy cut-rate Broadway tickets for a show that's running that day. Call ahead to find out when matinee or evening tickets start selling. In Chicago, get bargain tickets from Hot Tix. Visit TICKETplace for shows in Washington D.C. or AtlanTIX for Atlanta shows. Other major cities have similar outlets. Check your phone book to find out what your city offers.

If you love music, look for recitals by performing arts professors — or find out who the best local music teachers are and attend their student recitals.

For many extra tips about frugal dining, entertainment, and more, order *The Penny-Pinching Hedonist* e-book from *www.frugalfun.com*. The book comes as a computer file. You can read it with the free Acrobat Reader program available from *www.acrobat.com*.

5 ways to spend less at Christmas

You love Christmas, but hate what it does to your budget. Stop seeing red and keep more of those green dollars with advice from *Savvy Discounts* editor Rick Doble.

Shop year round. Go treasure hunting. Check thrift stores and consignment stores often. Doble recalls one case where a woman found a wet suit for her daughter who loves to surf. Another time, his wife bought a Chinese-style red silk dress for just $3. Yard sales can be treasure troves, too.

Get creative with cards. "With everyone having a computer these days, it's very simple to make your own Christmas cards," Doble says "You can get the kids to hand-color them — which gives it a nice, personal touch."

For last-minute card-sending, find one of the many free e-card sites on the Internet — or check *www.savvy-discounts.com* for a list of links. If you send a free e-card to Aunt Jane, she'll get an e-mail that tells her you've sent a card. When

Don't pay the whopping TV ad price for a new exercise machine. Wait and buy it used. Exercise industry reports suggest that many machines are used four times – at most. Look for used exercise machines at super discounts.

she clicks the link in the e-mail, she'll be able to view and print the lovely card you sent.

Stock up on paper goods. Buy Christmas decorations, wrapping paper, Christmas cards, and other holiday items at freshly slashed prices on December 26. You may even find spectacular Yule-oriented savings for several days running. Keep your eyes peeled for bargains on other products, too. In fact, Doble suggests that after-Christmas cash could be part of a Christmas gift. After all, that cash may go a lot farther in an after-Christmas sale.

Exchange gifts wisely. Sometimes you need to exchange an item after Christmas, but your courtesy receipt fails to list the price. Make sure you are credited with the before-Christmas price, Doble says. The after-Christmas price may be much less. Be sure no one "forgets" to include the before-Christmas sales tax as well.

For more of Doble's Christmas tips, visit the online *Savvy Discounts* newsletter at *www.savvy-discounts.com*.

Stretch your Christmas budget

Faye starts next year's Christmas shopping on December 26. At after-Christmas sales, she buys next year's wrapping paper and Christmas cards at 50 to 80 percent off. She won't settle for lesser markdowns.

Faye also purchases discounted Christmas ornaments, scented candles, gift sets, and other items to give as presents. She lists who each gift is for and stores them on her Christmas/birthday closet shelf. As Faye shops during the year, she adds to her gift stash. By December, she has few presents to buy and can enjoy the holidays.

Banking

Mastering the ins and outs of borrowing and lending

Wise ways to secure a loan

If buying a home is in your future, good budgeting includes saving to pay for as much of it as possible. When you've put aside a significant amount, your next step may be to secure a loan to cover the rest. It's important to do some homework so you'll get the right loan from the right lender. Jack Guttentag, also known as "The Mortgage Professor," says there are three basic rules to follow when you're looking for loans and lenders.

Know your niche. "Borrowers need to know which market niche they fall into. When you pick up a newspaper and see a price quote on a mortgage, the prices you see there are for a generic borrower with a whole range of features — all favorable from a lender's point of view."

Those advertised prices make assumptions about you, the customer.

- You've got great credit and enough income and assets to meet the lender's requirements.

- You can fully document your income and assets (a tough one, especially if you're self-employed).

- You're purchasing a single-family, detached house that will be your primary residence.

If you don't meet those requirements, you're out of luck. Those great advertised deals are for Mr. Generic Consumer — not you.

Before you set out in search of a loan, be sure you know how you deviate from that generic norm and in which borrowing niche you fit. Begin the process with realistic expectations. Those ads just set you up for disappointment.

Decide on a loan. Smart loan shoppers realize that lenders with the best deal on one type of loan may not have the best deal on another. Do some research. Do you want a fixed-rate or adjustable-rate ... a 30-year or 15-year term ... zero-point or three-point loan ... a large down payment or no down payment?

Figure out which type of loan suits you, and stick with it. Switching loan types and features in midstream can knock you back to square one.

Choose your lender. "The cardinal mistake," says Guttentag, "that gets people into trouble is not selecting a loan provider, but allowing the loan provider to select them. They are solicited."

The problem with letting yourself be solicited is that solicitous lenders are anxious to sell you a loan that will be profitable to them. If you do the choosing, you're in the driver's seat. "Victims of predators are almost always solicited," Guttentag says.

He knows that most people don't know how or where to look for honest, reputable lenders. That's

Mortgages, retirement plans, car and student loans, credit card balances, and savings plans need "tune-ups" to assure peak performance. Be sure you schedule regular visits with a financial advisor to get more mileage from your money.

why he created "upfront mortgage brokers" and "upfront mortgage lenders."

"Brokers are in the market every day. By acting as an upfront mortgage broker, he voluntarily gives up his opportunity to deceive borrowers and take advantage of changes in the market during the negotiations phase." That's why it's a good idea to do business with these folks.

Guttentag's Web site, *www.mtgprofessor.com,* provides free information about these reputable brokers and lenders, as well as a series of articles about "Mistakes to Avoid." For more advice on shopping for a mortgage, read Guttentag's book, *The Mortgage Encyclopedia.*

Don't play around with home equity

Taking out a second mortgage once meant you were in financial trouble. Today, people take out home equity loans, which is another name for a second mortgage, to pay for everything from home renovations to weddings. Although some people consider it a smart way to borrow money, this type of loan can be hazardous to your finances.

Equity is the amount left over after you subtract your home loan from what your house is worth. People think this type of loan is a great deal because you get better terms when pledging your home rather than an unsecured credit card or used car. Plus, the interest is tax deductible. Rising real estate values have created more equity in most homes, allowing people to borrow even more money.

But borrowing against your home may put you so far in debt that you'll never own your home free and clear. And consider these other pitfalls. Interest rates usually are not fixed so they can change as the economy changes. That means you have no control over future costs. And if the economy is bad, the lender can demand payment or a renegotiation of terms. On the other hand, if something happens to you and you can't pay, the lender can foreclose and sell your home to collect the loan.

So you need to consider this type of loan carefully and decide whether it's worth the risk of losing your home. In most cases, you're better off keeping your equity and working to pay off the remaining mortgage.

Truth in advertising remains a primary concern of today's Better Business Bureau (BBB). Among its other services are reports on charities and company reliability, complaint resolution and arbitration, and scam warnings. Before doing business with a company, check out the BBB Web site (*www.bbb.org*) or call your local BBB.

If you do have a serious reason to borrow against your home, you can do it in one of three ways.

Installments. The basic home equity loan is just a normal installment loan with a fixed interest rate and regular payments. It's a good way to borrow because there is built-in discipline. You take care of a set amount of debt over a set time period and at a set interest rate.

Line of credit. A home equity line of credit (LOC) is a revolving line of credit, just like a credit card. You set it up for a maximum amount and usually for a certain time period. You only have to borrow as much as you need at a time, then you can pay some or all of it off, and borrow it back again. You'll probably get a lower interest rate, but it will float up and down with current economic conditions.

Don't use an LOC to replace your out-of-control credit card. If you can't manage your spending with a credit card, you're likely to get into even more trouble with the extra freedom of a home equity line.

An LOC is good for things that don't require full payment all at the same time, like a long-term remodeling project or college expenses. It's also nice to have it ready for emergencies, like unemployment or hospitalization.

It's very important to have a payoff plan for an LOC. You don't want selling your house to be the only way of getting rid of the debt.

Refinancing. The third option is to refinance your original home loan. Pay off your first mortgage and write a new one for a larger amount, using the leftover cash instead of getting a separate loan. But that's only a good idea when current interest rates are lower than your old loan. In a rising rate situation, you're better off with a second mortgage.

Watch out for closing costs and other fees on both first and second mortgage loans. They are, after all, real estate loans that can require surveys, appraisals, and other documentation. Make sure the convenience and the interest savings are more than the extra fees. Sometimes you can find lenders so eager to make home equity loans that they will waive the fees or offer other incentives.

Escape zero-percent financing trap

If it sounds too good to be true, it probably is. Keep these words in mind when you're being enticed by ads for zero-percent financing (ZPF), and follow this advice from a pro.

Keep your guard up. ZPF is bait to lure shoppers into showrooms and encourage impulse buying, says consumer educator Joyce Cavanagh of Texas A&M University.

While seniors often show more restraint when shopping than younger consumers, don't let your guard down. Gimmicks like ZPF tempt you to buy now, before you have the money, and think you're getting a bargain.

"It is enticing," Cavanagh says. "It's a way of pulling people in and getting them to make a purchase they probably don't have the cash for. Most offers also include no payments for up to a year."

Beware of the "gotchas." Here are some common pitfalls you need to watch out for.

- Gotcha #1 — Sorry, you don't qualify. Check your credit score before you shop, because once you've invested an entire afternoon shopping and falling in love with that car, washer, or whatever, they've gotcha.

  Sales clerks are patient. They wait until you're hooked. "You go through the whole rigmarole of working with the salesperson," Cavanagh says. "Then they tell you, 'Oh! You don't qualify for zero percent, but we can give it to you for 5 or 6 or 9 percent.' Don't shop and then see if you qualify for ZPF," she says.

  "In most cases with major retailers, if you don't already have one of their credit cards, you'll have to qualify for one," says Cavanagh. And it's better to stay away from store accounts, which traditionally have high interest rates.

- Gotcha #2 — The fine print. Read the ZPF sales contract. Understand payment deadlines and grace periods. Making a late payment can have serious consequences. Cavanagh mentions one. "They make their payment. They think they're on time, but they've missed the deadline and find themselves responsible for interest covering the entire delayed period." Ouch! That's an expensive mistake.

- Gotcha #3 — Self-discipline. This trips a lot of people up, says Cavanagh. You intend to put money aside every month but it never happens. When the time comes to pay up, there's no money. Then you're hit with payments at high interest rates, and the good deal vanishes.

- Gotcha #4 — You may be charged a higher purchase price to offset the ZPF. For example, you may pay closer to sticker price on a new car.

Stay strong. "Ask questions before you get into the negotiating process," says Cavanagh, "and before you start investing lots of time and emotion."

If you have a hard time talking with sales clerks, use the phone or the Internet so you won't worry about offending the salesperson. Or have a friend who's good at negotiating and saying "no" go with you.

Proceed with caution. ZPF may be just the promo you've been waiting for. "For people who are already planning to make a specific purchase and have the money," Cavanagh says, "ZPF means they don't have to take the money out wherever it is. They can continue to earn a little bit of interest and make monthly payments because they have the money to pay for it." It can help in building a credit rating, too.

In any case, proceed cautiously. Ask yourself if you would buy the item if it wasn't being sold at zero percent. And consider whether it's just not smarter to pay cash after all.

Secrets for staying out of debt

All debts will be cancelled in heaven, and borrowing won't be necessary. If you find it's a necessary evil here and now, Joyce Cavanagh, professor of economics at Texas A&M University, has some great advice for changing that and staying out of debt.

Think twice about borrowing. Any time you owe money, you're carrying debt, whether it's the mortgage, your credit cards, or even utilities. You're enjoying something now and paying for it later.

"Normally, borrowing for homes, vehicles, and self-training is not a bad kind of debt," she says. A student loan, for example, is a debt that makes sense — an investment in human capital, something that's going to appreciate.

Getting a handle on bill collectors

Bill collectors who constantly hound retired people about debts they can't pay are often barking up the wrong tree. "Senior citizens frequently don't have any assets that anybody can take," says bankruptcy attorney Jerry Harper. He says some seniors declare bankruptcy just to get collectors off their backs.

Creditors can't take your household goods, car, home, or Social Security and pension payments to pay a debt unless you've signed them up as security. If that's all you have, then you are being badgered unnecessarily. See *Get debt collectors off your back* in the Consumer Credit chapter for help.

"A lot of parents don't want their children to graduate from college with any student loan debt. That's very noble. But in order to make that happen, sometimes they'll sacrifice saving for their own retirement."

Just remember, says Cavanagh, "Nobody is going to lend you money to retire, but they will lend you money to put your children through school."

And, she believes, "Students who know they're responsible to pay at least a portion of their education take school more seriously."

Use credit cards carefully. Credit card debt has reached epidemic proportions. "Before you put something on a credit card," Cavanagh says, "ask yourself, 'Will this thing be around, will it exist anymore, when my bill comes?' That automatically eliminates gas and food."

Evaluate your finances. Folks with limited and fixed incomes face special challenges. "People who are already retired obviously have to determine whether or not they can really afford to make the payment," advises Cavanagh. You need to determine what the monthly payment will be and see how it fits into your cash flow.

She also warns of the danger of paying for prescription drugs and medical co-payments with a credit card. "Your monthly cash flow may cover normal living expenses. But then you have to pay a couple hundred dollars for prescriptions each month. So if you're putting it on your credit card and just making the minimum payment each month, it may work for a while, but eventually you'll find your resources stretched."

When it comes to debt, make it work for you. Rein in credit card spending, and make sure you control it, not vice versa.

Expert advice for avoiding bankruptcy

Bankruptcy brings to mind a frazzled man in a tuxedo shouting "I'm ruined! Ruined!" before jumping from a high building after the stock market crash of 1929. Or at least it used to.

Nowadays, as people file for bankruptcy in record numbers, the prevailing attitude seems to be that it's no big deal. But it is. With bankruptcy, you can't wave a magic wand and make all your debts disappear. If you declare bankruptcy, it appears on your credit report for 10 years, making it difficult to obtain credit, except at very high rates. It may even affect your employment with many companies.

Always think of bankruptcy as your last resort — not as an easy way to escape your creditors. Take responsibility for your debts, and take action to avoid bankruptcy.

Budget, budget, budget. Make a serious effort to live within your means. Good planning and budgeting will go a long way toward keeping you safe from bankruptcy.

"People are usually in crisis mode when they come to see me," says bankruptcy attorney Jerry Harper. "In a few instances, it's because of poor management or going to the casino, but the overwhelming majority of cases it's because something unforeseen happens."

Expect the unexpected. Good planning can overcome unexpected setbacks. You never know when you'll need to go to the doctor or get your car repaired. When you make your monthly budget, set some money aside for medical bills and car maintenance so these "surprises" won't hit you as hard. Put some money into a savings account, which can be used for emergencies.

Sidestep credit card trap. Excessive use of credit cards contributes to most bankruptcies. Higher interest rates and extra fees kick in if you get behind. All of a sudden, you're maxed out and only making the minimum payment when another emergency comes along.

At reasonable rates and no new spending, it takes 10 to 20 years to pay off a credit card when you pay just the minimum payment. "If you can't make at least double the minimum payment, you've got a problem," Harper says.

Stay alert as you age. Think bankruptcy is just for the young and irresponsible? Think again. Harper believes the number of older people declaring bankruptcy is increasing.

"People are ending up in retirement with their finances not in order," he says. "And a lot file because of medical bills, especially drugs that aren't covered by Medicare."

Plan well. Make sure you'll be able to make ends meet when you stop working and your income drops suddenly.

"If you arrive at retirement age and haven't retired those credit card and other debts, you simply don't have the funds to pay them anymore," Harper says.

Keep in touch. If you can't pay your entire bill, do not hide from your creditors. Ignoring them now will only make it more difficult for you to deal with them later. Explain your situation honestly, and try to work out an acceptable plan. At least try to make partial payments.

Take stock of your situation. Getting close to the end of your rope? Try this. "Add up the debt and divide it by 48 (months)," Harper says. "If you can't pay it off in four or five years, then there probably aren't any good solutions. You've either got to reduce your expenses or increase your income — or both. If you're on a fixed income, it's just real difficult."

Think of some changes you can make. Maybe you can move to a smaller, cheaper house, sell one of your family's cars, or pick up a part-time job. It may sound drastic, but sometimes drastic change is the only solution.

Ask for help. Bankruptcy may seem appealing to provide relief from the bill collectors and the worry that comes with owing

---

2 choices in bankruptcy court

There are two chapters in the Bankruptcy Code that cover almost all personal bankruptcies.

Chapter 7 is straight bankruptcy. You surrender all your non-exempt assets. They're divided up among your creditors, and you're finished. The people you owe can't make you pay any more.

Chapter 13 lets you pay off things you want to keep — like a house or car — under a court-approved, three- to five-year payment plan. You can keep your belongings and creditors will leave you alone as long as you stick to the plan.

money you can't pay. But declaring bankruptcy doesn't mean your struggles are over. Unless you rebuild your life based on a sound budget and debt-free lifestyle, you'll find yourself in another financial mess all too soon.

A good credit counselor may help you restructure your debt, negotiate with creditors, and head off a bankruptcy. But be careful about who you go to, Harper warns. Many who call themselves credit counselors are just glorified collection agencies.

Groups like American Consumer Credit Counseling, who have been around a long time and charge only a modest fee, have a good reputation. The fee is a pretty good test, Harper believes. "If they want to charge you a lot of money to do this, then I worry that they're not in it to help people as much as they're in it to make money." Call them at 800-769-3571 for a free budget consultation, or check out their Web site at *www.consumercredit.com*.

Another reputable group, Crown Financial Ministries, provides Christian-based credit counseling. Go to the Web site *www.crown.org* to find contacts in your area. You may also want to check with your church. Many have trained financial counselors available as part of their ministries.

7 questions to ask your banker

Wouldn't you like to know what "service" means at your bank? Ask these questions to find out.

"How does the interest accumulate on an interest-paying checking account?" Banks must pay interest on the money in your account at the end of each day, but listen for the term "blended rates." If that's how they pay interest, they're shortchanging you.

"What's the penalty for falling below the minimum balance?" The answer should help you decide which of your bank's checking accounts is best for you. Don't choose an account that puts you in jeopardy if you dip too close to that minimum balance.

"Can you 'truncate' my account?" If they can, they'll send a list of the checks you wrote every month instead of the canceled checks. This saves the bank money, and they should pass the savings on to you.

"Will you remove my checking fees if I take out a loan with you or buy a certificate of deposit?" This is a good way to find out how much they appreciate your continuing business.

"Will you reduce my loan rate if I have my payments made automatically?" It makes sense. Making less paperwork for them should make you a preferred customer.

"How long before I can draw on deposits made to my account?" If you don't know how much breathing room they allow, you may face the scourge of unforgiving overdraft penalties.

"What fees will I have to pay?" Don't wait until you receive your monthly statement to discover fees you never knew existed. Once you know those fees are lurking in the shadows, beat them before they strike.

Stop banks from stealing your money

Bank mistakes can cost you money, and they usually aren't cheap. But what if you never notice the slip? Your cash could be gone for good.

They may not mess up often, but when they do, it's up to you to hold them accountable. Greg McBride, senior financial analyst with Bankrate.com, considers these the most common bank blunders.

Debit card fumbles. Bank cards make it easy to buy groceries, clothes, and other necessities — but stay alert. Sometimes the same charge goes through twice.

ATM errors. They provide fast cash, but be watchful. A withdrawal may post to your account more than once.

Overdraft protection failure. This special service transfers money into your account when you overdraw it, saving you expensive fees. However, the bank charges a fee every time you use it, and sometimes it may not work, and your check still bounces.

Deposit slip-ups. You know you deposited money, but your bank statement shows no sign of it. Banks may wrongly record deposits, or fail to post them at all, according to Bankrate.com.

You can't always prevent these errors, but you can catch them before they do too much damage.

- "Make note of all transactions immediately, especially if you frequently use a debit or ATM card," McBride advises.

- Save receipts for all your transactions, whether a debit charge, ATM withdrawal, or a check copy. These will help you balance your register, plus prove your case if the bank goofs up.

- "Take advantage of technology," he urges. Most banks let you track transactions by phone or Internet. You can get your balance, find out when checks clear, and stay on top of other details. You could catch errors weeks earlier than if you had waited for the monthly statement.

- Read your statements. It helps you keep up with changing fees and balance requirements. This way, you'll avoid penalties for dropping below the minimum balance or having too little cash for fees.

- Opt for overdraft protection. True, it occasionally fails, but McBride still recommends it. "Overdraft protection saves you the embarrassment of bouncing a check from time to time." It also saves you the expense of fees for insufficient funds.

- Consider direct deposit. "It not only saves you the hassle of going to the bank, it also reduces the risk for error," McBride says. Ask about getting paychecks, Social Security checks, and other payments directly deposited into your account.

Ultimately, the bank must return your money, not a merchant or other third party. Get them to correct botches with McBride's advice.

Make the call. "Start with a phone call to the bank." Go through customer service first. If that doesn't work, move up the chain of command. Keep asking to speak with managers until you reach someone willing to help you. Be sure to write down the name and title of the person you finally deal with.

Get it in writing. "Follow that call up with a letter." If the mistake takes more than 24 hours to fix, document it and your complaint in writing. Address your letter to the person who helped you on the phone. "You need to send it to someone specific, somebody higher up, and it helps if you actually discussed the problem with them." Include this information in your correspondence:

- your name and account number

- the date, time, and place where the transaction took place

- your contact information, including daytime and evening phone numbers

- copies of any documentation that proves your claim, like receipts from deposits, withdrawals, or debit charges or copies of checks

- if the problem involves an overdraft protection failure, a copy of the paperwork you received when you signed up for the service.

Save a bundle on banking fees

It's reasonable to assume a bank fee is the cost of a service provided by your bank. Unfortunately, you might be paying for services you don't want or getting stung by needless penalties — and you won't learn this from your banker.

Ask yourself if the services you're using make your account "user-friendly" and protect you from penalties for minor oversights or errors. If not, here's how you can fix the problem.

Choose wisely. The most important services your bank can provide actually eliminate unnecessary fees, says Dr. Walt Woerheide, vice president and director of the Irwin Graduate School at The American College in Bryn Mawr, Pa.

For example, automatic credits and debits — like direct deposit — can eliminate fees sometimes charged for personal visits to the bank and writing checks. "Many banks waive monthly fees if you use direct deposit," says Woerheide.

"Merchants are also providing the opportunity for direct debits for your bills. I sign up with my utilities company, and when it's time for the utility bill to be paid, they simply send a notice to the bank, and the bank issues a payment."

Beware of minimum balances. "Some banks really focus on senior citizens and offer them special checking accounts," says Woerheide. "But you can't always say they're a good deal."

"If your bank says you have to keep $2,000 in the account at all times, and for some reason you drop below that, a line of credit won't cover you. You could end up with a really stiff monthly fee."

Check out the competition. Maintaining an account that serves you well without unnecessary fees requires research, advises Woerheide. Bank fees are often the product of genius gone bad — monthly fees,

fees for writing too few checks, fees for not having overdraft protection. The list goes on.

"You should make a point, at least once a year, of looking into another bank to see what kinds of accounts, what kinds of programs are available — to make sure you're comfortable with your bank and getting a good deal," says Woerheide. "Shop around, and see what the competition is doing."

Don't pay useless fees. When you receive your bank statement, scan the debit column. Look for entries that don't refer to checks you've written, debit card purchases you've made, or authorized automatic debits. If anything else appears in the debit column, it's probably a bank fee. If that fee doesn't cover a service you need, call the bank and contest it.

Tips for using a debit card

Comparing plastic to paper at the store isn't about sacks anymore. People now use debit and credit cards more than cash and checks to pay for their purchases, according to a study by the American Bankers Association (ABA) and a Boston consulting firm.

Most people choose plastic because it's easier to give the clerk a card instead of dragging out a checkbook and identification. It's also safer than carrying cash.

Debit cards are used more often than credit cards. The pay-as-you-go system is best because it sidesteps the problem of running up excessive credit card debt and having to pay interest. But there are still a few things you need to pay attention to when using a debit card. The ABA has these suggestions.

Watch your account balance. It's a lot easier to let your balance get away from you when you don't keep track of every withdrawal, like you do in your checkbook. If you end up in the hole, you'll have to deal with returned checks, overdraft charges, or activation of your overdraft protection.

"You still need to keep track of your debit card transactions," says John Hall of the ABA. "If you don't write them down in your checkbook, then you need to have some other kind of register."

Keeping track is even more critical with a joint account. It's hard enough to figure a correct balance when there are two checkbooks without the complication of two sets of unrecorded debit payments. Be sure and check your statement as soon as you get it. Better yet, use online banking to help keep up-to-date.

Report fraud immediately. Checking your online and printed statements regularly is also a good way to guard against fraud and lost or stolen cards. You're more vulnerable with a debit card than a credit card because money is taken out of your account immediately. If an unauthorized withdrawal shows up, call and notify your bank right away. Federal law says $50 is the most you can lose if you report it within two business days, so it pays to be vigilant. If your debit card has the Visa or MasterCard label, you won't be out anything if you report the fraud in two days.

Save your receipts. Don't throw receipts away until you've checked them against your statement. If they show your account number, tear them up or run them through a shredder.

Keep PIN a secret. Memorize your Personal Identification Number (PIN), the ABA says. If you want to write it down, keep it completely separate from your card. The worst thing you can do is write the PIN on the card.

You can only use PIN-based debit cards at Automatic Teller Machines (ATMs) and other places that are set up with the proper keypad and equipment. Banks sometimes charge extra for PIN payments because they cost more to process.

Signature debit cards are good any place that takes credit cards. Most signature cards also have a PIN, so sometimes you can choose how you want to use your card.

New twist on ATMs

The automated teller machine, known as ATM, turned 30 years old in 2003. That's been plenty of time for it to prove its value, and that's exactly what it's doing.

Peg Bost, Director of Financial Industry Marketing for Diebold, Inc., one of the world's largest ATM manufacturers, is an ATM expert. She has exciting news about how ATMs can make banking easier and more secure.

User-friendly. Have you ever been confused by machines or the instructions on how to use them? If you have, you're not alone. "Now," Bost says, "ATMs have graphics on the screen that help you walk through the transaction." And some even talk you through it.

---

3 kinds of cards — what's the difference?

- Credit cards – Sign the slip and get a bill for all your purchases once a month.

- PIN-based debit cards – Key in your secret Personal Identification Number and the money comes out of your account immediately.

- Signature-based debit cards – Processed the same as credit cards, but the money still comes out of your account. Sometimes these also have a PIN.

Multi-talented. "About 78 percent of all ATM transactions are cash withdrawals," Bost says. But there's much more. You can make deposits, pay bills, view cancelled checks, and receive on-the-spot statements. "For a senior balancing a checkbook, that's a nice feature," Bost says.

Bost knows that blind transactions — the old method of sealing your deposit in an envelope and dropping it in the ATM — make many users nervous.

"Now, the ATM can actually image that check, display it, tell you the amount, and print the image on your receipt. This removes the opportunity for error by miss-keying an amount. The amount is verified and confirmed."

Safe and sound. While it's safe to use an ATM for your banking needs, there are things you should know to help keep your accounts secure. Bost offers three ATM security tips for safety's sake.

- Don't pack your PIN (personal identification number) with your ATM card. Keep it safe, secure, and separate.

- When you key in information at the ATM, use your body as a shield so no one can watch, even people at a distance. Keep your transactions private.

- If something about an ATM looks unusual, like an extra gizmo attached to it, leave. Don't use it. Alert your bank or the police to anything you feel is strange or threatening.

So stay alert. Be smart. And let today's super-convenient ATMs make life a lot easier for you.

Checklist for better checking

Maximize the effectiveness of your checking account with these helpful tips.

- Buy cheaper checks. If your bank doesn't offer you free checks, use a check printing service instead of your bank. Or, better still, eliminate the cost of checks by using a check card.

- Endorse checks correctly. An endorsed check is just like cash to its possessor. Write instructions on every check, like "for deposit only" or "pay to the order of."

- Secure a signature card. This ID card will keep transactions secure, reduce theft, and eliminate hassles when you're doing business somewhere other than your home branch.

- Report theft immediately. If your checkbook is lost or stolen, alert your bank as soon as you realize it's gone. You may know it the moment it's stolen, or it may not dawn on you until your monthly statement arrives. But act without delay

How to balance your checkbook

- Regularly enter each deposit and withdrawal in your check register, and calculate your current balance. This will help you avoid overdrawing or dropping below your minimum balance.

- Compare your check register with the monthly bank statement.

- Figure in interest payments, direct deposits, automatic withdrawals, and fees. They're included on your monthly statement.

- Flag checks that haven't cleared the bank. Notify the payees. Make sure the checks haven't been lost.

While success at balancing a checkbook is surprisingly satisfying, consider taking advantage of help if it's available. Some banks offer checkbook balancing as a courtesy service to senior citizens.

to minimize losses. It's the bank's job to defend your account against invasion by forgery, but you must let them know so they can take action.

- Stop payment on checks you shouldn't have written. It's legit when you've been hoodwinked, tricked, fooled, or even if you've made a simple error and overpaid on your utility bill. Know your bank's rules on its stop-check service.

- Bank "automatically." Take advantage of automatic deposits, debits, and fund transfers. It'll save you time and money and remove the stress of worrying that payments and deposits are being made on time.

- Know when you can draw. How long will it be before you can draw on funds you've deposited in your account? This alone may save you the expense of overdraft penalties and the embarrassment of bounced checks.

- Debit with plastic. A debit card is a plastic check, not a credit card. Be sure to tally debit card purchases in your checkbook ledger.

- Guarantee payment with certified checks. Sometimes it's necessary to pay by certified check. Many banks provide them free to their account holders.

- Keep up with your accounts. Avoid unhappy surprises by staying current with each account you have with your bank. If you're late with a payment on a loan, the bank may debit your checking account to satisfy that outstanding obligation. One problem will lead to another.

- Choose an account that suits you. If you know you can maintain a healthy balance in your checking account, make sure your account lets you collect interest on it. If you only keep enough to pay the bills, use an economy account — no bells and whistles, no penalties for dropping below the minimum balance. Talk with your banker about which of their checking accounts is best for you.

Pay bills online for more free time

If you're responsible for paying the bills, you know what's involved — paperwork, clutter, and lots of time. Wouldn't it be great if you were never bothered with tedious bill-paying chores again?

Judy Wicks, vice president of CheckFree, an online bill-paying service provider for over 1,200 banks, has great news for those who yearn to be free from bill-paying bondage.

Here are five good reasons to pay your bills online.

Convenience. "The average household pays 12 to 15 bills a month. You write a check and send it to the same company every month. That process takes two to four hours each month. You can cut that to literally 10 to 15 minutes," claims Wicks.

What's more, you can even download payment records from your bank's Web site into Quicken or Microsoft Money so you don't have to manually redo it all.

Control. Ever been charged a late fee? You may know you paid on time, but you can't prove it. Once you've dropped that check in the

Meet an online believer

"I'm a true believer in online financial services," says Bob Glantz, Vice President of Access Communications. "When I was a renter, my landlady lived right below me. I'd pay her every month via CheckFree. It was easier than writing a check, walking down the stairs, and slipping it under her door.

"It also lets me do things like send my nephew $20 on his birthday. It's a very cool service. No stamps, no envelopes, no muss and fuss."

mail or after-hours drop box, you have no control over the payment process.

"With CheckFree, if you want a bill paid by the 22nd, schedule it to be paid by the 22nd, and it's guaranteed to get there on time. You control when money comes out of your account, you're protected by a guarantee, and you have a more detailed history than you keep by hand. It's automatically recorded," Wick says.

Protection. "When you bank online, you're protected by a lot of legislation and regulations. Banks are responsible for protecting you at an even greater level than with checking. When people hear about identity theft, they assume the criminals are getting the information off the Internet. But they're getting your information from credit card statements and your mail — means that are a lot more accessible than trying to hack into a bank's Web site," Wick says.

"It's very, very safe. The banking system has been moving money among banks and merchants for years. Bank Web sites give you a level of convenience and efficiency you can't get from the paper system," she says.

Flexibility. "Use the service to send you reminders," says Wicks. Online bill paying has a cousin — e-billing. Bills are sent to your bank's Web site. "The e-bill can meet you at the bank's secure Web site." And you can ask them to send an e-mail to let you know when it arrives.

"And even if someone could get to your e-mail, all they can really do is pay your bill. They can't take money out of your account," Wick says.

"Your cable bill, for example, is the same every month. You can set it up to come out automatically. You get a notice. If you want to change it, you may. You can cancel it. You can change the amount — whatever," she says.

Simplicity. "Just go to your bank's Web site," says Wicks. "All the information is there. Good sites will lead you through the enrollment process. We make it easier and easier all the time."

But if you'd like someone to talk you through it, the people you know and respect at your bank will be glad to help you.

It's a great service. And bill paying is just the start. Have a child in college or a grandchild you'd like to send an allowance? Online banking services allow you to pay them just as if you were sending payment to a company, complete with better records than you could ever hope to keep in your checkbook ledger.

Consumer credit

Take charge of spending to end debt forever

Control credit for stress-free living

It's easy to get credit. Unfortunately, it's even easier to misuse it. But credit doesn't necessarily lead to debt and despair if you use it responsibly. Just make sure you have a budget that provides a cushion for unexpected expenses.

As important as it is to live a debt-free life, there may come a time when you need to establish credit. One simple way to accomplish this is to save a certain amount of money, say $2,000, then apply for a loan equal to that amount, using your savings as collateral. For a small amount of interest, you'll establish credit without putting yourself into debt. Just make sure you pay back the loan on time.

Once you establish yourself as a good credit risk, you'll probably receive credit card offers in your mailbox. Now comes the hard part — using that credit in a responsible manner.

Remember, a credit card does not give you a license to spend lavishly, and credit card debt usually carries a high interest rate. So stick to your budget. Use your card primarily for emergencies, for renting cars and other transactions that require a credit card, and to build your credit rating. If you control your credit instead of letting it control you, you'll free yourself of unnecessary stress.

You'll also avoid the downward financial spiral that many people sink into.

Noted personal finance expert Larry Burkett offers these three guidelines for using credit wisely:

- Never use a credit card to buy anything that is not in your budget for the month.

- Pay the entire credit card bill each month.

- The first month you find yourself unable to pay the total charges, destroy the cards.

Follow that advice — and the helpful tips in the following stories — and you'll be a credit to credit users everywhere.

Choose card carefully for best value

Don't be enticed by "pre-approved" credit card applications you get in the mail, even if your favorite team is proudly displayed on the card. If you decide you need a credit card, follow this advice from an expert.

Get the features you need. "Someone who pays the balance in full every month is looking for entirely different features than someone who carries a balance and is looking to reduce their interest charges," says Greg McBride, Senior Financial Analyst for Bankrate.com, a leading provider of consumer financial information.

If you carry a balance, interest rates and fees are most important. "Find a card with a low interest rate," says McBride, "and keep in mind that an annual fee is not automatically a deterrent."

Read the disclosure agreement. Look beyond the big bold letters advertising the interest rate and study the disclosure agreement. Be especially alert for policies that punish certain actions. Will one late payment throw you into a much higher rate cycle? These differ among both card issuers and the various cards they offer.

"The disclosure agreement is more important than the annual percentage rate (APR)," he warns. "The smaller the print, the more important the words."

McBride says to look at the day-to-day procedures. "What kind of billing cycle do they have? How much of a grace period do you have to get the payment in? And if you are doing a cash advance or balance transfer, how do those policies differ from that of purchases?"

Switching credit cards makes sense if you can get a lower interest rate. But watch out for high balance transfer fees, low introductory rates that skyrocket in six months, and any other fees that will make the move costlier than keeping your old card.

Weigh the fringe benefits. "Rewards and rebates really only benefit those who pay the balance in full every month," says McBride. "If you're carrying a balance, you should not be looking at these cards." Remember that rewards are not confined to frequent flyer miles or cash back anymore, so shop around.

Other differences in credit card features include insurance and warranties. Again, check the fine print for protection against rental car damage and flawed merchandise.

"It varies from card to card," McBride says. "If there's something of value to you, make it a point to investigate the specifics of it."

Consider all types. According to McBride, as long as the other terms are similar, the name on the card doesn't make a difference. MasterCard and Visa are credit card networks that license individual banks to issue cards. Discover is both a network and a card issuer. American Express and Diners Club are basically charge cards. You have to pay your bill in full every month, although they are beginning to add some credit options.

"It's the terms that really matter when you're comparison shopping," McBride says. "Things such as the interest rate, the fees, the grace period, the perks earned on rebate or reward cards."

'Can't miss' tips for using credit cards wisely

The Bible says the love of money is the root of all evil. Others might argue that credit cards deserve this distinction.

With a credit card, it's all too easy to live above your means. Want something? Just whip out your card. Before you know it, you'll find yourself buried in debt, unable to get any more credit, and seriously considering bankruptcy.

To remain debt free, you have to know when — and how — to use them. Here are some guidelines to help you use your plastic wisely.

Display discipline. Pay off your balance in full every month to avoid finance charges. If you discipline yourself, you get the benefit of a short-term, interest-free loan. That's assuming your card has a grace period. Look for one that does.

Pay promptly. Even if you don't pay in full every month, always pay on time. This will help you avoid hefty late fees and interest rate hikes. Always pay more than the minimum if you can afford it.

Take advantage of protection. Credit cards give you more protection than you get with cash, check, or debit cards. If something goes wrong, it's easier to resolve the problem and get your money back.

One area where credit cards come in handy is travel. In fact, you often need a major credit card to reserve a hotel room or rent a car. It's also safer to carry a credit card than large amounts of cash. And if your travel agency or airline goes bankrupt, you're protected if you used a credit card to book your trip.

Beware of hidden credit card penalties

John had a high balance on his credit card, but the low interest rate made it possible for him to manage his monthly payments. When the bank tripled his interest rate without warning, he was almost forced into bankruptcy.

A practice called universal default allows credit card companies to change your terms without notice. If you commit an error such as missing a payment, they can slap you with a penalty rate as high as 28 percent. And if you're late with a payment, you can now incur a hefty $39 fee.

Creditors can also monitor your credit report and raise your interest rate if they see you've made late payments on other accounts. Play it safe, and read the fine print of your credit card terms. If your account is subject to universal default, you may want to close it.

Reach your goal. Some cards feature rebates or other rewards. Maybe you'll earn free airline tickets or get cash back. If you're planning to get a card, you may want to consider one of these, but you still want to be careful. Don't make unnecessary purchases just to earn rebates. And make sure you pay the balance in full each month. Otherwise, you're putting yourself in debt for a freebie.

Shop around. Even if you're satisfied with your current credit card, keep your eyes open for better deals. You might save a significant amount of money by switching to a different card with better terms.

Watch out for traps. There are plenty of sneaky, but perfectly legal ways your credit card company can sock it to you.

For example, different methods of calculating your balance can make a big difference in how much you pay. The two-cycle average daily balance method can be the most costly.

Don't be seduced by wily credit card companies that want to take your money. Defend yourself against hidden charges.

One sneaky trick is to raise your credit limit. It might seem like your credit card company is doing you a favor, but it really wants you to charge more — and pay more in interest. Proceed with caution.

Those low "teaser" rates that companies use to lure you to a new card often skyrocket when the introductory rate expires. Also, watch out for over-limit, cash advance, balance transfer, and transaction fees.

Make sure you understand what you're getting into when you sign up for a credit card, and change cards if you're not being treated fairly.

Get what you want from credit card companies

Dissatisfied with the terms of your current credit card? Pick up the phone. Scott Bilker, author of *Talk Your Way Out of Credit Card Debt*, explains how you can get banks to waive fees, lower your interest rate, or increase your credit limit.

"Anyone can do it," Bilker says. "It takes persistence, organization, and patience. You also need to have credit options. You need to be able to transfer your balance to another card and fire your current credit card bank."

Get tough. Often, you just need to ask. You'll be surprised how easy it can be to get what you want. Other times, you might need to get tough and threaten to take your business elsewhere.

"Make it clear to them that you will transfer your balance to another credit card and close your account if they do not comply with your demands," Bilker says. Be prepared to follow through with your threat or else it has little power.

High cost of credit card freebies

It's great to get airline miles, cash back, free shipping, and other perks just for using your credit card. But these rewards programs can become a punishment if you're not careful.

Every time you get a new card, you're tempted by more credit. Give into the temptation and you could find yourself in debt. Resist it and you could hurt your credit rating by not using an open line of credit.

Never make freebies the main reason for choosing a card. If you have a card with a rewards program, keep things in perspective. Don't charge more than you can afford just to get a free DVD.

Climb the ladder. Don't take your first "no" for an answer. The first person you talk to might not have the power to change your terms — or any motivation for doing so.

"Never give up! Always ask to speak to a supervisor," Bilker says. "Make it clear that you are prepared to take your business — that is, their profits — to another bank if they don't do something. You may not be able to get the bank to reduce your rate by 10 percent, by why not 2 percent?"

Stay on their good side. You have a better chance at success if you've never been late with a payment and your account is in good standing.

"If you have a good relationship with the bank, then it should be fairly easy to get them to comply," Bilker says.

Study successful strategies. Bilker's book includes transcripts of 52 phone calls dealing with several types of negotiations. Not all of them worked, but all of them can shed valuable light on the haggling process.

"I wrote this book to prepare people for the call, and I have since received many responses from people that have saved thousands of dollars by calling their banks," Bilker says. "Nothing prepares you better than reading through actual calls that are similar to the one you're about to make."

For anonymity — and added amusement — the names of the banks in Bilker's book have been changed to dog breeds and the names of their representatives have been changed to bugs.

Make a pitch. You don't always have to threaten your bank. You can always offer another one your business — in return for favorable terms. That's why having available lines of credit comes in handy.

"Call a credit card bank that you have that has a zero balance and say, 'Hey, I'll transfer $1,000 to my account from another bank right now if you give me zero percent for six months with no transfer fees.' You might be surprised to find that you have existing low-rate deals available right now!" Bilker says.

"The bottom line — you must punish the banks that are charging you a high interest rate by transferring your balance to banks that treat you well and deserve your business."

Stop pre-approved credit offers

It's hard to handle rejection. But with dozens of pre-approved credit card offers cluttering your mailbox, it's hard to handle acceptance, too.

These offers are dangerous in two ways. Not only can the temptation of easy credit spell disaster to your budget and financial security, but the risk of identity theft rises with every credit card offer drifting through the postal system.

The solution is to "opt out." This means you stop the offers of pre-approved credit cards at the source — the credit bureaus. You have the choice of getting your name removed from the mailing list for two years or permanently.

You can opt out by calling toll-free 888-567-8688. You will be asked for personal information including your name, telephone number, and social security number. Don't get nervous — these details remain confidential and are only used to process your request.

Or opt out in writing. The Federal Trade Commission has even developed a sample letter you can use (see page 84). Send it to each major credit bureau at these addresses.

Contact: Equifax, Inc.
Options
P.O. Box 740123
Atlanta, GA 30374-0123

Experian
Consumer Opt-Out
701 Experian Parkway
Allen, TX 75013

TransUnion
Marketing List Opt Out
P.O. Box 97328
Jackson, MS 39288-7328

Guide to settling credit card disputes

What do an umbrella, a shield, and a credit card have in common? They all provide protection.

Sample opt-out letter

(Today's date)

To whom it may concern:

I request to have my name removed from your marketing lists. Here is the information you have asked me to include in my request:

FIRST, MIDDLE, and LAST NAME

(List all name variations, including Jr., Sr., etc.)

_____

CURRENT MAILING ADDRESS

_____

PREVIOUS MAILING ADDRESS

(Fill in your previous mailing address if you have moved in the last six months.)

_____

SOCIAL SECURITY NUMBER

_____

DATE OF BIRTH

_____

Thank you for your prompt handling of my request.

_____

(Your signature)

A credit card won't keep you dry during a rainstorm or block your enemies' swords and arrows, but it does come in handy if you have any disputes with merchants.

For example, maybe you were billed for an item you returned or never received. Maybe you were charged twice for the same item. Or maybe you noticed unauthorized charges on your bill.

Thanks to the Fair Credit Billing Act, you can fight back with a chargeback. Here's how it works.

Send a message. Pick up a pen, or sit down at your computer, and compose a letter to the creditor disputing the charges.

Make sure you write to the address for "billing inquiries." Include your name, address, account number, and a description of the billing error. Include copies of sales slips or other documents that support your position.

Send the letter certified mail, return receipt requested, so it arrives within 60 days after the first bill containing the error was mailed to you. The creditor must acknowledge the complaint within 30 days and resolve the dispute within 90 days.

Hold out. During this process, you don't have to pay the portion of the bill you're disputing, but you must still pay the rest of the bill. Disputing a bill will not hurt your credit rating.

If your bill did contain an error, the creditor must send you a letter explaining what corrections will be made. Your account will be credited and all finance charges and late fees related to the disputed item will be dropped.

On the other hand, if the creditor determines that the charges are correct, you'll receive a letter detailing how much you owe and why. You have a right to request documents that support this claim.

If you disagree with its findings, you can alert the creditor in writing within 10 days. You can make it clear that you refuse to pay the disputed amount. The creditor might begin collection procedures and report you as delinquent to the credit bureaus — but must also note that you don't think you owe the money.

Benefit from mistakes. If the creditor doesn't properly follow the settlement procedure, it cannot collect money from you, even if the bill is correct.

Possible infractions include taking too long to acknowledge or resolve your dispute and reporting or threatening to report your failure to pay during the dispute period.

Top tips to escape debt

Drowning in debt? Get practical advice from the experts for repairing your finances and your credit. Here are 10 steps you can take.

- Pay off credit card with the highest interest rate first.
- Consolidate your debt on one low-rate card.
- Try to pay more than the minimum due.
- Always make payments on time.
- Stick to a budget. Cut out unnecessary spending.
- Get a second job and put the money toward your debts.
- Sell investments or use your savings to pay off debts.
- Talk to a reputable credit counselor.
- Enroll in a debt management plan.

Work it out. If your problem does not involve a billing error, but rather a dispute over the quality of the goods or services you purchased, you still have some protection with a credit card.

In fact, you can take the same legal actions against your credit card issuer as you can against the seller under your state law.

To qualify for this protection, you must have made the purchase, for more than $50, in your home state or within 100 miles of your billing address. But these rules don't apply if the seller is the card issuer or the two have a special business relationship.

You must also make a good faith effort to resolve the dispute with the seller before taking any other action.

Dig your way out of credit card debt

Every time you pull out a credit card, it's like digging a deeper hole. Start climbing out of the hole and back onto solid financial footing.

April Lewis-Parks, educational and community outreach coordinator for Consolidated Credit Counseling Services, offers these tips to help you end credit card debt.

Stop charging. This is an obvious first step. Use your credit cards only for emergencies. Use cash or a debit card instead.

Find extra money. Take a close look at where your money is going. Chances are you'll "increase" your income simply by minimizing expenses.

"Track your spending and carefully prepare a budget including fixed and flexible expenses," Lewis-Parks says. "Many people are often surprised at how much money they spend on unnecessary or miscellaneous items. Once you are aware of money holes, use those savings to pay off your debts."

Shuffle your cards. While you're at it, list your cards by the interest rate they charge.

"Keep the one card with the lowest interest rate and cut up the others and close the accounts," Lewis-Parks says. "If you don't have a card with an interest rate of less than 14 percent, get one."

Transfer your high interest rate balances to one card with a low interest rate. It's a good way to end credit card debt fast without paying more each month.

Speed things up. Of course, paying more works even better. Paying only the minimum you owe can keep you in debt forever. If you owe $1,000 on a card with a 17-percent interest rate, it might take 12 years and cost over $900 in interest by the time you pay it off.

"Calculate how much you can pay over the minimum. Really stretch your budget," Lewis-Parks says. "For instance, let's suppose the minimum payments on your credit cards total $350 a month. What could you pay if you really stretched? How about $750? No pain, no gain."

Think big. If you don't — or can't — transfer your balances to a low-rate card, prioritize.

"Apply all your additional funds toward the card with the highest interest rate," Lewis-Parks says. "If two cards have the same rate, put the additional money on the card with the largest balance. Pay the minimum on your lowest interest rate credit cards until you've paid off the balance on the more expensive cards."

Raid the piggybank. If you have savings, use that money to get out of debt.

"Sure, it sounds harsh," Lewis-Parks says. "But if you put together a balance sheet, your debt would cancel out your savings anyway. If they're in the bank, you're earning just over 3.2 percent to carry debt at 18 percent or more."

Get help for buying addiction

Like alcohol, drugs, or gambling, buying on credit can be addictive. It can also keep you buried in debt. Luckily, if things get out of control, you can get help with Debtors Anonymous.

Based on the principles of Alcoholics Anonymous, this organization also features a 12-step program and regular meetings. Its stated purpose is "to live without incurring any unsecured debt one day at a time and to help other compulsive debtors achieve solvency."

Find a D.A. meeting near you by visiting its Web site at *www.debtorsanonymous.org.* Or send an e-mail to new@debtorsanonymous.org.

You can also write to Debtors Anonymous General Service Office, P.O. Box 920888, Needham, MA 02492-0009 or call 781-453-2743.

Get help. Sometimes, even your best efforts fall short. If you need help, you can contact a credit counselor. A good one will offer budgeting and money management education as well as a debt management plan.

With a debt management plan, the credit counseling agency works with your creditors to reduce or eliminate interest rates and fees. You make one monthly payment to the agency, which then pays your creditors. It's a customized plan to get you out of debt in one to five years.

"To avoid any of the bad things you may have heard about credit counseling, make sure you choose a nonprofit agency that spends at least 60 minutes discussing your situation and discloses to you all fees and payments required of you before you sign an agreement," Lewis-Parks says.

"Insist on getting a spending plan or budget as part of the process. Any agency that will not provide such a plan is not interested in you — it is interested only in fees. Don't do business with them. They can complicate your life more than you can imagine."

Get debt collectors off your back

You get a sickening feeling every time the phone rings. You dread picking it up because a debt collector might be calling. Again.

"Owing money to creditors that you cannot afford to pay is stressful enough," says Consolidated Credit Counseling Services spokeswoman April Lewis-Parks.

"But being hounded by debt collectors about your unpaid debts can make life a living hell — especially if the debt collectors use threats and scare tactics to get you to pay up."

Fortunately, the Fair Debt Collection Practices Act (FDCPA) protects you from such tactics. Under the FDCPA, debt collectors cannot:

- Call you at an inconvenient place or time, such as before 8 a.m. or after 9 p.m., unless you give them permission to do so.

- Call you at work if they know your employer does not want you to be called there. Also, they cannot contact your employer about your debt.

- Contact you by postcard or use an envelope that makes it clear it was sent by a debt collector.

- Try to scare you into paying a debt by sending you a letter that appears to have come from a government agency or a court of law.

- Call you repeatedly within a short period of time — every hour during an afternoon, or day after day, for example.

Pay back your pals

There are advantages to borrowing from friends and family. If they charge you interest, chances are it will be much lower than what you'd get from a bank. They won't report you to a credit bureau if you can't pay them back.

But you still must treat this debt seriously. Your credit rating is one thing, your personal relationships are quite another. Don't risk damaging them over money. Be as committed to repaying them as you are to repaying your credit card company. If you can, pay them back first.

To make things more official, put the terms and conditions of your personal loans in writing. And make sure to honor them.

- Contact your neighbors, relatives, friends, or other people to get information that can help them collect the money you owe.

- Use profanity when communicating with you.

- Threaten to ruin your reputation, harm you or your property, or throw you in jail unless you pay your debt. They can threaten to sue you, assuming they are willing to follow through on their threat.

- Order you to accept their collect calls or pay for their telegrams.

- Collect more than the amount you owe, unless it is allowed under your state's law.

- Deposit a post-dated check before its date.

- Take your property or threaten to take it unless they are legally entitled to.

Best of all, you can put an end to phone calls from debt collectors. Send them a letter, and they have to stop calling. It's the law.

Sample debt collector letter

(Your name)
(Your address)
(Your city, state, and zip code)

(Today's Date)

(Name of the contact person, if you have one)
(Company name)
(Company street address)
(Company city, state, and zip code)

Dear (contact person) or To whom it may concern:

(Company name) has contacted me regarding a debt you say I owe to (name of original lender). I do not want you to call me again regarding this debt.

As you should know, the Fair Debt Collection Practices Act, a federal law, says you may now contact me only to say there will be no further contact or to notify me that you or the creditor intends to take some specific action.

Sincerely,

(Your name)

(Your account number, if applicable)

"Write the debt collector to state that you do not want to be contacted again. The debt collector must comply with your request," Lewis-Parks says. "However, it can send you a notice confirming that it won't contact you again or informing you of a specific collection action that it intends to take."

Remember, you still owe the debt. You just won't be constantly pestered to pay it. You can use the sample letter above as a guide.

Rebuild your credit rating

The Motion Picture Association of America rates movies as G (General Audiences), PG (Parental Guidance suggested) or R (Restricted).

If you have a bad credit report, these letters could stand for Gruesome, Pretty Grim, and Rotten. But that doesn't mean you'll always be a flop at the box office.

April Lewis-Parks, spokeswoman for Consolidated Credit Counseling Services, offers these tips for rebuilding a bad credit rating.

Review your report. First, you need to look at your current credit report. Since the three major credit bureaus — Equifax, Experian, and Trans Union — don't share information, it's a good idea to order a report from each one. Scour each report closely for the following problems.

- mistakes in personal information, including your name, Social Security Number, or addresses

- mistakes in account listings, such as late payments that aren't correct, outdated balances, or duplicate listings of the same account

- negative items, including bankruptcies, judgments, liens, collection accounts, or late payments

- inquiries from companies you don't recognize

"When a company reviews your credit report, it creates an inquiry," Lewis-Parks explains. "While they may be legitimate, inquiries into your report from companies you don't know can sometimes indicate fraud."

Dispute mistakes. If you do find mistakes or incorrect information in your report, make sure to act. Contact the lender, court, or collection agency that furnished the information and ask them to investigate it. Or contact the credit bureaus and ask them to verify the information. If they can't confirm the information you dispute, it must be removed from your report.

"If the information is old, the account has been sold, or the creditor is simply too busy, it may simply be removed when you challenge it," Lewis-Parks says. "There's no guarantee that will happen, but it does sometimes work."

Take your time. If you have negative, but accurate, information on your credit report, time will heal your credit wounds.

"As the negative information becomes older, it will be less important," Lewis-Parks says. "This is especially true if it is more than two years old."

If you have unpaid tax liens or judgments, you must pay them before the clock starts ticking for them to be removed from your report.

Cosign at your own risk

Mike just wanted to help his son Nick buy a new car. He ended up doing more harm than good – to his own credit rating.

By cosigning the loan for Nick's car, Mike put himself at risk. When Nick, not the most responsible young man, stopped making his car payments, the lender came after Mike.

Eventually, the car was repossessed. The whole experience damaged Mike's once-perfect credit rating and made it harder for him to get a loan when he needed it.

"If I had it to do over again," Mike says, "I'd think twice before cosigning."

Order your free credit report

An update to the Fair Credit Reporting Act, effective Dec. 1, 2004, allows you to get one free credit report annually from each of the three major credit bureaus by contacting a central third-party organization.

This service is being implemented gradually across the country. Check the Federal Trade Commission Web site at *www.ftc.gov/opa/2004/06/freeannual* for information on when it will be available in your state.

If you need your credit information right away, Experian offers a free report once per year at its Web site *www.freecreditreport.com.*

Establish good credit. You can speed up the process by taking some action while you wait. Positive credit references will help improve your report.

That means having three or four active accounts, including credit cards, car loans, and mortgages, and making payments on time each month.

"If your credit report is damaged and you are having a hard time getting credit, consider a secured card," Lewis-Parks says. These cards require you to put up a security deposit with the issuer. Then use the card like any other credit card. If you pay on time, you can eventually get your deposit back.

Ask for a break. Hard times can hit anyone. Maybe an unexpected illness, a brief period of unemployment, or some other crisis forced you to fall behind on your bills.

If you've paid on time for at least three months since then, you might be able to get the lender to remove the negative information, a process called "re-aging" the account.

"It may take a few phone calls to find the right person who can help, so be patient," Lewis-Parks says.

Give your credit score a boost

When it comes to credit, you should know the score. Your credit score, that is. A credit score is a three-digit number from 300 to 850 that serves as a snapshot of your credit report at any given time.

Ryan Sjoblad, spokesman for Fair Isaac Corporation — the company that created the credit, or FICO, score — explains how this important number works.

"The higher the number, the less likely you are to go delinquent on your accounts in the next 90 days," Sjoblad says. Lenders often just look at your credit score rather than wade through your entire credit report to determine if you're a credit-worthy risk. You get better rates with higher scores.

Take a peek. Who gets to see this magic number? You can look at your own score. So can lenders preparing to offer you a loan or companies about to offer you credit. Your employer might even sneak a peek.

"Sometimes employers will take a look at the score to see if you're a risk to be handling their company's money, especially if you're applying for an accounting job or something like that," Sjoblad says. "They might take a look at you and see if you're responsible with your own money. Then you'll probably be responsible with your company's money."

But no one else can look at your score without permission. Make that scores. You actually have three credit scores, one from each of the three major credit bureaus.

"A lender is not required to send information to any of the bureaus, let alone all three of them. Information from the bureau level can be slightly different, and so your FICO scores can be different," Sjoblad says, "If you're getting ready to apply for a loan, it's always a good idea to check all three scores."

To do this easily, all in one place, go to *www.myfico.com*. The median credit score is 720. That should be high enough to qualify you for the lowest rates — but it depends on each lender's own cutoff.

Learn the recipe. What goes into a credit score? "It's solely from information that's available in your credit report," Sjoblad says. "Factors that don't go into your score are things like income, age, race, sex, location, that sort of thing. Those things do not factor into the score."

Now, here's what does factor into your credit score.

- Payment history, the biggest factor, comprises 35 percent of your score. "How you paid in the past is a good indication of how you're going to pay in the future," Sjoblad says.

- Amount owed counts for 30 percent. This includes all your balances on your credit cards. "For example, if you have a whole bunch of credit cards that are near maxed out, that's not going to factor as well as if you have a $100 balance on your credit cards and you paid it off at the end of the month," Sjoblad says.

- Length of credit history is worth about 15 percent. "It makes sense that somebody just coming out of college or just coming into the workforce and has no length of credit history might be a bigger risk than somebody who has been out for a while and has established a long credit history," Sjoblad says.

- New credit counts for 10 percent. Applying for new credit in the past 60 to 90 days has the biggest effect. "If people are going out and all of a sudden getting six, seven, eight new credit cards all at once, it may be an indication that something might be going on with them financially. You kind of keep an eye on that. It may lower your score," Sjoblad says.

- Types of credit used makes up the final 10 percent. You want a healthy mix of credit. "Somebody who has, for example, a mortgage, an auto loan, and maybe two or three credit cards, that's a pretty good, responsible use of credit," Sjoblad says. "Somebody who has no mortgage, no auto loans, and 25 maxed-out credit cards, for example, shows less responsible use and that may factor into your score."

Improve your score. If your credit score seems a little low, don't worry. You can take steps to correct that.

"The good thing about credit scores is that, unlike a credit report, you can change it over time. It's something you can take action on. You can improve it," Sjoblad says.

Sjoblad suggests trying these three tactics to boost your credit score.

- Pay your bills on time.

- Pay down the balances, especially on credit cards.

- Take out credit only when you really need it.

Then let time handle the rest. "The farther you get away from your bad history, the less and less influence it's going to have on your new history," Sjoblad says. "The recent history is the most important history."

How to foil 'card' sharks

You're probably wise enough to stay out of high-stakes poker games with shady card sharks. But every day, you're gambling with a different set of cards — your credit cards.

Credit card fraud makes up a whopping 33 percent of all identity theft crimes, according to a Federal Trade Commission study. That's because there are so many ways someone can steal your credit card information.

An identity thief might snag a credit card offer from your mailbox or trash can and get a card in your name. Or he might simply steal your wallet, find that credit card you lost, or use the telephone or Internet to trick you into revealing your credit card information.

One of the sneakiest tricks is called "skimming." Betsy Broder, assistant director of the FTC's Bureau of Consumer Protection, explains how this works.

"We've seen skimming used in places, like restaurants, where you give your credit card over and it disappears. You give it to the waiter and they process it. Some corrupt waiters may be carrying a skimmer, which is really no larger than a pager, in a pocket," Broder says.

"They process your meal expense, but then they also run your credit card through this device, which captures all of the data on the magnetic card and enables them to create new cards with your credit account number and all of the stored data in that mag strip."

That could lead to a very expensive meal — one you'll be paying for long after it's been digested.

"If you choose to use credit cards in transactions, the card will be out of your sight and there's no way to control how someone's going to use it," Broder says. "You can't follow the waiter back to the kitchen as they're processing your credit card. But you can protect your rights after the fact."

Thanks to the Fair Credit Billing Act, you are not liable for fraud-ulent use of your credit card. There is a $50 deductible, but Broder says that's usually waived. The key is to spot the fraudulent charges and act quickly.

"The best way to protect yourself is to review very carefully your statement every month," Broder says. "If you see that there are charges on your account that you did not make or authorize, you dis-pute them with the credit card issuer immediately and in writing."

Not all identity thieves resort to high-tech gadgets. To thwart these common pickpockets, the advice is simple — don't carry around extra credit cards.

"We're just carrying too much documentation, too many credit cards that we rarely use. Limit what you carry," Broder says. "If your whole wallet gets stolen, it's much easier to call one or two creditors rather than seven or eight."

Protect your identity from thieves

It sounds like something out of a science-fiction movie, "Invasion of the Identity Snatchers," but identity theft is a very real crime.

Could someone steal your identity to get to your money? It hap-pens all the time. And about 50 percent of the victims don't even know how their information was stolen.

"Identity theft is often an invisible crime," says Betsy Broder of the Federal Trade Commission. "People don't know how it hap-pened, when it happened, unless there's a definite event such as having your wallet or purse stolen."

Has someone stolen your identity? Find out how it's done and what you need to do to protect yourself.

ID theft complaints by year				
1999	**2000**	**2001**	**2002**	**2003**
1,380	31,117	86,212	161,836	214,905

Source: Federal Trade Commission

Know your enemy. Besides the most common method of stealing your wallet or purse, here are just some of the ways identity thieves operate. They might:

- rummage through your trash for personal information.

- steal your mail, including bank and credit card statements, pre-approved credit offers, new checks, and tax information.

- fill out a change of address form to divert your mail to another location.

- obtain your credit report by posing as a landlord or employer.

- trick you into giving out information by posing as legitimate companies or government agencies.

- get your information from a place of business, either by stealing files, bribing an employee who has access to your files, or hacking into electronic files.

Once they get your information, they can run up charges on your credit card account, open new credit card or bank accounts in your name, make counterfeit checks or debit cards and drain your account, establish phone or wireless service in your name, take out auto loans in your name, and generally make a mess of your credit rating. You might even find yourself being arrested for crimes committed by your "evil twin."

So now that you know how identity thieves can acquire and misuse your personal information, how do you protect yourself? You can't guard against everything, but you can take some simple steps to make identity theft less likely.

> Identity theft costs time and money. According to a recent Federal Trade Commission survey, the average victim spends $500 and 30 hours to resolve problems related to the crime.

Safeguard your SSN. "Keep your private information private," Broder says. "First of all, open up your wallet and look at what you're carrying around. You shouldn't be carrying around your Social Security card. And try to avoid carrying anything that has your Social Security Number on it."

Speaking of Social Security Numbers, don't be too social with yours. Over 290 million Americans have one of these — the main target of identity theft. Know the law. Many may ask, but only these three need to know your Social Security Number.

- your employer

- your bank or any financial institution that's involved with taxes or income

- credit bureau, when you're requesting a copy of your credit report. Also, if you're opening a credit account, the company might want to check your credit record and will need your Social Security Number.

Some states, but very few, still require your Social Security Number for your driver's license. "If you ask to have another number used in place of the Social Security Number, generally they will accommodate you," Broder says.

Other companies might ask for your Social Security Number, but you're not legally compelled to give it to them. Keep in mind they can refuse to do business with you if you decline.

Skip ID theft services

With all the dire warnings about identity theft, you might be tempted to invest in identity theft insurance or subscribe to a credit report monitoring service.

Consumer Reports says don't bother. These services generally aren't worth the money. Insurance costs up to $50 a year but provides limited coverage that rarely includes the money you lost from the crime.

Instead of paying up to $150 a year for someone else to monitor your credit report, just order an annual report from each of the three major credit bureaus. You're entitled to one free report each year.

Look before you leap. You might be a generous person, but when it comes to your personal information, be stingy.

"Be careful how you give out information, making certain that when you do provide information, you know who you're giving it to and how it will be used," Broder says.

Watch out for slick telephone scams. For example, you might get a call from someone claiming to be a representative of your bank who needs to verify some information, like your credit card number.

"Call back at a telephone number you know is associated with that institution and confirm the legitimacy of that phone call," Broder says. "You just need to be very wary when people ask for your information."

Here are some other steps the FTC recommends to make things harder for identity thieves.

- Guard your mail. Promptly remove mail from your mailbox. Deposit outgoing mail in a post office collection box or at the local post office. Put a hold on your mail if you're going on vacation.

- Tear or shred mail that contains personal information. Don't just toss this junk mail in the trash. This includes receipts, medical statements, bank statements, insurance forms, expired charge cards, and pre-approved credit offers.

- Pay attention to billing cycles. If your bill is late, contact your creditor. An identity thief may have changed the billing address on the account.

- Place passwords on your credit card, bank, and phone accounts. Don't use an easy-to-guess password, like your mother's maiden name or your date of birth.

- Make sure personal information is in a safe, secure place in your home, especially if you employ outside help or are having service work done.

Act fast to limit identity theft damage

Over 30,000 people had their identities stolen in the year 2000 alone. By the time most of them realized what had happened, over a year had passed.

Even though you must spend your own time and money repairing the damage, it's essential you do so. Identity theft can ruin your life. You could be denied credit, mortgages, jobs, educational opportunities, and even arrested for crimes committed in your name.

The international non-profit network Call for Action urges you to watch out for these warning signs that someone has stolen your identity.

- You suddenly stop receiving monthly bank statements or credit card bills.

- You start getting bills from companies you don't recognize.

- You are denied loans or credit for no reason you can think of.

- Collection agencies begin contacting you about debts you didn't create.

Acting fast is key in limiting the damage. Take these emergency steps set out by the Federal Trade Commission (FTC) as soon as you suspect your identity has been stolen.

Ask for fraud alerts. Notify the fraud department of one of the three major credit bureaus and ask them to place a fraud alert on your credit file. They will notify the other two bureaus and have them do the same. This alert flags your file so creditors will contact you before they open any new accounts in your name or make changes to your existing accounts.

This initial alert will expire after a certain amount of time, and you must call each bureau to renew it. Contact them at these numbers to report the fraud.

Equifax	800-525-6285
Experian	888-397-3742
TransUnion	800-680-7289

Look over your credit reports. As soon as you have placed fraud alerts, each bureau will send you a free copy of your credit report. Look it over carefully for suspicious activity — like accounts you didn't open or unexplained debts.

Sample credit bureau dispute letter

(Date)
(Your name)
(Your address)
(Your city, state, and zip code)

Complaint Department
(Name of credit bureau)
(Their address)
(Their city, state, and zip code)

Dear Sir or Madam:

I am writing to dispute the following information in my file. The items I dispute also are circled on the attached copy of the report I received. (Identify which items you are disputing by the name of the source – such as creditors or tax court – and the type of item – such as credit account, judgment, etc.)

I am a victim of identity theft, and did not make the charge(s). I am requesting that the item be blocked to correct my credit report.

Enclosed are copies of (mention any documentation you are including – such as a police report) supporting my position. Please investigate this matter and block the disputed item(s) as soon as possible.

Sincerely,

(Your name)

Enclosure(s): (List the documents you are enclosing.)

Order your reports periodically the first year following the crime, then at least once a year after. Use the sample letter from the FTC on the opposite page to dispute fraudulent activity on your report, and send it to the bureaus at these addresses.

Contact: Equifax
P.O. Box 740241
Atlanta, GA 30374-0241

Experian
P.O. Box 9530
Allen, TX 75013

TransUnion
Fraud Victim Assistance Division
P.O. Box 6790
Fullerton, CA 92634

Close your accounts. Contact credit card companies, utility companies, banks, lenders, and other creditors, and ask to speak with someone in their security or fraud department. First, close any existing accounts you know the thief tampered with, as well as any new accounts he opened. Next, open new accounts with different passwords and PINs (personal identification numbers). Don't go for the obvious — like your mother's maiden name, your birthday, phone number, or the last four digits of your social security number. These are too easy to guess.

Write letters to dispute debts. Phone calls aren't enough. It's crucial to tell your creditors about the fraud in writing. Otherwise, they could still hold you liable for the bad debts.

- To challenge charges made to one of your existing accounts, mail a dispute letter to the creditor telling them which charges are fraudulent. Use the sample letter in this chapter from the FTC.

- To dispute new accounts a thief opened in your name, fill out an ID Theft Affidavit — a form put out by the FTC — and mail it to the creditor. You can print the Affidavit off the Internet at *www.consumer.gov / IDTheft / recovering_idt.html*. Or order a copy by calling toll-free 877-FTC-HELP.

  Some creditors may require you to fill out one of their own fraud forms. Ask which they prefer when you call.

- Insist the creditor send you a letter saying they have forgiven the fraudulent debts and closed the unauthorized accounts. You may need this information in writing if these same bad debts reappear on your credit report.

File a police report. An official police report builds your case and may protect you from creditors collecting on fraudulent debts. Give the police as much information as you can, then get a copy of the report. Your creditors may need proof of the crime to forgive the debts. Plus, the credit bureaus will automatically block or erase any fraudulent activity from your credit report if you send them a police report.

Complain to the FTC. File a complaint about the crime with the FTC. This government agency tracks trends in identity theft and gathers information to help solve future cases. Filing a complaint also helps government officials understand how widespread this crime is. Call the FTC's Identity Theft Hotline toll-free at 877-438-4338, or file a complaint through their Web site at *www.consumer.gov / idtheft*.

Organize correspondence. You could spend weeks or even months undoing the damage from ID theft. The FTC offers these tips to help keep you organized.

- Keep a notebook. Write down the name and company of everyone you speak with, what they told you, and the date of the conversation.

- Follow up all phone conversations in writing.

- Make copies of every piece of correspondence you mail regarding your case.

- Only mail copies — not originals — of police reports, sales slips, or other supporting documents. Keep the originals in your own files.

- Send all correspondence by certified mail and request a return receipt. This way you can prove the date a creditor received your letter.

- Save your files, even after you think the case is closed. Problems could crop up later.

You are never alone when dealing with identity theft. Many consumer groups offer counseling and step-by-step help.

Contact: Call for Action
301-657-7490
www.CallForAction.org

National Fraud Information Center
800-876-7060
www.fraud.org

Identity Theft Resource Center
858-693-7935
www.IDTheftCenter.org

Outsmart high-tech thieves

Computers and the Internet make your life easier in many ways. Unfortunately, they also make identity theft easier for high-tech criminals.

"A lot of identity theft is still pretty low-tech. People go through your trash," says Betsy Broder of the Federal Trade Commission.

"But on the other hand, the Internet makes it easier sometimes to gain, to gather information. And you can open up credit accounts online without having to validate your identity or show any other identifying information."

Here's how to protect your private information while using your home computer.

Play it smart with passwords. You need plenty of passwords while computing. Make it harder for computer criminals to guess yours and access your information. Pick passwords at least six characters long. Use a combination of letters and numbers, and mix uppercase and lowercase letters. Don't use any part of your name or any significant numbers, like your birthday or telephone number. Don't use the same password for everything.

Snatch a patch. Check for the latest security patches. They're usually free from the software maker's Web site. They prevent hackers from taking advantage of new security holes in browsers and other software.

Fight back with firewalls. One problem with a continuous Internet connection, like you have with DSL or cable, is that you leave your computer open to anyone on the Internet who wants to get into your system and cause mischief. Block them out with a piece of software called a firewall. It will protect your files from tampering.

Vanquish viruses. Install anti-virus software, such as Norton Antivirus or McAfee's VirusScan. Keep the software enabled and running. Make sure to get virus updates several times each month.

Remain detached. Don't open an e-mail attachment if you don't recognize who sent it to you. You could be opening a can of worms.

Accept no imitations. Sometimes e-mails and Web pages that look legitimate really aren't. Beware of a clever scam called "phishing."

With a phishing scam, you receive an e-mail that appears to come from your credit card issuer or Internet service provider, telling you there's some problem with your account. You then click on a link that asks you to provide identifying information. It might ask

Avoid being a victim of identity theft

Angela retrieved the box of new checks from her mailbox without suspecting her life was about to change. She wasn't aware someone had stolen a booklet of checks from the box. The thief forged checks, got a fake ID in Angela's name, and passed bad checks all over the state.

Angela didn't realize her identity had been stolen until she started receiving nasty calls from creditors. She filed a police report, documented everything, and reported any fraudulent activity right away.

"Acting quickly and staying on top of things made it easier to deal with problems as they came up," she says. Eventually, she was able to restore her good name. But she stays vigilant to avoid being a victim again. She has also made one important change. "Now I pick up my new checks at the bank rather than have them sent to my home," she says.

for your Social Security number, bank account number, bank routing number, credit card number, or PIN.

"It looks as if you're putting this information into a legitimate form sponsored by your bank or service provider," Broder says. "In fact, most likely it's going into someone's database from which they will create new accounts or misuse your existing accounts. It is certainly a growing problem."

Contact your bank or service provider before responding to this kind of message.

Shop safely. It's hard to beat the convenience of online shopping. That's one good reason to avoid it. If you do decide to buy something online, remember to follow these guidelines.

- Stick to familiar companies. Avoid companies that don't have a phone number, street address, or other contact information readily available.

- Check with the Better Business Bureau before ordering if you're not sure about a company.

- Look for a secure server. You can tell if a Web site is secure by the unbroken padlock or key symbol in the browser corner. You might get a Security Notice dialog box that says you are entering a secure page. Or you may see "https" in the address line. Make sure the site uses encryption, or a secret code, to store your information.

- Read the site's privacy policy. Only do business with sites that won't share your personal information with other businesses.

- Don't register with the site if you don't have to. If you choose to register, fill out only "required" fields on the registration form. Never give out your Social Security number. No shopping site should need it.

- Print out a copy of your transaction with proof of payment listed, and keep it with your records.

Communicate cautiously. Take the following precautions to help your private e-mails stay private.

- Don't share the password to your e-mail account with anyone. Always sign out when you close your e-mail connection.

- Read and compose messages offline, then go online to send them. Less time online means less danger.

- Save copies of personal e-mails on a floppy disk or CD and store them in a private place. If you leave them on your computer, a hacker may find them.

- Check out your mail program's encryption option. It scrambles messages between your computer and that of the recipient so no one else can read them.

- Never e-mail your Social Security number or credit card number to anyone. In fact, think twice before you send anything in an e-mail you wouldn't post on a bulletin board.

Zip your lip. Chat rooms are a great way to meet people and make new friends who share similar interests. But don't be too chatty.

Never give your real name, address, or other personal information in a chat room. Even if you don't intentionally reveal yourself, you'd be surprised at the clues you can innocently drop into a conversation — where you live, if you live alone, when you plan to be away from home, even your financial status.

The problem is, people can pretend to be anyone they choose online. That friendly grandmother you share family stories with could really be a 30-year-old male con artist. But that shouldn't keep you from enjoying online connections. Just don't be too trusting.

Essential financial advice for women

One common symbol of wealth is the tuxedoed and monocled Monopoly man. But making money is not a game, and men shouldn't have a monopoly on financial knowledge.

Janet C. Bechman of the Purdue University Cooperative Extension Service specializes in women's financial issues. Here's her advice for becoming more comfortable handling money.

Learn the basics. It's tough to win at Monopoly if you don't play — or even know the rules.

"One of the most important steps for women to take is to be involved in financial decisions and management," Bechman says. "They can ask questions of spouses and make sure they understand how and what is happening with the household finances."

Various publications, workshops, classes, programs, and Web sites can all help you with basic and more advanced information. Look for financial management programs through your county's Cooperative Extension Service or a local financial institution or nonprofit organization.

"Some of these programs are targeted specifically for women to help them learn the basics in a nonthreatening environment," Bechman says.

Do it yourself. Do you have a joint checking account with your spouse? Believe it or not, you also need an individual checking account. Here's why.

"Many women are on their own at some point in their lives. They need to know how to manage checking accounts and credit cards along with other financial tools to reach their goals and provide adequate financial resources for themselves," Bechman says.

"Women outlive men, which means that many married women will be widows and will be responsible for financial decisions."

Bechman also notes that 50 percent of marriages end in divorce and approximately 20 percent of women choose to remain single throughout life.

Get organized. Enter the world of money management without a map, and you'll end up wandering aimlessly. "It's important to set goals, have a plan for reaching goals, and review the goals and plans on a regular basis," Bechman says. "Good recordkeeping can be an asset in financial management."

Discuss dollars and cents. Take an active interest in your money and ask questions. "Good communication among family members and financial advisors is critical," Bechman says. "Don't be afraid to ask questions and keep asking until the answers are clear and understandable. Don't procrastinate about learning about finances. Don't turn over all financial decisions to someone else and not pay attention. No one else cares as much about your money as you do."

Overcome obstacles. Some people still have the old-fashioned notion that it's not a woman's role to manage money. But often the biggest obstacle is your own attitude.

"Having a positive attitude about managing money can have a big effect on how well people do managing money," Bechman says. "Being involved in financial decisions and practices is the best way to learn and gain confidence in financial skills."

Take small steps. You don't have to become a financial wizard all at once. Just make slow, steady progress. "Set a specific money management goal for this week or this month," Bechman says. "Set a goal to read an article about financial information. Go to a one-hour class on a financial management topic. Ask someone to explain how to balance a checkbook or to read a credit card statement or investment report. Find a friend who also wants to learn about financial matters and sign up for a class together."

The important thing is to start now — no matter what your age. "It's never too late to learn and begin taking control of your money," Bechman says.

Home and auto

Savvy strategies for paying less and saving more

Pay off your mortgage faster

You own a $150,000 home and a 30-year mortgage. So the house cost you $150,000, right?

You don't really believe that, but you'll be stunned when you see how much it actually costs. If you have a fixed rate of 6.64 percent, you'll end up paying an extra $196,304 in interest alone.

But wait — you don't have to pay that much interest. Mortgage prepayment is the solution you've been hoping for.

How it works. "Mortgage prepayment reduces the amount of money you actually owe," says family economics specialist Nancy Granovsky of Texas A&M University. "By prepaying, you reduce the principal on your overall mortgage. You can't owe interest on principal you've already paid down."

How it's done. "The method most people use involves paying additional sums applied to the principal each month. But make sure the financial institution allows for prepayment," says Granovsky. Before you send the check, find out if there's a prepayment penalty written into your contract.

"For people who send a coupon with their monthly payment, there's often a line on the coupon that says 'additional payment toward principal.' If they fill that out correctly and make it clear they've added $100, then it should be credited correctly."

Some lenders recommend that the regular mortgage payment and the prepayment be sent on separate checks, with a special designation, "for prepaid principal," in the memo blank of the prepayment check.

If your mortgage payment is automatically withdrawn from your checking or savings account, prepayment may be a little more complicated since you may not know where to send an extra check. So first thing, find out where to send your prepayment check.

What it takes. You'll be rewarded for whatever prepayment you make. Some borrowers may have enough monthly income to double

Prepaying pays off

If you chip away at the principal, loans don't linger as long. Just ask Joe and Judy Collaro.

When the Collaros bought a vacation home at the shore, they decided to send a little extra money with each mortgage payment. They accounted for this extra expense in their monthly budget — but didn't realize just how effective their strategy would be.

In fact, they ended up making too many payments because they paid off their mortgage much more quickly than expected. Finally, the bank gave them the good news that they owned their home — and a hefty refund check for the amount they had overpaid.

"What a pleasant surprise," Judy says. "We paid off our mortgage early and had some bonus money to celebrate the occasion."

their regular mortgage payment. Others may pay an additional $50 or $100.

There are other possibilities, as well. "Early retirees or people who are in a pre-retirement planning phase," says Granovsky, "may have elderly parents who eventually pass. They are perhaps going to come into a little bit of money. That means they'll have lump sums of money they may want to use toward the principal on their own mortgage."

What's the point? "The advantage of paying off a mortgage early is that you'll have money to do other things," Granovsky says. "It's for people who need money for retirement. Maybe they haven't maxed out on their contributions to individual retirement accounts. Paying off a mortgage early can free up enough money for people to go on a savings binge for a while."

Save big with a shorter mortgage

You've got another home in your plans. This time it'll be in a community with the amenities and services you'll need to live comfortably throughout your golden years.

Remember when you bought your first home? You probably had a 30-year mortgage. That final payment must have seemed a long way off.

But things are different now. You have lots of equity in your home, and retirement is near. But new homes can be expensive, and you're not interested in another 30-year loan.

Keep it short. It's time to consider a 15-year, or shorter, mortgage. Your monthly payments may be higher, but you'll pay a lot less interest. One thing is for certain — when you choose a shorter term, you'll save thousands of dollars.

Texas A&M University professor and family economics specialist Nancy Granovsky says, "I think anybody who is 60 or even 65 and in pre-retirement could be considering a 15-year mortgage. If they have the financial wherewithal for it, and it fits their budget, the likelihood that they'll qualify for a 15-year mortgage is pretty good."

> A lender who shaves a single point off the interest on a 15-year, $100,000 house loan will save you around $100 every month and nearly $20,000 over the life of the loan.

Save a bundle. Bankrate.com offers a sample comparison on their Web site of a 30-year and a 15-year mortgage on $150,000 that makes the savings really clear. The monthly payment on the 30-year loan is $961. On the 15-year plan, you'll pay $1,274 — a difference of $313 a month. If you can handle that difference, it will reduce your overall interest payout by $117,001.

But even if a 30-year mortgage is all you can qualify for, there are more ways than one to shorten the term, whittle away at the principal, and substantially reduce the interest you pay on your mortgage. (See *Pay off your mortgage faster* earlier in this chapter.)

However you do it, shorten your mortgage and you'll save a bundle. You're sure to find better ways to spend $100,000 than on mortgage interest.

Maximize your refinancing options

Refinancing can be a shrewd move if it will actually save you money. But there are some cautions to consider first.

Look before you leap. "Normally," says Nancy Granovsky, family economics specialist with the Texas Cooperative Extension, "if you're within the first seven years of the mortgage, and you can get an interest rate at least two full percentage points lower than what you have presently, then there's reason to refinance." But remember — there are refinancing charges on home mortgages. Don't leave them out of the equation.

"If you're getting down to the end of the repayment road, you aren't going to be saving that much more." Granovsky adds, "I'd recommend you talk to a lender or financial adviser to see if a refinance would actually save you money."

Choose wisely. "Where I'm concerned right now," says Granovsky, "where people have to be cautious is getting mixed up between conventional mortgages and ARMs — Adjustable Rate Mortgages. Those ARMs can appear to have the lower mortgage rates.

"The danger for anyone interested in refinancing, or even somebody buying a house for the first time, going into an Adjustable Rate Mortgage is what happens if inflation really starts revving up again. The Feds will undoubtedly respond by raising interest rates. If that happens, when it's time for your ARM to roll to its next level, it could be much higher than what a conventional mortgage would have been," she says.

Seek advice from a pro. Granovsky knows there's no works-for-everyone prescription for refinancing. "You may think this could be a good time to refinance. But that depends on your individual situation, even as interest rates start to go up."

Granovsky recommends seeking advice from a professional. "Run things by your tax accountant to find out if your decisions might have adverse tax consequences. Visit your financial planner to make sure you're maximizing your resources."

Think twice about taking cash from your home

If you're at least 62, you may be eligible for a plan that puts thousands of dollars in your pocket now that you never have to pay back — as long as you don't move or sell your house.

This plan, called a "reverse mortgage," allows you to borrow cash from your home based on your age and home equity, not income or credit history. You can receive the money in a lump sum, monthly check, or line of credit.

But don't jump into this type of deal too quickly. Depending on where you get your loan, you could end up paying thousands of dollars in fees. And when you sell the home, move out, or the last borrower dies, someone must repay the loan with interest.

Consider whether you're better off selling your home and moving, or staying in your home and making things work within your current budget. Do your homework before you make any decisions. A good place to start is the AARP Web site *www.aarp.org/revmort/*.

Triumph over devious lenders

Your home. It's one of your biggest investments — your most valuable asset. Safeguard your home's equity by recognizing trouble before you sign a loan agreement. The Federal Trade Commission has identified seven scoundrels who are after your precious equity.

Equity strippers. These crooks know your income may be limited. But they also know you have equity in your home. Since conventional loans may be tough to get if income is short, equity strippers offer to make borrowing easy. These lenders will show you how to doctor the books to improve your income figures. Then they'll float you a loan based on this fictional income.

They really don't care if you can't keep up with the repayment schedule. As soon as you fall behind, they'll pounce and strip you of the equity you've spent years building.

Fine printers. You decide to refinance your mortgage. Along comes a lender offering you a fantastic plan — super interest rates, low monthly payments. Wow!

For the best deal on a mortgage, compare at least six lenders. It's easy. Just make sure you ask for the same size, length, and type of loan so you're comparing apples to apples.

But wait. What's this fine print? It says you'll only be paying the interest. In the end, you owe what you originally borrowed — all at once. If you can't make this balloon payment or arrange to refinance again, they'll seize your equity.

Loan flippers. You've had a low-interest mortgage for years — one that fits your budget. But you need some extra cash. You're approached by a lender who promises extra cash if you'll refinance with him. You're persuaded. He makes the arrangements.

A little later, he approaches you again with another refinancing proposal. This time he offers more cash. The cycle continues. Each time this "loan flipping" occurs, you pay points, fees, and higher interest rates, and you fall further in debt. If you can't pay, you could lose your home.

Home "improvers." These people are more interested in enlarging their bank accounts than renovating your house. They offer a great deal on a home improvement job, like a new roof, siding, or windows. You know you really can't afford it, but the contractor assures you he can secure affordable financing.

You yield. He begins the job. Then he arrives with his pile of paperwork. You discover he's arranged a home equity loan. You sign on the dotted line, and suddenly the unthinkable happens. The contractor becomes scarce. His work is shoddy. You complain, but he's been paid. He disappears. The lender demands your payments, and you never get what you paid for.

Benefits brokers. At the closing on your home equity loan, the lender wants you to sign papers authorizing payment for "benefits," like credit insurance. He makes it seem like the benefits he's packed into your loan are a necessary part of the package. If you refuse them, you're told they'll have to start the loan application process again. These benefits favor him, not you.

Service abusers. You've gotten your home equity loan. Then letters from the lender start arriving. You find out your payments are higher than you thought. And you learn that an escrow account is being created for your taxes and insurance, even though you agreed to take care of that yourself. Then you receive a notice saying late fees are due, and you know you've paid on time, every time. This kind of service abuse can make the repayment of your loan a nightmare and threaten your equity.

5 ways to find the right lender

- Call your realtor. He knows the lenders and rates in your area.

- Read newspapers. Many print lists of lenders and their rates.

- Search the Internet for mortgage lenders.

- Consult a mortgage broker. Their job is to match borrower with lender and make the borrower happy.

- Order the Homebuyer's Mortgage Kit from HSH Associates, Financial Publishers. The kit includes current mortgage rates from lenders in your area and additional information about shopping for a mortgage. Call HSH at 800-873-2837.

Deed grabbers. You've suffered setbacks, and the threat of foreclosure looms. Along comes a "lender in shining armor" who offers to bail you out, if only you'll deed your property to him. Of course, it's only temporary. Beware! Once he's set the hook and secured your deed, he treats what was yours like it's his. And you're out of a home.

Don't fall prey to predators

Predatory lenders can steal your home out from under you and do it legally. Learn how to protect your home from loan fraud.

If there's anyone who knows how to deal with predatory lenders, it's Donna J. Gambrell, the FDIC's Deputy Director for Compliance and Consumer Protection.

According to Gambrell, senior citizens are vulnerable to predatory lenders because they're more inclined to trust people who seem to be looking out for them. And many seniors live on fixed incomes, leaving them short of money.

Keep your eyes open. There are predators among the ranks of lenders, appraisers, mortgage brokers, and home improvement contractors. These unscrupulous people could easily:

- encourage you to borrow more than you can afford to repay, lie on your loan application, or accept high-risk loans, like loans with balloon or interest-only payments and steep prepayment penalties.

- milk you by charging high interest rates based on your age or race, by convincing you to solve your financial problems by refinancing your home, or by selling you property for more than it's worth by using false appraisals.

- pressure you to purchase home improvement services at high interest rates, charge you for unnecessary or nonexistent products and services, or change the terms of your loan or the sale price of the house at closing.

• assure you that the government is going to protect you against loan fraud and property defects.

Defend yourself. Don't be conned by predators, says Gambrell. "When pressured, walk away, close the door, hang up the phone. Check references of anyone who wants to work on your home before you sign a contract and before they start work."

In addition, only provide account numbers, birth dates, and social security numbers in person or on the phone to legitimate organizations — and only when you initiate the contact. "When in doubt, say you want to take their proposal to a relative, friend, or lawyer to discuss before signing. Only a highly questionable lender would object," Gambrell says.

Make wise choices. "Predatory lending has been a problem with nonbank companies that specialize in marketing to people with poor credit histories," Gambrell warns. "Obviously, not every lender is unscrupulous, but senior citizens need to be informed so they can avoid doing business with those who are."

Pay rock-bottom for your next car

It's incredibly simple, and you won't learn this from an auto dealer. The secret to getting the best price on a new car is to know exactly what you want.

Car-buying expert Kurt Allen Weiss, author of *Have I Got a Deal for You!*, offers this profound insight. "Not having a good idea of what you want before you enter a dealership leaves you open to being sold something. Car salespeople are professionals in the art of persuasion. If you leave it up to them, they'll sell you what they want to sell, not necessarily what you want to buy."

Save a bundle by refinancing

It's one of the auto industry's best-kept secrets. Refinancing your car loan can reward you with huge savings.

Online lenders, like E-LOAN and Capital One Auto Finance, offer lower interest rates. And they won't sting you with points, fees, and penalties.

If you can beat your present loan by a single percentage point, it could save you $100 or more every month! Yes, even if you have credit problems.

Prove it to yourself. Go to *www.eloan.com* or *www.capitaloneauto.com* and use their free online calculators to figure out how much you'll actually save.

Of course, you want a great price. But what's the secret to finding a bargain? Conventional wisdom suggests you'll have to master the art of hard-nosed negotiating and challenge the salesman to a duel on his turf. But if that's your approach, you'll probably never win.

Do your homework. Veteran salesman Weiss says the key to buying the car you want is educating yourself, doing your homework. The only way you can gain the advantage over the professional car salesman is by changing the rules of the game. Play by your rules, not his.

Know exactly what you want — make, model, color, trim package, accessories — and the dealer invoice of that car before you set foot on the lot.

You'll find a host of sources, especially on the Internet, describing available options and providing the dealer cost of every car and accessory. You can even learn about rebate offers and sales on trim packages.

Beware of back-end costs. "Back-end profits," says Weiss, "are where most dealers make their money." Back-end products include things like extended warranties, alarm systems, pin striping, window etching, and special floor mats.

"Fend off back-ending by simply stating you're not interested in the add-ons," Weiss advises. Resisting the impulse to buy and refusing to pay for these extras is the key to saving money and getting a great deal.

Stick to the plan. Be a smart shopper and stick to your shopping list. Refuse to buy on impulse or yield to the salesman's enticements.

Online auto shopping offers great deals

The next time you buy a car, use the Web. It has everything you'll need to find the right car at a great price.

Begin with a visit to an information site, like Edmunds.com or Kelley Blue Book (*www.kbb.com*), for comparisons, prices, and up-to-date research.

Then start shopping. Try any of the many popular, reputable buying sites:

- Autobytel.com
- AutoTrader.com
- Cars.com
- CarBargains.org
- CarsDirect.com

If car auctions and bidding are your thing, try it online at *eBayMotors.com*. But have a mechanic check the car before purchase if possible, because cars auctioned online are frequently lemons.

Enter the dealership knowing exactly what you want. This will help you make a reasonable offer.

Develop a good relationship. Getting a rock-bottom price is just the beginning of true customer satisfaction. By developing a good relationship with your car dealer from the start, you'll end up with the car you want at a good price and a friendly relationship with the service department for years to come.

Find a car loan that fits your budget

Since paying cash usually isn't an option for most new car buyers, financing may be a necessity. But take heart. The process of shopping for a loan has changed for the better in recent years.

Car loan expert Steve Carpowich with Capital One Auto Finance has some important tips for taking advantage of these changes and finding a great deal on vehicle financing.

Use online lending services. The advent of the Internet is a boon to borrowers. "Consumers may be surprised at the range of money-saving options available to them," says Carpowich, "now that the Internet allows them to easily comparison shop for interest rates and quickly secure their own low-rate, no-obligation loan before shopping."

Steer clear of dealer financing. Surveys by the Better Business Bureau and the Consumer Federation of America show that hassles related to car dealerships top the list of consumer complaints. "New options, such as online financing, can help improve consumers' car-buying experience by giving them the power of a cash buyer, which puts them in control of the process," says Carpowich.

Using Capital One as an example, Carpowich describes the potential for greater bargaining power at the dealership. "Consumers fill out an online application in about 10 minutes, and 15 minutes later they receive a reply. Those approved can receive a no-obligation blank check in the mail as early as the next day, which they use like a personal check at the dealership to purchase the vehicle of their choice. If the dealer offers a better rate, the consumer can take it with no penalties or fees."

Look before you leap. Here are some things you should consider before making a decision.

- Check your credit report before you apply. One lender trick is to tell you your credit score is worse than it is. Arm yourself with the facts.

- Compare auto interest rates using the Internet — *www.bankrate.com* is a good source.

- Explore your options — online lenders, credit unions, and banks. They all want your business.

- Secure your own no-obligation financing before visiting the dealer. It's your guarantee for the best rates, and it's your bargaining chip to see if the dealer can beat it.

- Treat the transactions as three "mini-deals" — vehicle price, trade-in value, and financing rate. Do this to maximize your negotiating power.

- Avoid ending up with an "upside down" loan, owing more than the car's worth when the time comes to trade in on your next new car. Don't take out a loan that lasts longer than you plan to keep the car. And don't end up owing more than the car is worth.

Steer clear of car repair rip-offs

Make car repair a pleasure rather than a pain by heeding the advice of veteran mechanic Ken Smith, owner of Smith's Auto and Truck Service, a NAPA Car Care Center in Fayetteville, Georgia.

The best way to find a good repair shop, he says, is to shop around. "Go by word-of-mouth recommendations," he suggests.

"Look for some certification — ASE in particular — and their time in business. Check their affiliation with a reputable parts distribution and repair network." A network — such as NAPA — will assure you the service center has:

- the parts you need.
- the latest repair information for every vehicle.
- good warranties on parts and service.
- access to technical hotlines for hard-to-solve problems.

No one likes "misunderstandings" when he's having his car repaired. Smith, who has been in the auto repair business since 1962, has several suggestions to improve communication and prevent unpleasant surprises.

Describe the problem. Don't leave it up to the shop to discover the symptoms. "An accurate description of the problem or service needed is good at the onset," says Smith. Describe that noise or vibration, and they'll quickly pinpoint the cause.

Expect honesty. One clue that you've found a good shop is their willingness to point you to a specialty shop or dealer. "A reputable, honest repair facility would refer you to a dealer if it's necessary," says Smith, "especially if the repair involves warranty work." If he can't or shouldn't make the repair himself, he'll refer you to someone who can or suggest a choice of service providers.

Schedule an appointment. Avoid a long wait or unnecessary delay. "Scheduling allows proper time for the service or repair to be performed," Smith says.

Keep in touch. Give the shop a way to contact you. Leave phone numbers in case a problem arises during the repair. A reputable shop will hold off making further repairs if they discover a new problem beyond the scope of your work order and can't reach you.

Save money at the pump

- Check Web sites such as *www.GasBuddy.com*, *www.FuelMeUp.com*, and *www.GasPriceWatch.com* to find the cheapest stations near you.

- Keep to the speed limit. You essentially pay an extra 10 cents a gallon more for every 5 mph you drive over 60. Stay steady at 60 and improve your gas mileage 7 to 23 percent.

- Nix those jackrabbit starts and aggressive driving moves to save yourself another 5 to 33 percent.

Be reasonable. Allow adequate time for your repair, and understand that in the auto repair industry there are few quick fixes. "If you've got to have your car back today, and you've got a repair that's going to take two days, naturally, that's not going to happen," Smith says.

Don't procrastinate. Some drivers delay having their cars serviced or repaired because they're worried about the cost. "There needs to be some communication and some understanding," Smith advises. "If you're limited with how much you can spend, let the repair facility know that to start with." Then they will know what you can afford and take whatever steps are necessary to make your car roadworthy — within your budget.

Lots of problems can arise in the world of car repair. "If you have repairs that exceed the car's value, we certainly don't want the customer unhappy." Smith believes that a good shop will assume the responsibility of explaining what your options are.

Stay in the driver's seat. You can expect a good repair shop to do the following things:

- diagnose your car's problem.

- estimate how long a repair will take and its cost.

- give you expert advice.

- repair your car so it's safe to drive.

But it's your car and your responsibility to make sure things are done right. So be sure to communicate with the shop, and stay informed about what your mechanic is doing each step of the way. You'll drive away a happy, satisfied customer.

Learn the 'games' car dealers play

Car dealers' tactics may vary, says Jeff Ostroff, CEO of CarBuyingTips.com, but you can protect yourself by knowing the scams they're likely to try.

VIN window etching. Don't believe them if they say you won't get the loan without it. That lie could cost you $300 to $900. The bank does not need it, and you can have the vehicle identification number (VIN) etched yourself for around $30.

Denied financing. You signed for a low interest rate and thought your worries were over. Now, two weeks later, they're saying you didn't qualify, and they'll be raising your rate and your monthly payments. Next time read the fine print that says "subject to financing."

False credit score. "Your credit score is 580," they say, "so we can only give you 10.9 percent APR." Good thing you have proof your score is 780, which qualifies you for the best rates. Not knowing your score may cost you the difference between a low rate and a much higher rate over the life of your loan.

Forced warranty. The bank does not require an extended warranty. That could cost at least $2,000.

Dealer prep. They might say, "Our dealer prep fee covers the cost of getting your car ready to drive off the lot." This fee is $500 for a job that only takes the dealer two hours. That's $250 an hour! Why are you charged when the factory already pays the dealer to do this?

Additional dealer markup (ADM). This is padding, pure and simple. It doesn't even pretend to be the cost of a service or benefit. The ADM "hides" on a little orange sticker next to the MSRP sticker. Cost — $2,000.

Loan pay-off. They may offer to pay off your loan, but the amount you owed, plus the penalties for breaking your loan contract, is folded into your monthly payments. The dealer doesn't pay it. You do. This huge added fee lies hidden in your monthly payments, spread out over 60 or 72 months.

Bounced bank checks. You arrive at the dealership with a draft from your bank, credit union, or lender. The dealer says, "We don't take their checks. They always bounce." The dealer then offers you its own financing package, but at a higher APR. Cost — higher payments over the life of your loan.

Forced credit application. You come prepared to pay cash, but they insist you complete a credit application. Contrary to what the salesperson says, there is no state law requiring you to fill out a credit application, and "everybody" doesn't do it. If he claims it is company policy, then, according to Ostroff, maybe you need to find another company to deal with.

Remember, you are in control of the deal, not them. Any time you encounter one of these scams, or feel uncomfortable in any way, simply get up and take your business elsewhere.

Steps to take when donating a car

What could be worse than bestowing a blessing on someone and having it return as a curse? It can happen if you're not careful.

Here's the scenario. You decide to donate your car to charity. You complete the "seller's" part of the title or registration papers — odometer reading, seller's name, and date of sale. However, you leave it with the charity to complete the portion having to do with the "buyer." The benefactor drives away with your car. You feel good. You've given to a worthwhile cause.

Unfortunately, two weeks later, you get a call from a wrecker service. They say you owe $400 for towing and storage fees — and you need to come get "your" car. It was found abandoned. "But I gave it to charity!" you plead. They reply, "That's nice, but the car is registered in your name. You owe us for towing and storage."

The point here is certainly not to sow seeds of distrust for charitable causes or a fear of being benevolent. This situation probably doesn't happen very often. It's simply a caution — the best of intentions can be rewarded with ungratifying results when you overlook rules designed to safeguard you against such problems.

Robi Turner, office manager for the Coweta County Tag Department in Georgia, recommends a few simple steps to take when you donate a car to charity.

Document the transfer. "Make copies of the title once it's assigned to the new owner," Turner says. Until the "buyer" registers the car in his name, the vehicle is yours for all practical purposes — unless you have copies documenting the transfer of registration or title. Without those copies, you have no way of proving that you are no longer liable for traffic violations, parking tickets, collision damage, or other mishaps involving your old car.

Make sure information is complete. Those copies need to include the name, address, signature of the person or organization to which the vehicle is being given, and the date of the sale. That information will enable authorities to locate those liable for any mishaps your donated car may be involved in after the sale.

Check with your tag office. Details concerning the proper way to transfer auto ownership vary from state to state, Turner says. So inquire at your tag office about canceling your registration, removing or transferring license tags, and notifying your insurance company — before the transfer takes place.

Taking these steps will assure you that your generosity won't be spoiled and your gift car won't come back to haunt you.

Property insurance

Smart ways to protect your possessions from disaster

Great strategies for buying insurance

The hassle of shopping for a new insurer ties people to policies they don't need and companies they don't like. But bad service and skyrocketing rates could change all that.

Jeremy Bowler, Director of J.D. Power and Associates, says there's never been a better time to shop around. "It may well pay for you to shop, because carriers are raising premiums by drastic amounts for the first time in a decade." Follow these steps to get the best service at the right price.

Answer these questions. After surveying thousands of people, Bowler has reached one conclusion — "No single company is best for everybody." Ask yourself a few questions to narrow your search.

- Are you a bundler? Some people like to buy all their policies from the same insurer. Trouble is, this limits your choices since certain companies only sell one or two kinds of insurance.

- Are you willing to split up your policies? "Many customers might if it will save them some money," Bowler notes.

- Do you want an agent? More and more companies deal with customers through the Internet or by phone rather than in person. Do you like walking into a building and speaking with an agent? Or are you comfortable dealing over the phone or computer?

Learn the basics before you shop. Get a crash course in insurance on the Internet. Learn the terminology and read answers to common questions on Web sites, like *www.InsWeb.com*. You'll have more control when you shop and a better idea of what you're buying.

Get referrals. Ask friends, family, co-workers, and other people you trust how they feel about their insurers. Then make a list of the best companies and find out more about them.

Review the ratings. "We polled 18,000 households, asking them what they like and don't like about their insurance companies," says Bowler. Then J.D. Power graded insurers based on the answers. Ratings like these give you a snapshot of how other customers feel about their insurance companies. View the newest rankings online at *www.JDPower.com/cc*.

> You should receive a copy — but not a photocopy — of a new insurance policy 30 to 60 days after buying it. If you don't, call your insurance company immediately.

Check for complaints. Contact your state's insurance department. They track complaints against insurers, compare rates among companies, and can tell you if an agent holds a license to sell insurance in your state.

Use your connections. Membership in groups such as AARP or USAA has its privileges. Reputable organizations like these may sell insurance themselves or through carefully chosen partner companies. You could end up with cheaper, better service than you would shopping on your own. Plus, you can complain to your organization if the insurer treats you unfairly.

Read the policy before you buy. In his research, Bowler found that one in five people don't know what kind of homeowner's insurance they have. So why did they buy it? One in three say because their agent recommended it. Unscrupulous agents could sell you insurance you don't need just by suggesting it. Know exactly what you're buying before you sign the papers. "My advice to anybody who is concerned about fraud — be informed, read the policy."

Ask questions. Don't stop there. Question any details in the policy you don't understand. "If you have any questions, it's the agent's job to explain," Bowler argues. If an agent shrugs off your questions or pressures you, simply leave. "I would say, 'Thank you for your time,' and walk away."

Creative ways to shop for insurance

Old-fashioned insurance companies aren't your only choice. These days, you can buy policies through the Internet and even discount stores.

It pays to shop because prices usually differ, explains Bob Hunter, director of insurance for the Consumer Federation of America. Web sites such as *www.InsWeb.com* and *www.insurance.com* let you comparison shop several companies all at once.

One-stop stores, like Costco, are in on the action, too, offering auto and homeowners insurance through American Express Property Casualty companies. "I wouldn't discount them, even though they are a discount store," laughs Hunter. So shop around, and consider all your options.

Coverage for hard-to-insure people

Rising insurance costs have hit everyone, but if you're a high-risk customer, you could feel the biggest bite. Getting dropped, cancelled, or denied a policy is no laughing matter.

Fortunately, you needn't cry either. You might have trouble getting insured, admits Bob Hunter, director of insurance for Consumer Federation of America (CFA). But it's not impossible. In some cases, you can even prove your innocence. You just need to know how the system works.

So what raises your risk in the eyes of insurance companies? Here's Hunter's breakdown.

- number of accidents and tickets — A few of these and your auto insurer will dub you an irresponsible driver. "Almost every company looks at this," he says.

- home condition — Maintenance concerns, such as outdated wiring or badly needed repairs, make homes more hazardous.

- credit history and rating — Insurance companies claim a link between bad credit and insurance risk. Hunter thinks that's bunk. "If I get laid off and fall behind on some bills, why am I a worse driver or homeowner?" Unfortunately, many insurers think there's a connection.

- previous carriers — Who insured you in the past? If you bought costly insurance from high-risk insurers, your new company may count that against you.

- age — Older adults often earn price breaks on their homeowners insurance, but their auto generally goes up after age 70, says Hunter.

Check your credit reports. The CFA recently reviewed 500,000 credit scores and discovered 20 percent of them were wrong. "We found all kinds of errors in the credit scores," he says. An insurer might refuse you or drop your policy based on these mistakes.

Review your report at least once a year to make sure it's accurate. Learn how to order credit reports and fix errors in *Rebuild your credit rating* in the Consumer credit chapter.

Shop around. "Some companies don't use your age or credit scoring, so it pays to shop around," explains Hunter. He suggests getting quotes from at least three regular insurers, even if you think you're high risk. Most major carriers operate high-risk companies, too. So if the regulars turn you down, ask about their higher-risk counterparts.

Complain to your insurance company. Getting dropped or cancelled doesn't doom you. Mistakes happen and insurers are no exception. "They may have the wrong facts," Hunter notes. This can happen if they used your credit report. First, ask them why they denied you. Then write a formal letter of complaint. Keep copies of any correspondence you send or receive.

Take it to the state. You probably don't have cause for complaint if you have had multiple accidents or tickets, or if you are nearly blind. But if a carrier denies you coverage based on age or credit score, or cancels your policy after only one claim, you have every right to fight back.

Contact your state insurance commissioner's office. You can file a complaint with them by phone, fill out an online form, or mail a letter detailing what happened.

Whichever you choose, explain the situation objectively, Hunter advises. Don't lose your temper. Simply state the facts as you understand them. You may want to include copies of any correspondence between you and the insurer regarding your coverage.

Guard against unexpected losses

Think your homeowners policy protects you from loss? Think again. "A lot has changed from a few years ago," warns Michelle Rupp, CEO of The Rupp Group, an independent insurance brokerage in Seattle.

Insurance companies have not only changed what they cover, but how much. Unexpected losses can hit hard where it hurts most — in your wallet. Here's how you can protect yourself from unpleasant insurance surprises.

Understand the basics. Homeowners policies offer two types of coverage — replacement cost and actual cash value. The first pays for you to rebuild your home at today's prices. The second pays based on the depreciated value of your home.

Policy checkups ward off woes

Review your homeowners policy every five years with your insurance agent, and reevaluate your needs.

- Have you spent $5,000 or more remodeling your home? Consider insuring it for more.

- Did you get a dog? Some insurers no longer extend liability coverage to certain breeds.

- Do you run a business from home? Your policy may not fully insure tools, computers, or other business equipment.

- Do you own expensive jewelry, coins, or collectibles? Homeowners insurance protects them from fire but not necessarily from theft, unless you add it.

Unfortunately, not many insurers offer full replacement cost policies anymore. Now most of them cap their payments, say 120 percent of its insured value. It sounds like enough until the house burns down. "Insurance companies have not done a good job of keeping up with property values," says Rupp. Because of that and rising construction costs, you could pay much more to rebuild the home than what you insured it for — with the difference coming out of your pocket.

"We recommend people get guaranteed replacement cost coverage that has no cap if they can find it," she says. If you can't, then shop for the policy with the highest cap.

When you buy a house with less than 20 percent down, you must purchase private mortgage insurance (PMI) for a monthly fee. PMI insures the lender – not you – in case of default, and premiums are an unnecessary expense. A new law says the lender must drop PMI once you have 22 percent equity in your home, based on the original property value. But you can – and should – ask them to cancel it when you reach 20 percent.

Protect what's inside. She sees another common mistake — plenty of coverage for the home's outside, and not enough for the inside. "Not a lot of houses burn to the ground. But smoke damage can destroy everything inside, even if you can rebuild."

Generally, homeowners policies insure the contents up to a percentage of the house's worth. For instance, your policy may replace everything inside — up to 70 percent of your home's insured value. "That sounds like a lot until you have to replace every spice in your cabinet, every single item you owned."

As with the building, Rupp suggests you choose a policy with replacement cost coverage on your personal contents instead of actual cash value. "Again, that should be a no-brainer." Then decide realistically how much it would cost to replace all your belongings and get a policy with a percentage that fits the bill.

Defend against disasters. The standard all-risk homeowners policy insures against all perils except those it specifically leaves out. Trouble is, that laundry list can get long, and the exclusions vary from one part of the country to another. In areas hit hard by high winds, policies may not cover wind damage. Those in another region may limit hail damage claims.

Your basic homeowners policy may exclude floods, earthquakes, hurricanes, hail, wind, mold, and termite damage to name a few, but that doesn't leave you out in the cold. You can buy back some coverage, like earthquake protection, by adding riders, or endorsements, to your policy. Or you could buy flood insurance from the Federal government through your insurance agent. Consider the risks where you live and get insured against them.

Safe homes save cash

A few safety measures around your house could shave 5 to 20 percent off the cost of homeowners insurance. Ask your agent if adding these features would lower your premiums.

- smoke detector
- burglar alarm or other security system
- dead-bolt locks
- sprinkler system
- updated heating, electrical, or plumbing systems
- reinforced or fire-retardant roofing materials
- storm or hurricane shutters
- hurricane-resistant glass windows and doors

Types of homeowners policies

Policy type	Property type	Rating	Description
HO-1	Homes	Poor	Very basic coverage. Only protects against the few specific perils it lists.
HO-2	Homes	Good	Also basic coverage. Insures against all the risks covered by HO-1 plus six more. Again, it only protects against the listed perils.
HO-3	Homes	Better	The most common homeowners policy. Protects your home, other structures, and loss of use against all perils except the ones it specifically excludes.
HO-4	Renters	N/A	Insures personal contents against specific perils, but provides no structure or liability coverage.
HO-5	Homes	Best	The most comprehensive policy. Covers your home, other structures, loss of use, and personal contents against all risks unless it specifically excludes any.
HO-6	Condominiums	N/A	Protects the condo's interior structure, the part condo owners are responsible for, but offers no liability coverage.
HO-8	Special homes	N/A	Insures historic, expensive, or irreplaceable homes as well as houses of little value in isolated areas. Only insures against perils listed in the policy, and only pays actual cash value.

Beef up liability. The comprehensive personal liability portion of your homeowners policy pays medical bills and damages if someone gets hurt on your property.

Most policies come with either $100,000 or $300,000 liability limits. Rupp suggests buying more. "We recommend people get the highest available. That's usually $500,000." And you could pay as little as $10 a year for the increased protection.

First, figure out how much your assets are worth — home, cars, savings, retirement, and other funds, she says. Then purchase at least enough liability to cover them.

Stay informed. Pay attention to the notices your insurance company mails, says Rupp. These letters often point out important changes in your policy. Read them and call your agent if you have questions.

Expedite your homeowners claim

Here's how you can limit your losses and get the money you're owed the next time you file a homeowners insurance claim. Just make sure you don't file a claim for an amount that's mostly within your policy's deductible because this may affect your future coverage or rate.

Jump start a recovery. Spring into action right after trouble happens.

- Call your insurance agent. If crime caused the property loss or damage, call the police and then your agent.

- Take pictures of the damage.

- Prevent the damage or loss from getting worse. For example, cover that hole in the roof. If this requires spending money, keep receipts. You might be reimbursed.

- Once you've prevented further harm, don't repair, replace, or discard damaged property until you've cleared it with your adjuster.

- Find your insurance papers. If they were destroyed, ask your insurer for replacements.

- Ask your agent if you must complete your claim by a deadline.

- Start a list of destroyed or damaged items for the insurance claim. Ask how to establish replacement value.

- Find your records of what you own. If you have no inventory of items owned, use backgrounds of family pictures to jog your memory and prove your losses to the insurance company. To establish item values, contact retailers and credit card companies for purchase records.

Each time you talk with insurance employees or a contractor, note the date, time, person's name, and contact details. Also write down what was said or what happened. Keep copies of all receipts, correspondence, and paperwork.

Phoning in your claim may be fast, but you also need to put it in writing to protect your rights with the insurance company. Ask your agent or insurer how to file a written claim.

Keep things moving. "The more involved you are in the claim process, the sooner it's going to get taken care of," says Steve Sparkes, certified insurance counselor and independent insurance agent with Barker Uerlings Insurance. If the insurance company requests information, get it to them quickly.

Ask your claim adjuster what you can expect to happen and when to expect each event. Find out what she expects from you, too. Then get the adjuster's name, toll-free number and extension, and your claim number.

If you know the damage report has been submitted to the company but a week passes with no results, call the claim adjuster. Ask about the status of your case. Find out whether the company is waiting for anything else.

"Keep the lines of communication open between the contractor, or whomever is doing the repair work, the claim adjuster, and the homeowner so everyone knows what to expect in a timely fashion," Sparkes says.

Be prepared. For best results, make a few preparations before disaster happens.

- Study your homeowners policy as best you can so you'll know what you should expect.

- Find out whether you should contact your agent or call the company's toll-free line.

- Put insurance documents, your items-owned inventory, deeds, and other property ownership records in a safe deposit box or mail copies to a friend or relative.

Cut your losses with an inventory

Use a regular camera or video camera to make a record of what you own, recommends insurance agent Steve Sparkes. Go room by room and document every item. Open drawers, look in closets, go outdoors, and go into your attic, garage, and outdoor storage. Insurers may also accept written lists, especially if you include such details as serial numbers, make, model, purchase date, and purchase price. Ask your insurer about a home inventory form to make the process easier.

Save big bucks on car insurance

Most people spend hundreds of dollars a year on car insurance. You can slash your insurance costs by as much as 50 percent by paying attention to the things that influence your premiums.

Follow these tips from the National Association of Insurance Commissioners and the Insurance Information Institute and start saving money today.

Get more than one quote. Rates can vary a great deal between insurance companies, so get quotes from several. Talk to friends, relatives, or your state insurance department for recommendations. Take into consideration the financial stability of the company, how well it takes care of its customers, and how fairly and efficiently it settles claims.

Some companies have agents that provide exclusive representation, some work through independent agents, and others sell directly over the phone or on the Internet. Make sure you're comfortable with this arrangement.

Ask for special discounts. These vary in different states and with different companies. Ask your agent or customer service representative about discounts for:

- insuring more than one car or combining your auto and homeowner's policies.

- being a longtime customer.

- anti-theft devices and safety equipment, like airbags or anti-lock brakes.

- mature drivers, good students, or college students away from home.

- driving fewer miles or carpooling.

Remember, it's possible a company with fewer discounts can have a lower overall price.

Raise your deductible. If you're willing to pay the first $500 of collision or comprehensive losses instead of just $200, for instance, you could save 15 to 30 percent of the premium. If you can afford more, ask about a $1,000 deductible.

Even better, think about dropping physical damage coverage altogether on older vehicles. It may not be worth it to insure cars worth less than 10 times the cost of the coverage. Figure how much you'd get on a claim — minus the deductible — and compare it to the amount of the premiums.

Of course, if you have a loan on the car, the bank may require a certain amount of coverage. Review your coverage at renewal time to see if you want to make any changes.

Who's covered to drive your car?

As you age, you may rely more on friends or family to run errands, sometimes using your car. You trust them, but will your insurance company pay if they have an accident?

Yes, says Keven Craiglow, a spokesperson for Nationwide Mutual Insurance Company. "Most policies should provide coverage. It's fairly standard." The only rules – you must give the person permission to drive, and your policy cannot specifically exclude them. And if the same person drives your car often, you should add them to your policy.

"Policies and coverages can vary by state and insurance company," Craiglow warns, "so it is always best to check with your insurance agent about your specific coverage."

Maintain good credit. Insurance companies find that drivers with long, stable credit histories have fewer accidents. That means a favorable credit report can almost guarantee you'll get better rates.

Buy the right car. Companies charge more to insure cars that cost more to repair, offer less protection or cause more damage in accidents, or are more likely to be stolen. When shopping for a new or used car, check to see what the insurance rates are before you buy and avoid an expensive surprise.

Be a safe driver. Don't get traffic tickets and avoid accidents, and you'll receive better insurance rates. Sometimes a defensive driving class will count.

Get the most from a car accident claim

Car accidents can be stressful and confusing. Don't make a mistake that could jeopardize your claim. Build your case and get all the insurance money you're entitled to by following these steps.

Take notes right away. A police report should include most of the important information, but it may not be available for several days. Jot down your own notes at the scene as backup.

- Personal information. Go to all the other drivers in the accident and get their names, addresses, and telephone numbers, including their home, work, and cell phone numbers. Then do the same with all the passengers.

- Driving details. Write down their drivers license numbers, as well as the color, make, model, and license plate numbers of every car involved.

- Insurance specifics. Check the insurance card of each driver and get the insurance company name, policyholder's name, and policy number.

- Police particulars. Once the police arrive, note the names of the officers and the police department. Ask for the report number, too, if they fill one out.

- Bystander basics. Catch any witnesses who saw the accident, and ask for their names, addresses, and telephone numbers.

- Damage facts. Make detailed notes about the damage done to each vehicle.

Amica Insurance warns you to take care in discussing the accident with the other people involved. Answer the police officers honestly, but don't admit anything to the other driver. It could affect the resolution of your claim.

Be sure to share your own license, insurance, and contact information with the other drivers, too. If someone was driving a car that did not belong to them, or if the insurance policy is not in the driver's name, you should get the name, address, phone number, and insurance information for the actual owner or policyholder.

Write your own report. Record your own account of what happened as soon as possible after the accident, while the details are fresh in your memory. You may want to include specifics such as:

- exactly where the accident occurred.

- how fast you and the other cars were traveling, and in what direction you were heading.

- what the weather was like.

- who braked, who honked, who swerved, and when.

- any other information you think is meaningful.

Notify your insurer. Tell your insurance company about the accident immediately. Most have a toll-free phone number to call, or you can contact your agent to file a claim. Give them contact information for any witnesses and injured people.

Don't fix your car. The insurance company will want to see the damage first and appraise it. Need a temporary fix-it? Your insurer should pay for one in the meantime. But make sure the repair is just enough to protect your car from further damage. If you make permanent repairs before they look at your car, they may not pay your claim.

Send in the paperwork. You should receive a police report shortly after the accident. Send copies of this and any legal papers you receive to your insurance company.

You don't have to accept the insurer's first offer if it seems too low. You have room to negotiate. And if you think an insurance

---

Post-accident emergency steps

The Texas Department of Insurance recommends these emergency steps after an accident to protect your life, your car, and your rights.

- Move your car out of the flow of traffic to prevent further damage to it and other vehicles.

- Call the police for even a minor accident, but especially if someone has been injured or killed, or if you cannot move your car.

- Sit tight and call the police if your car is struck by a hit-and-run driver. In some states, you must report this kind of accident to the police, or your insurance company will not pay for the damage.

---

company has treated you unfairly, complain to your state's insurance department.

Dodge rental car rip-offs

You could slash your car rental bill nearly in half by skipping the expensive rental insurance. "The amount of money rental car companies charge for their insurance easily can cost as much as the rental price of the car," according to Tom Schneider, a partner in Schneider Insurance Agency in Gahanna, Ohio.

These companies sell almost as many kinds of insurance as insurers themselves. But do you really need it? This action plan can keep you from getting taken for a ride.

Review your coverage. Not everyone has homeowners or auto insurance, and in that case, paying extra for rental car coverage makes sense. "People without a policy should buy every damage and loss waiver they can from the rental company," advises Schneider.

On the other hand, if you have auto and homeowners policies, you may not need car rental insurance. "Most policies cover the majority of things that could go wrong when you rent a car," he says. Yet, a few leave gaps.

Ask your agent. Don't assume you have the coverage you need. Schneider says, "Check with your agent. You might have a substandard policy or limited coverage." He recommends asking three specific questions.

- Does my policy pay for damage to the rental car, or replace it if it gets stolen? "Almost 99 percent of the time, the answer is 'yes.'"

- Does my policy cover loss of use to the rental company if I wreck the car? Otherwise, you may have to pay for the rental while it gets fixed.

- Is there anything my policy doesn't cover on a rental car? "Put the heat on your agent," Schneider advises. And if he doesn't know, ask him to call your insurance company and find out.

Check your credit card. Some cards offer free rental insurance along with other benefits. But beware — it only covers damage to the car, not personal liability. "Heaven forbid you're in an accident and you injure someone badly — that's liability," he says. Visa or MasterCard won't pay that portion.

Your auto policy still provides primary coverage, but a credit card could boost your protection. Call your credit card company to find out if you have car rental insurance and exactly what it covers.

Share the responsibility. Add the names of anyone else who will drive the car to the rental agreement. It may cost a few dollars more per day, but Schneider says it's worth it, if only for liability's sake. Then you aren't the only one responsible for damage or liability. "It brings their credit cards in. Otherwise, if it's in your name solely, you're the one responsible for it."

International travelers should ask their insurance agent if their auto policy covers rental cars in other countries. If not, you can add an endorsement, which covers you to drive or rent a car internationally.

Inspect the car yourself. Look the rental over before you drive away and again when you bring it back. "It's so important to inspect your rental car before you leave the lot," says Schneider. Check carefully for prior damage, like scratches, scuffs, and dents. Point it out to the salesperson, and make sure he documents the damage in writing. "You've got to cover yourself, so you don't get blamed when you take it back."

Eyeball your balance. If you do wreck a rental car, watch your bank account and credit card balances. The rental company may automatically charge one of these accounts for damage or loss of use. That could spell bounced checks or maxed out credit if you don't pay attention.

Protect vacation home from disaster

Many people struggle to own one home, but others play their cards right and wind up with a lake cabin or vacation hideaway. If you've worked hard all your life to earn this type of luxury, you want your investment to be safe. What protects your home-away-from-home from storm damage, theft, or other losses?

If you think it's the insurance policy on your primary house, think again. That policy only partly protects your vacation home, says Kip Diggs, a spokesperson for State Farm Mutual Insurance Company. Here's what's covered — and what's not — by your main homeowners policy.

- Personal liability. If someone slips and falls on your vacation property, the insurance on your first home would cover the claim.

- Contents. Not so for all the furniture and personal belongings in your vacation home. "If you want coverage for the home's contents, you need to get a separate homeowners policy," warns Diggs.

- Structure. The same goes for protecting the building from damage. If a tree falls on the roof of your second home, your first home's policy won't cover the repairs. "Basically, you're out of luck," he says.

Buying a separate homeowners policy for a vacation home makes sense for most people, and the lender may require it if you carry a mortgage. Generally, you'll need the same kind of policy as you have for your primary home, and you can shop for it the same way.

Check with your current insurer. "I'd say it's almost a no-brainer to start there," says Diggs, "especially if you are satisfied with the level of service and what you are getting for your money." You might also snag a discount buying both policies from the same company.

Shop around. "On the other side of the coin, it might be a good time to look at another insurer," he adds, "since you are doing the research anyway." Compare prices for the same policy with several other insurance companies. You may find better value and service with another carrier.

Consider additional insurance. Homeowners policies have limits on what they cover. Diggs warns that if you keep costly items like jewelry, antiques, or a boat on your vacation property, you may want to insure them separately. A personal articles policy, for instance, would cover certain valuables. Your agent can help you decide if you need a specialty policy, and which kind to buy.

Umbrellas keep you high and dry

People entering retirement may own sizable assets for the first time in their lives – a home, an RV, cars, a retirement savings account. These valuables are important to your livelihood, so carry plenty of liability coverage to safeguard them.

Your homeowners and auto policies provide personal liability, but it may not be enough to protect your assets if you get sued. Umbrella policies give you another layer of liability coverage. "Get an umbrella with a liability of at least a million dollars, if not more," recommends Steve Sparkes, an independent agent with Barker Uerlings Insurance in Oregon. You'll sleep easier at night.

The right way to insure your 'toys'

Play it smart. Make sure your recreational vehicles (RVs), boats, golf carts, and other fun things are protected. But beware — your auto and homeowners insurance might not offer full coverage.

You could end up paying out of pocket if you have an accident, break down, or hurt someone. Worse yet, if someone sues you over an injury and wins, they could take most of what you own, including your retirement savings.

Insurance shelters you from these financial catastrophes, says Steve Sparkes, a certified insurance counselor and independent agent with Barker Uerlings in Oregon. Having the right coverage is crucial to your retirement plans.

RVs. A recreational vehicle is part auto, part home. As such, a patchwork of policies protect it. "Some auto insurance companies will put motor homes on their auto policies and cover it like a vehicle." This gives it collision, uninsured motorists, comprehensive, and liability coverage, Sparkes explains. But not all will, and they may not cover the RV while it's parked.

Consider buying a special roadside assistance package for your RV, Sparkes says, since your auto policy will probably not cover the full cost of towing a motor home. Shop for one that also includes paying for your hotel while the vehicle gets fixed.

Your homeowners policy insures your personal belongings, like clothes or a television in the motor home. But chances are, it does not extend personal liability protection, especially if you live in the vehicle a significant amount of time each year. That means if someone falls on the RV space you are leasing, you might have to pay their medical bills and even face a lawsuit.

Sparkes suggests you buy a special insurance policy to fill in these gaps if you spend a lot of time in your RV. Progressive, Foremost, and other specialty insurers sell policies tailor-made for motor homes that provide auto, contents, and personal liability coverage.

Boats. Basic homeowners insurance may provide personal liability coverage on watercraft, like boats, Sparkes says, but with a horse-power limit. If you exceed the limit, you're uninsured.

"I would recommend purchasing watercraft or boat insurance. You can probably modify your homeowners policy to pick up liability coverage and damage to the boat itself," he notes. Yet, a separate boat policy will offer more comprehensive protection. If you plan to water ski, he warns, shop for a policy without liability limits on water skiing accidents.

Sniff out shady insurance agents

Don't fall for clever cons. Take this advice from the National Association of Insurance Commissioners.

- Send aggressive agents packing. Someone who pressures you into buying a policy, calls you repeatedly, or makes you uncomfortable does not have your best interests at heart.

- Ask for advice. Talk to a trusted accountant or financial advisor before you put down a large sum of money for any policy.

- Do your homework. Contact your state's insurance department to find out if an agent is licensed to sell insurance in your state – and if he really represents the company he claims to work for.

Golf carts. Once again, regular insurance provides a patchwork of protection. Your homeowners insurance generally shields you from personal liability while the cart is on your property. The course's insurance covers you while you're on the golf course. But between home and the course, you may have little or no coverage.

Ask your agent how your homeowners policy insures your golf cart, and how you can improve the existing coverage. "Make sure your homeowners policy covers you not just on the golf course or on your property, but in between, as well," advises Sparkes. Consider adding personal liability and damage coverage for the cart, he says, or buy a separate golf cart policy with these protections.

Collectible cars. These classics need insurance like your other autos, but Sparkes suggests shopping with an insurer who specializes in classic cars. If you have an accident, they will pay you the total collectible value of the car, as opposed to your regular auto policy, which will pay the depreciated value.

The company will need documentation before issuing you a policy, so be ready to provide proof. "The insurer will require photos from all sides, inside and out," he explains. "Most of them require everything be original."

Personal insurance

Getting the most coverage for the least expense

Guard your family's financial future

Live life to the fullest. Grab life by the horns. Just make sure your life is insured.

Here's the lowdown on life insurance — its perks and perils. Find out why you need it, how much you need, and which type best suits you.

Support your survivors. "Remember this about life insurance — it's the only vehicle that delivers a set amount of money at a specific point in the future," says Certified Financial Planner Bob Weigand.

While you won't be around to collect it, that money can help pay off your mortgage, put your children through college, cover estate taxes, or just help your family make ends meet.

Consider buying life insurance if:

- you have dependent children
- you support your parents
- your spouse depends on your income

On the other hand, if you're single with no dependents and limited assets, you probably don't need life insurance.

It's a good idea to examine your life insurance policy every few years to make sure it's still sufficient. If you refinanced your home or borrowed more money, you might need to adjust the policy's value.

Account for the amount. How much life insurance do you need? One popular rule of thumb is to figure seven times your annual salary and purchase that amount of insurance. But Weigand says that rarely reflects your true need.

The better approach is a thorough analysis that takes into account your loans, obligations, and current coverage.

"You really need to understand your needs and purposes and then purchase accordingly," Weigand says. "You need to find an insurance agent who's willing to take the time to sit down and explore your needs and not just throw a couple of numbers in a computer program and say, 'Here's what you need to have.' "

Pick your policy. There are two basic types of life insurance — term and whole life. Each has its pros and cons.

- Term insurance lets you specify the amount of coverage you want for a given time — in 5-, 10-, 15-, 20-, 25-, and 30-year periods. Experts say to buy guaranteed renewable full-term insurance. Your premiums won't change, and your beneficiary receives the full value anytime during the term of the policy.

  This is the cheapest life insurance you can buy and the most popular. Term's main drawback is that it's temporary. Once the policy expires, the money you spent on premiums is gone.

- Whole life insurance has higher premiums because you're buying an investment that offers lifelong coverage. As long as you pay your premiums, a percentage is set aside and invested. As your policy grows tax-deferred, you can make withdrawals or borrow against it. If you cancel the policy, you can receive some or all of the cash value back.

These permanent policies, which include variations such as universal life or variable universal life, act as a forced savings and help protect your assets. High costs and investment risks are among the drawbacks.

> Because term insurance is so cheap, a lot of people suggest buying term and investing the difference to make more money. "The problem is, when people do that, they usually don't invest the difference. They find something different for it," says agent Tom Ahart. "They spend it."

If your insurance needs change, you may be able to convert your term policy to a permanent policy, as long as you do it through your current insurance company. But be careful whose advice you take.

"The agents that sell policies make a whole lot more money on permanent policies than they do on the term, so the advice they give may be suspect," Weigand says.

Ask some questions. That's why it's important to find the right company and agent. Here are some things to consider when shopping for life insurance.

- Strength of the company. What's its rating? How many claims has it paid out?

- Qualifications of the agent. How long has he been in business? How many companies has he worked for? Have there been any ethics complaints against him? What are the characteristics of the majority of his client base?

- Is the agent a captive agent who sells for only one company or is he an independent agent? "Truly, I would search out the

163

How long will you live?

Following is an excerpt from the Commissioners 2001 Standard Ordinary Mortality Table, which is used to help determine premium rates for life insurance.

Life expectancy years			Life expectancy years		
Age	Male	Female	Age	Male	Female
50	28.23	31.74	76	8.83	11.53
51	27.34	30.85	77	8.28	10.91
52	26.46	29.96	78	7.75	10.30
53	25.58	29.08	79	7.25	9.72
54	24.72	28.21	80	6.76	9.14
55	23.86	27.34	81	6.30	8.59
56	23.02	26.49	82	5.87	8.06
57	22.19	25.65	83	5.45	7.55
58	21.37	24.82	84	5.06	7.07
59	20.55	23.99	85	4.69	6.60
60	19.75	23.18	86	4.34	6.16
61	18.96	22.37	87	4.02	5.74
62	18.18	21.58	88	3.73	5.34
63	17.42	20.79	89	3.45	4.98
64	16.67	20.01	90	3.20	4.64
65	15.94	19.24	91	2.98	4.29
66	15.23	18.48	92	2.76	3.94
67	14.53	17.73	93	2.56	3.61
68	13.84	16.99	94	2.38	3.29
69	13.16	16.27	95	2.21	3.02
70	12.50	15.55	96	2.06	2.79
71	11.84	14.84	97	1.91	2.61
72	11.20	14.15	98	1.77	2.43
73	10.59	13.48	99	1.64	2.23
74	9.99	12.81	100	1.53	2.03
75	9.40	12.16			

independent agent," Weigand says. "I refer my clients to independent agents particularly because they have a lot more flexibility."

- How does the agent get paid? Most of them are going to get a commission. The buyer has a right to know how much money the agent is going to make on this policy.

Protect your future earning power

Fall off the roof and your financial plan may crash with you, says Jane Bryant Quinn in her acclaimed book *Making the Most of Your Money*. A terrible accident can leave you unable to earn a living and quickly sap your savings and investments. Fortunately, disability insurance can provide a dependable source of income.

Insurers usually offer policies that cover only a portion of your income — often anywhere from 40 to 70 percent. That's why you need to look for the best value. Quinn says to forgo the bells and whistles. Your objective is a policy that meets your reasonable needs.

Think long term. Many policies pay benefits only for a year or two. These are not too expensive and Quinn says only about 10 percent of disabilities last longer than that. However, the best — and more expensive — insurance policies will provide for you until you turn 65, when you are eligible for Medicare and Social Security.

Lock in security. A "noncancellable" policy guarantees the same premiums and benefits over your lifetime, so it's expensive. "Guaranteed-renewable" coverage is more common. Your benefits won't change, but your rates might.

Pay now, less later. If you can afford to pay higher premiums now, choose a fixed rate that lasts the life of the policy. On the other hand, an annually renewable disability-income (ARDI) policy starts low and gradually increases every year. If your income also increases, Quinn says that's not too bad a deal.

Consider your occupation. You'll come across terms like Own Occ (own occupation) and Any Occ (any occupation) when researching policy payouts. But Quinn says the best choice is an income replacement option. This covers you for a certain level of income regardless of the job you get after an injury.

Collect enough to work less. Sign up for Residual Benefits if you choose an Any-Occ or Own-Occ policy, and you'll receive the difference between your previous and your current benefits.

Don't pay after pain. Make sure your insurer will waive your premium once you're disabled. Otherwise, factor this cost into the income you need to insure.

Cut costs with details. All the choices may seem intimidating, but Quinn says some of them can save you money.

- Buy into a unisex plan if you are a woman. This can save you up to 50 percent, since women usually pay higher premiums than men.

- Ask for the non-smoker discount.

- Choose the longest elimination period you can afford. If you can wait six months to receive benefits, your policy may cost 30 percent less.

- Skip add-ons that don't increase the value of your policy – such as presumptive disability, accidental death and dismemberment, hospital income, and premium refunds.

How to find the best health insurance

They say when you have your health, you have everything. That's not quite true. You also need health insurance, just in case.

Don Brain, chief executive officer of Corporate Benefits Consulting in Overland Park, Kan., offers the following tips for finding the best health insurance.

Choose a good company. Look at the strength and quality of the underwriting carrier. "What's their financial rating? How long have they been in business? What is their commitment to the health insurance marketplace?" Brain says. "Clearly you want one that is a long-term player."

Pick the right plan. "You want to make sure the policy terms really match up with your needs," Brain says. For example, you might not want to pick a local HMO group if you won't be in the area for long periods of time. "Usually, there are out-of-area services, but sometimes if you own a second home or you're traveling all the time, that could make it a lot more inconvenient to get those services."

Figure out finances. You can find a wide range of contracts, ranging from those with first-dollar coverage to those with high deductibles — and lower premiums. Choose the financial design that makes the most sense for you.

"Don't take a high-deductible program to save money if you can't, in fact, afford to withstand that cost," Brain says. "And it may not just be for you. It may be for multiple members of your family in any particular year. So you really have to weigh all the financial ramifications of the kinds of contracts you select."

Think big. Don't focus too much on a plan's everyday perks. Make sure the network your carrier uses will provide the best care when you need it most.

"Something may look attractive from a routine care standpoint, but they may not have the acute care center or the specialist that you would want," Brain says. "Then I would opt for a different plan.

"Because the most critical time, really, is not the routine care, it's not the office visit co-pays and the convenience of a particular pharmacy or whatever — it's the times you're going to need it for critical illness."

Manage on your own. Perhaps you've heard horror stories about managed health care. With these plans, you must go through a primary care physician in order to access specialists, and someone besides your primary care physician makes sure that the care you receive is appropriate.

"Most of the carriers are moving away from managed care plans," Brain says. "There's really less need for it on an ongoing basis today."

Seize control of your health care

Looking to save a bundle on premiums and take charge of your own health care? Open a Health Savings Account, or HSA.

Don Brain, CEO of Corporate Benefits Consulting, describes an HSA as a "medical IRA." Used in combination with a high-deductible major medical plan, an HSA lets you sock away pretax dollars to use for your health care expenses.

Best of all, the money carries over from year to year. Once you turn 65, you can use it for anything without penalty, but if you use it for nonmedical expenses, you will have to pay taxes.

"I think it's a marvelous vehicle to really turn patients into consumers," Brain says. For more information on HSAs, check out The HSA Insider at *www.hsainsider.com*.

He says consumer and regulatory backlash, as well as the fact that the medical establishment has adopted many of the pathways of managed care, has caused most carriers to move to open-access plans.

Join the group. If your employer offers group insurance, take it. "Because it's going to be employer subsidized, it really makes sense for most people to participate in those plans rather than buy an individual plan," Brain says.

Most companies will offer a choice of plans. Choose the one with the plan design and network that best fit your needs.

Preserve your group health insurance

Saying goodbye to your job doesn't mean having to say goodbye to your benefits. Two federal laws, COBRA and HIPAA, see to that. Here's how they work.

COBRA. Thanks to COBRA (Consolidated Omnibus Budget Reconciliation Act), you can temporarily keep your previous employer's group health coverage.

You can keep your coverage for 18 months and sometimes even longer. Your spouse and dependent children can also continue in the group health plan for up to 36 months, depending on the situation.

Just be prepared to pay a pretty penny for this privilege. Without any further contribution from your employer — and with an extra 2 percent fee for administering the plan — it can cost you up to 102 percent of the full premium.

That's why Don Brain, chief executive officer of Corporate Benefits Consulting of Overland Park, Kan., says most people are better off getting an individual health plan and establishing a Health Savings Account instead.

"It rarely makes sense to take COBRA," Brain says. "The exception to that, obviously, is just the situation where somebody is in ill health or has a condition that would prevent them, from an underwriting standpoint, in getting issued. Then they may be forced to take COBRA until they can get on a new employer's plan on a guaranteed issue basis."

Whether you choose COBRA or not, the most important thing is to have continuity of coverage. Otherwise, you run the dual risk of not being covered if you get sick or not being covered for pre-existing conditions once you join your next employer's group health plan.

Length of COBRA coverage

Qualifying event	Employee	Spouse	Dependent child
Loss of job	18 months	18 months	18 months
Reduction in hours worked	18 months	18 months	18 months
Divorce or legal separation	–	36 months	36 months
Death of employee	–	36 months	36 months
Employee enrolls in Medicare	–	36 months	36 months
Dependent child no longer meets plan's definition of dependent	–	36 months	–

Certain disabled individuals may be eligible for an additional 11 months of COBRA coverage in order to serve as a bridge to Medicare.

"You want to have coverage for everything — not be covered for anything except those pre-existing conditions, which are the ones you really need coverage for," Brain says.

Timing is everything. Once your company says you qualify, you have 60 days to elect the COBRA continuation option and 45 days from that date to pay the first premium.

When COBRA benefits run out, you may be able to convert the group insurance to an individual policy.

HIPAA. Thanks to HIPAA (Health Insurance Portability and Accountability Act), it's easier to switch jobs when you or your family members have health problems that otherwise would keep you trapped in your old job.

If you meet the requirements for HIPAA, you cannot be denied coverage or charged higher premiums because of present health problems or pre-existing conditions.

As long as your previous group insurance plan meets criteria set by HIPAA, you get credit for that coverage, which helps lower or even eliminate any waiting periods.

When moving from one group insurance plan to another, make sure you don't go more than 63 days without coverage. To move from a group plan to individual insurance under HIPAA, you must first accept COBRA if it's offered and use up the benefits.

Clear up Medicare and Medicaid confusion

Government health insurance programs are hard to keep straight. Discover basic differences between Medicare and Medicaid and learn about your federal health plan options.

	Medicare	Medicaid
Who can use the program?	People 65 or older and people of any age who have selected disabilities or end-stage renal disease (kidney failure) are eligible.	Requirements vary by state, but depend on income, age, and if you are disabled or pregnant.
Who is in charge?	The Federal government manages Medicare.	Generally, each state decides who is eligible, which benefits to offer, and how much services will cost.
How does it help you?	Medicare Part A (Hospital Insurance) helps cover inpatient hospital care. Medicare Part B (Medical Insurance) helps with outpatient care, doctors' services, and possibly some items not covered by Part A.	Although coverage varies by state, certain services must be covered in order to receive federal funds. Other services, many items that fall between the Medicare cracks, are optional and decided upon by each state.
How much do you pay?	Part A: no premiums, but a deductible and copayments; Part B: premiums, a deductible, and copayments	You may pay a small copayment or have a small deductible, depending on your state and status.

Although Medicare won't cover all your medical expenses, you don't have to qualify for Medicaid to fill those gaps. As long as you have both Medicare Part A and Part B, either Medicare + Choice or Medigap policies may help with out-of-pocket medical expenses.

- Medicare + Choice Plans are offered by private companies with Medicare's approval. They include the same coverage and protection as Medicare, but often with more choices or more benefits.

- Medigap policies, also called Medicare Supplement Insurance, are not part of Medicare. Private insurance companies sell these heavily regulated policies to cover such Medicare costs as copayments. If you already have Medicare + Choice, you don't need a Medigap policy. In fact, it is illegal for anyone to sell you one.

Call 800-MEDICARE or go online to *4.medicare.gov* to find out more about Medicare or to get details on Medigap and Medicare + Choice plans available in your area.

For more information about Medicaid, check entries under "United States Government" or "Community Services" in your local phone book or visit them on the Internet at *www.cms.hhs.gov/medicaid*.

Smart way to fill health coverage gaps

Medicare helps seniors handle the high costs of health care. But it doesn't cover everything.

That's where Medigap comes in. As its name suggests, Medigap, also known as Medicare supplement insurance, fills the gaps in your Medicare coverage.

"I generally recommend people purchase Medigap policies because I think they tend to offer a nice protection, particularly for prescriptions and those sorts of things," says William J. Browning, past president of the National Academy of Elder Law Attorneys.

Here's how to go about finding the right Medigap plan.

Compare plans. Medigap policies come in 10 standard varieties, ranging from A to J. Plan A covers only the basics, while Plan J provides the most coverage.

Personal insurance

Every plan covers at least the following:

- the Medicare Part A coinsurance amount for days 61-90 and days 91-150 of a hospital stay

- coverage of up to 365 more days of a hospital stay during your lifetime after you use up all Medicare hospital benefits

- the coinsurance or copayment amount for Medicare Part B services after you meet the yearly deductible

- the first three pints of blood or equal amounts of packed red blood cells per calendar year, unless this blood is replaced

Coverage for extras, such as skilled nursing, at-home recovery, foreign travel emergencies, and preventive care, vary from plan to plan.

Use the accompanying handy chart, developed by the Centers for Medicare and Medicaid services, to help you decide which policy to get — and which to avoid.

Find a trusty company. Browning says many people go through AARP for Medigap insurance. Major insurance companies also tend to offer good polices. Before choosing a company, check out its ratings.

For more information about Medigap, visit *www.medicare.gov.* Its Medicare Personal Plan Finder can help you find Medigap policies in your area. You can also read the 92-page publication "Choosing a Medigap Policy."

Keep in mind that premiums vary from plan to plan and even company to company. Make sure the policy you want can be sold in your state.

"Shop smart," Browning says. "A lot of people have a trusted insurance adviser they use. It's a good time to use him."

Medigap Plans A Through J

A	B	C	D	E	F	G	H	I	J
Basic	Basic	Basic	Basic	Basic	Basic	Basic	Basic	Basic	Basic
		Skilled	Skilled	Skilled	Skilled	Skilled	Skilled	Skilled	Skilled
	Medicare	Medicare	Medicare	Medicare	Medicare	Medicare	Medicare	Medicare	Medicare
		Medicare			Medicare				Medicare
					Medicare Part B	Medicare Part B		Medicare Part B	Medicare Part B
		Foreign	Foreign	Foreign	Foreign	Foreign	Foreign	Foreign	Foreign
			At-Home			At-Home		At-Home	At-Home
							Basic Drug	Basic Drug	Extended Drug
				Preventiv					Preventiv

Plans F and J also have a high deductible option.

This chart doesn't apply if you live in Massachusetts, Minnesota, or Wisconsin.

Start looking immediately. When you turn 65, you have a six-month open enrollment period. That means you can't be turned down for any Medigap policy.

The six-month period begins on the first day of the month in which you turn 65 and are enrolled in Medicare Part B. This is the time to shop for your plan. After six months, you might have a harder time getting insured.

"Do not wait till you get sick," Browning says.

Beware of scams. Never buy more than one Medigap policy. You'll just overlap your coverage. In fact, it is illegal for a company to sell you a policy if you already have one.

However, you can buy a second policy if you put in writing that you intend to cancel the first. Don't cancel your first policy until the second one is in place. You have 30 days to decide whether to keep the second policy.

Get more Medicaid money

Medicaid may help you in illness, but it could have devastating consequences for your spouse. To qualify for Medicaid, you often must spend your own money first — leaving your spouse with very little.

William J. Browning, past president of the National Academy of Elder Law Attorneys, explains how spousal impoverishment laws work.

"In many states, they don't give much by way of protection for the well spouse," Browning says. "The minimum in many states is $18,552. They'll let you keep your house and a car — and $18,552 is the minimum amount they'll protect for you. So that's not very much."

But you're never too rich to qualify for Medicaid if you know the right way to go about it. Here are some steps you can take to protect your spouse and your money.

Buy a new house. Make sure your spouse has a decent place to live when it's time for you to go to a nursing home. Consider buying a house or condo that's easy for an older person to manage. "I think that's a legitimate thing to do, and for the most part, the states are not opposed to that," Browning says.

Renovate your home. If you like the home you already live in, make some home improvements. For example, you can install handrails along stairs, add ramps, move the bedroom and bathroom downstairs, adjust the height of kitchen cabinets, or replace doorknobs with levers.

"You're really trying to make sure that the man or woman who's living in the home can stay there as long as possible. You really want to promote their independence," Browning says.

Turn assets into income. Convert some of your assets into a source of income, such as an annuity. This is especially helpful if your spouse has very low income. But buy only from a reputable company, and make sure the annuity will provide enough income for your needs.

"Some of the states are really cracking down on those plans, mainly because I think there's been some abuses," Browning says.

But you can do it on the up-and-up. Browning often works with middle-age men who have amyotrophic lateral sclerosis (ALS) — better known as Lou Gehrig's disease — and know they don't have much longer to live. Often they have a wife and young children. One way to help the family is to annuitize the husband's IRA or 401(k).

"So the husband gets it for the rest of his life and then his wife gets it for her life. It allows them to support the wife and any minor children," Browning says. "That, I think, is very different than taking an 80-year-old who has $500,000 and buying an immediate annuity and asking for Medicaid the next week."

Give it away. Maybe you thought about setting up a trust for your kids to protect some of your money. Think again.

"Trusts in many states don't work very well. There's a much longer look-back period for trusts, and a lot of states will challenge any trust you would try to set up, particularly if you're a beneficiary of that trust," Browning says.

On the other hand, you can gift money to your children. But you'll be ineligible for Medicaid for some period of time. While the general

---

The latest Medicaid math

Three couples — the Smiths, Joneses, and Johnsons — live in the same state with the same spousal impoverishment rules. The well spouse can keep a minimum of $18,552 and a maximum of $92,760.

Not counting their house, car, and prepaid burial, the Smiths have $100,000 in assets. This gets divided in half regardless of title. The well spouse keeps $50,000, and the ill spouse must spend $50,000 toward his care before qualifying for Medicaid.

The Joneses, who have $30,000 in assets, still divide them. But because of the minimum, the well spouse gets to keep $18,552 — more than half. On the other hand, the Johnsons have $200,000 in assets. Since the maximum is $92,760, the well spouse keeps less than half.

The Clarks, who live in a state with a minimum of $92,760, have $100,000 — just like the Smiths. But the ill spouse only has to spend $7,240 before Medicaid kicks in.

rule is 36 months, this can vary from state to state. For smaller gifts, the time period may be shorter.

"If you start actually gifting money to your kids, you'd better be very sure your kids are going to treat you right if you ever need anything and don't have the money," Browning says.

"It doesn't happen very often, but you see or read about circumstances where the kids end up with a new boat and a nice fancy car, and Mom is left with barely enough to survive. While she may be in a nursing home, the quality of life in a nursing home can be greatly enhanced if the kids are willing to spend some money."

Get the right advice. If you have any questions about these strategies, Browning recommends talking to a certified elder law attorney who gets paid a flat fee or by the hour for his advice rather than someone making commissions on what he's selling you. "Sometimes advice not to buy something is the best advice you ever get," he says.

He also warns not to count on straight advice from state agencies, which may be more concerned about cutting their budgets than helping you.

"A lot of older people are pretty sure they can trust the government until they've been taken advantage of, and then they feel a little differently," Browning says.

Long-term care checklist

Expect you'll have to go to a nursing home? Believe it or not, the expense won't be covered by Medicare. And it can be quite an expense. Nursing home costs are nearly $200 a day — and rising. That can eat up your savings in a hurry.

But a nursing home policy can protect your home and other assets. Even if you don't need to go to a nursing home, you or your spouse might require expensive long-term health care at home. Don't just wonder how you can prevent a spouse's care from driving you to bankruptcy. Find out how long-term care insurance can help.

J. Derieck Hodges, president of Albrecht-Hodges, Inc., an insurance and investment firm in Cape Girardeau, Mo., offers the following expert advice on long-term care.

Evaluate your needs. First of all, you have to determine whether you need long-term care insurance at all.

"I don't know that it's something everybody needs," Hodges says. "I think it's something probably everyone should consider."

Someone with a very low or very high net worth might not need to purchase it, Hodges says. "But that leaves a whole big group of people that probably do need to look at it."

If you are at least 62 years old and own your home, consider a reverse mortgage to help finance your long-term care. Instead of paying the bank, as with a traditional mortgage, the bank makes payments to you. Find out more about reverse mortgages and other ways to finance long-term care at *www.ltccounselor.org*.

Hodges recommends doing a "needs analysis" to determine how much money you're likely to need for long-term care and how much money you have available to pay for it.

Do some research. Considering a long-term care insurance plan? Discover the best daily benefit amount — it will cover 100 percent of your costs.

It all depends on where you live. The average daily cost of long-term care varies greatly from region to region. Find out what it costs in your area or the area where you plan to retire. Then plan accordingly.

Keep in mind that high rates of inflation — in the neighborhood of 6 to 8 percent — can drastically alter this number in years to come.

Make some adjustments. One way to make sure your daily benefit increases each year to keep pace with medical inflation is to get a cost-of-living adjustment rider, or COLA rider, in your policy.

"That's what's going to make sure that if you buy a policy today that it's worth what it needs to be 10, 15, 20 years down the road from now," Hodges says.

Hodges admits that COLA riders aren't cheap. But they're worth it — and most people end up buying one even if they initially balk at the cost.

"If somebody's 50 and they don't buy it, I'm not really sure what they're going to get when they're 75. It's not going to make a very big dent in their long-term care expenses," Hodges says.

It's also important for most people to have home health care benefits included in their long-term care policy.

Wait a little longer. With most policies, you become eligible for the benefits when you can no longer perform several designated activities of daily living, such as bathing, feeding, or dressing yourself.

But you can save on your premium by choosing a longer waiting period between the time you need care and the time your benefits kick in.

"Obviously, the longer the waiting period, the cheaper the premium," Hodges says. "It goes back to that needs analysis. If somebody knows they've got $100,000 of ready cash, why pay an insurance company when you can just self-insure that a little bit?"

Stick with the pros. Fretting about which long-term-care insurance company to choose? Hodges offers some good guidelines.

"Weed out some of the companies that may not have been in the long-term care business very long or have questionable financial strength," he says. "I'd want to buy from a real premier company that has a lot of experience with this product."

Start looking now. It's never too early to start thinking about long-term care. Hodges, just shy of his 40th birthday, already bought a long-term care insurance policy.

"Generally speaking, though, most people start looking at it some-where after 50. It seems like more and more people I'm talking to are already past 60, and what they're finding is the costs are pret-ty high," he says. "I just encourage everyone to start the discussion earlier. It doesn't mean you need to buy it now, but you can at least start getting the prices."

You can also take advantage of policies that let you prepay your premiums while you're in your peak earning years. Instead of

Wait longer, pay more for LTC

Unlike fine wine, long-term care insurance premiums don't get better with age. Just ask sisters Esther and Marjorie.

They each bought a long-term care insurance policy from the same carrier. Both plans include a $100 daily benefit for nurs-ing home or home health care, a waiting period of 90 days, a lifetime benefit period, and a 5-percent compounded cost-of-liv-ing adjustment.

Marjorie, 50, pays a monthly premium of $193. But Esther, who is 10 years older, pays a whopping $274.

paying a premium every year for the rest of your life, you pay for 10 or 15 years. You're charged a higher rate, but at the end of that time period, you're all paid up. Then, when you're retired and on a more limited income, you don't have to worry about insurance premiums.

Go high-tech to get quotes

Computers might not make insurance any more exciting, but they make shopping for it a lot easier.

With the Internet, you have quick and easy access to a wealth of insurance information. Whether you're looking for life, health, homeowners, or auto insurance, you can find quotes, agents, and helpful tips on the Web.

Sample some sites. Explore the following Web sites to compare quotes and do some research. They are just a sampling of the many resources available online.

4BestQuotes	www.4bestquotes.com
eHealthInsurance	www.ehealthinsurance.com
Insure.com	www.insure.com
LocalInsurance	www.localinsurance.com
MostChoice	www.mostchoice.com
Tigerquote	www.tigerquote.com

Pause before you purchase. While some Web sites let you buy insurance with just a few clicks of your mouse, that might not be the best approach.

Certified Financial Planner Bob Weigand points out the following drawbacks of buying term life insurance online.

- Time is not on your side. It may take a long time — sometimes as much as six months to a year — before your application gets processed.

- Price is not always right. Make sure you're placed with an A+ or higher rated company, not just the least expensive one.

- Help is not on the way. When you buy insurance online, you might get a good price — but you might not get the assistance you need when making a claim.

  "They will do everything they can not to pay the claim. That's their motto. That's what they're out to do," Weigand says of

---

3 ways to pay

Before you decide how to pay your insurance premiums, consider these options.

- Pay the total premium and save money on monthly payment fees, stamps, and the headaches of writing checks every month.

- Select direct billing if you don't have money to pay your insurance costs in full. Unfortunately, you will be charged a monthly payment fee.

- Set up an automatic bank withdrawal for the convenience of monthly payments, and choose the date you want the money withdrawn. The payment fee each month is two to three times less than the per month cost of direct billing.

---

insurance companies. "You've got to have somebody going to bat for you, who knows the ins and outs and who knows the paperwork that needs to be submitted."

Combine the best of both worlds. Use the Internet to gather information and compare quotes, but purchase the insurance through a trusty agent.

Keep an eye on automatic withdrawals

Paying your bills by automatic withdrawal can make life easier. You give the insurance company your bank account number, and they deduct your premium when it comes due. No checks, no postage, no forgetting to pay. But all too often companies overbill you, leaving you with bounced checks and bruised credit. Here's how to spot the mistakes and fight for your money.

- Read your bank statements carefully, and compare them to the receipts or billing statements you get for automatic withdrawals.

- Call the bank and the company responsible as soon as you find an error, within 60 days of the bank statement's date.

- Write a letter detailing the mistake, and mail it to both the bank and the guilty company. Send it certified mail, return receipt requested, and keep a copy for yourself.

- Once you tell the bank, it has 10 days to investigate the unauthorized debit. After that, it must return the money to your account.

- If the same company continues to make unauthorized withdrawals, you may need to close that bank account and open a new one.

You can also put a "stop payment" on regularly occurring automatic debits, such as a monthly insurance or health club payment. Call the bank at least three days before the withdrawal to issue a stop payment, and follow up with a written request within 14 days.

When to buy travel insurance

Traveling can be fun, exciting, relaxing, sometimes even exasperating — but it's rarely cheap.

You want to save money whenever possible, but you don't want to risk losing the money you spent on your trip if you need to change your plans or have a medical emergency while traveling. Should you spring for travel insurance or not?

In some cases, it makes sense. In others, you're probably duplicating coverage you already have. Many policies offer baggage protection and legal assistance, along with travel arrangement and medical protection.

Here's what to do before buying travel insurance.

Consider the risk. Costly trips to faraway, potentially dangerous places are more likely to call for trip-cancellation insurance.

Trip-cancellation/interruption policies should protect you if a medical emergency or death in your family forces you to cancel or cut short your trip. Make sure you're also covered if your travel agency goes out of business. It's a good idea to look into terrorism coverage as well.

"If I was going overseas, I'd buy it," says independent agent Mike McCartin of Joseph W. McCartin Insurance in College Park, Md. "Certainly in the current state of things, the further you're going and the more money you spend, it's probably a pretty good deal."

Examine exclusions. What if you become seriously ill while traveling? It's important to realize what your travel medical insurance does not cover. You might not be as protected as you think.

"You've got to read the fine print," McCartin says. "The big print looks good. It's the fine print you've got to be concerned about."

For example, your travel medical policy likely excludes any pre-existing conditions as well as many popular vacation activities, such as inline skating, jet skiing, mountain biking, scuba diving, snorkeling, skiing, snowboarding, water skiing, and whitewater rafting.

McCartin recommends calling your corporation's benefits person or your insurance agent and finding out what's covered and what's not under your health plan.

"They're not going to give you a perfect answer. There's no way to predict the exact scenario, but I think they can give you some generalizations that would at least give you enough info to make an intelligent decision," he says.

One of the most important things to determine is what happens in the event of a medical evacuation. Make sure if you need to be flown back to the United States for medical reasons, either your health insurance or travel medical insurance will cover it.

Check homeowners policy. Worried about your possessions while on vacation? You can add a personal effects floater to your travel insurance. But before you do that, check your homeowners policy. Chances are you're already covered.

"If you have a decent homeowners policy, you've got coverage anywhere in the world," McCartin says. "In most cases, most people are pretty well protected."

Business property is probably not covered, and there are limits for jewelry. If you're unsure, call your agent and discuss the situation. If you need to, you can probably make the appropriate adjustments to your homeowners policy.

Talk with an agent. Many travel agents also sell travel insurance. Ask about it when you're planning your next trip.

"We can help you understand travel insurance and what might be the best program for you," says Tim Kangas, owner of the Cruise

Planners franchise in Sharpsburg, Ga. "Insurance is optional and recommended, but not mandatory. It's a personal decision," he says.

Stay away from these policies

Proper insurance coverage is a godsend when you need it, but there are some policies you'll probably never use. Here are 10 insurance plans experts say you don't need.

Life insurance if you're single. Life insurance provides money to live on if the breadwinner dies. If you have no dependents, your death won't create a financial hardship. The same is true if both spouses have ample individual income or an adequate retirement plan. Here's a rule of thumb — if your income won't be needed, don't buy life insurance.

Should you fetch insurance for Fido?

You want to take care of your beloved pet, but is pet insurance the answer? Usually, no. Put the money you would spend on premiums into a savings account to pay for pet care.

If you would do whatever it takes to save your pet, pet insurance might make sense. Recent advances in pet care give you many treatment options. Insurance can help defray these costs.

When shopping for pet insurance, compare policies as you would for any other type of insurance. Pay attention to deductibles, co-pays, and annual caps. Realize that pre-existing and hereditary conditions are usually excluded, and older pets cost more to insure.

Air travel insurance. If you die suddenly, it doesn't matter if it's from an airplane crash or a heart attack. Your family will still need financial support, so get regular life insurance with full coverage. Besides, most credit cards offer free coverage if you charge the tickets.

Mortgage-life insurance. These policies protect your lender if you die, since proceeds can only be used to pay off your loan. A better — and cheaper — choice is straight term insurance, which can be used for anything.

Private mortgage insurance. PMI is a special case, because you usually have to get it when you buy a home with less than a 20-percent down payment. The cost of PMI simply becomes part of your loan payment. However, once you owe less than 80 percent of the value of your home, you can, and should, ask to cancel it.

Credit-life insurance. These are policies attached to bank and credit card loans. They pay your loan off if you die, or make your payment if you are sick, hurt, or out of work. It is very expensive insurance and sometimes you don't even know you're getting it. Buy term life insurance instead and forget about the disability or unemployment policies, because their payouts are so low.

Life insurance on children. The death of a child has less financial impact than the loss of a breadwinner. High amounts of life insurance may not be necessary.

Cancer insurance. Unless you're pretty sure you're going to get hit by a particular disease, spend your money on more comprehensive health coverage. In any case, read the fine print closely. Many of these, and other one-disease policies, are cheap because they don't cover a lot.

Dental insurance. Unless your employer pays for it, this might not be worthwhile. Dental insurance normally only covers two cleanings and exams each year and limits payment for more expensive work.

Daily hospitalization insurance. Policies that pay a certain amount, such as $500 a day, for hospital expenses sound practical. But it's better to have a comprehensive, or major medical, health insurance policy that covers all your expenses, which can total much more than $500 a day.

Rental car insurance. This really isn't even insurance. Rental car companies call it a "collision damage waiver." It's very expensive and your own car insurance or your credit card company probably covers you. Check to be sure, especially if you'll be renting a car in a foreign country.

Pros and cons of credit card insurance

Credit card insurance pays off your credit card balance when you die. It also makes monthly payments if you're disabled. Sounds practical, but is it?

This insurance is more expensive than regular life insurance or disability insurance. And the beneficiary is your credit card company. All in all, it's not a great deal for you.

In most cases, it's smarter to get a life insurance policy and let your heirs use it to pay off any debts. However, if poor health prevents you from getting a life insurance policy, consider credit card insurance. Its open enrollment policy means you can't be turned down.

Real estate

Expert choices for buying, renting, and selling

7 secrets to hiring the best agent

A good real estate agent can make or break your home buying or selling experience. The good ones are willing to work hard for their money — and you. Don't waste your time with an agent who isn't. Separate the best from the rest in seven easy steps.

Choose a respected company. "Deal with a company that has a good reputation in your community," advises Dorcas Helfant, principal broker and managing partner for Coldwell Banker Professional Realtors in Virginia. Respected real estate firms will have a vested interest in the area and its property values, and most likely have better trained agents than their competitors.

Check professional standing. "Is the agent a member of the National Association of Realtors (NAR)?" Helfant asks. These agents tend to have more training than other real estate agents and must stick to a strict code of ethics. Look for the Realtor designation on the agent's business card, or simply ask if they belong to NAR. Also, contact the governing agency in your state. Ask if the agent is in good standing and holds an active real estate license.

Search for a specialist. Many agents have areas of expertise. Buying land? You may want an Accredited Land Consultant.

Searching for a home? Look for a Certified Residential Specialist. A Certified International Property Specialist can even help you set up house in another country. The list goes on. Ask the agents you interview what area they excel in, or search by specialty on NAR's consumer Web site at *www.realtor.com*.

Ask about free services. Agents work for larger companies, many of which offer free services to their clients. Ask what their firm can do for you beyond putting a sign in your yard or driving you around to look at homes. You may like the extra benefits that come with using certain companies.

Judge presentation. On their first meeting with you, a qualified agent should outline their strategy for selling your home or helping you buy one. "They should have something for you to understand their services, their firm, what they offer in the community, and how they can assist you." If they don't, she replies, "keep interviewing until you find a presentation that meets your standards."

Interview references. "Good professional people in our business live on their referrals," says Helfant. Ask all the agents you interview for a list of past clients, then call those people. "Talk to some of the references," she says. Ask how well their agent served them, and if they would choose that person again.

Not all real estate agents are REALTORS. This word applies only to agents who are members of the National Association of REALTORS (NAR) and follow NAR's strict Code of Ethics.

Get to know your agent. Spend time with them before you sign an exclusive contract. "You've got to figure out if the chemistry is right," Helfant explains. "You must really like the agent and trust them. That comes first." Likewise, a good one will want to spend time with you before asking for a commitment. "Anyone who pressures you or makes you feel uncomfortable — don't work with them."

After all this, you may wind up loving your real estate company but not working well with your agent. In that case, says Helfant, talk to the firm's manager and ask her to assign a new agent to you.

Get the best deal on a dream home

You could buy the house of your dreams — at the smartest price — when you use these essential tips.

Know your market. Get to know the local housing market. For example, learn how long homes take to sell and whether conditions favor buyers or sellers. "Visit open houses, read ads, even before you are ready for serious house hunting," says Edith Lank, author of *The Homebuyer's Kit*. "After you've done some serious house hunting, you become an expert for a short time. You probably know more than anybody else in the world about the right price for the right house in a given neighborhood."

Recognize the right price. Don't check property tax appraisals to learn what price a house should sell for. "No matter how earnest an effort the taxing authorities make to keep the assessments fair, they are nowhere near as accurate as what the buying public has paid for the house down the street," Lank says. Either your Realtor or city records can help you unearth how much similar houses in the area sold for.

Understand the seller. Sniff out whatever you can about what's important to the sellers. Talk to them directly or ask your Realtor about them. Understand the sellers' point of view, and you'll probably make better decisions when you make your offer.

Negotiate wisely. "Try to avoid little step-by-step negotiations," advises Lank. Before you set the terms of your first offer — or respond to counteroffers — review what you know about the sellers and remember this. "Brokers know that once you get past one or two counteroffers you're not going to make the deal," Lank says. "It becomes an emotional issue. Somebody says, 'it's not the money, it's the principle of the thing' and that's a good way not to get the house."

Get it in writing. If you meet the sellers or their agent, Lank warns against chatting about price. In real estate, she explains, the sellers aren't legally obligated to keep a verbal promise until it's in writing.

Prevent a nightmare. Even if the house is newly built, get a home inspection, Lank advises. To keep your dream home from becoming a nightmare, make your offer contingent upon the home inspection results.

Sweeten an offer cheaply. Even if you've offered the highest price you can, you can still tempt the seller with two low cost extras. Choose a closing date that helps the sellers, if you can. "Sometimes, that is the one thing that will make the deal," says Lank.

Pre-qualify for a loan before you start house hunting. This will help capture a seller's interest when you finally make an offer. "I wouldn't necessarily tell them how much my mortgage commitment is for, but I would tell them that I have a firm commitment for the money I need," says Lank. "Some banks will issue a commitment and blank out the amount so you can present it along with your offer without revealing your top chips."

Although you might spend money on pre-qualifying, you could pay out nearly as much for the loan after an offer is accepted. Spend the money early and you may gain two advantages. "You are a much stronger buyer and in a much better negotiating position," Lank says.

Evaluate your condo options

Many retirees and empty nesters have struck gold in their golden years by settling in condo communities. Once the realm of single young people, these developments now gear themselves to mature adults, offering many of the luxuries people crave in retirement.

"Understanding yourself and what will make you happy is very important," says Dorcas Helfant, a Realtor and managing partner for Coldwell Banker Professional Realtors in Virginia. Condos are a lifestyle choice, she says, perfect for some but not for everyone. Consider these pros and cons before you take the plunge.

- You get more for your money. Condominiums come with all sorts of extras for an active retirement — a clubhouse, gym, swimming pool, hot tub, tennis courts, sometimes even a golf course. That's far more than most people could afford on their own.

- Someone else does the work. The management hires groundskeepers and maintenance crews. No more fixing your own roof, trimming the hedges, or cleaning the pool. Many consider that a benefit. "You have less to worry about, yet more to enjoy," Helfant says.

- You pay for the luxuries. The amenities and maintenance aren't free, however. You pay monthly or annual fees to the homeowners association. Be prepared, she warns. "Condo fees will go up as the years go by." Remember, the same would happen with any home — as it aged, you would spend more to maintain it.

- Community rules keep everyone in line. "The condo offers many protections. That's the wonderful part about a condo," says Helfant. "The rules are for everybody. Some things you won't like or won't agree with. You will have to compromise," she says.

Ready to dive in? Here's Helfant's advice for finding the condominium of your dreams.

Decide where you want to live. Pick a geographic area, the broader the better in the beginning. "You'll have more options if you are willing to leave your area and go elsewhere." However, you may not have to change towns. Condos are popping up everywhere as they become more popular.

Choose a community. They come in all styles — high-rise condos, stand-alone homes, and something in between. Answer these questions to help narrow your search.

- Do you want to live in an urban area, close to the theater, opera, and shopping?

- Or would you rather retire to a golf course community with idyllic greens, or a lakeside development with a marina?

- Do you like being outdoors, or do you enjoy coming home to a lobby, an elevator, and a hallway?

- Would you prefer living with other retirement-age adults in an over-55 community?

- How high up are you willing to live? Some people want the top floor in a high rise, while others like modest buildings with two or three levels.

- Will you need an elevator to get up and down those floors, and if so, is one near your unit?

You can buy a condo as a seasonal home, but read the fine print. The homeowners association may let you rent it out for a year but not allow short-term leases. If you buy in an age-specific community, you also face age restrictions on who can rent there.

Do your homework. Once you've decided on an area and style, research the local condos that meet your criteria. "You need to do a lot of reading and talking and chatting and walking in advance," says Helfant. "When the opportunity comes to purchase, you might have to move quickly." Homes in some communities sell almost as soon as they go on the market. "You don't want to be rushed," she explains, so start investigating early.

4 tips for buying a second home

Vacation getaway. Family retreat. Investment property. Retirement home. Think of the possibilities of a second home.

Veteran real estate agent Alan Gilbert has been in the real estate business for over 30 years and now teaches agents how to help seniors with their real estate needs.

When you're considering a second home, says Gilbert, four things should figure into your choice — your priorities, location, health needs, and the right agent.

Know what you want. Priorities vary widely among homeowners, but studies show that seniors like water. "Water is the number one amenity seniors are looking for," says Gilbert.

But water alone won't cut it. Seniors like second homes to be reasonably close to their primary residence. They also prefer to be near a favorite vacation area and close to family. "There was a time when people thought about heading to Florida or Arizona. But now they're becoming much more family oriented. They're turning back toward their families," says Gilbert.

Another important consideration is the second home as an investment. "The second home market has been getting stronger, particularly with the baby boom generation and those who are older," says Gilbert. "They're seeing the second home as a true investment. Having an investment home with an eye toward having it as a vacation or retirement home makes a lot of sense."

Pick a location. This shouldn't be too tough. Where do you like to vacation? That's where many seniors turn their eyes when they retire.

College towns also have a special attraction. Gilbert says the atmosphere and amenities of college communities have become drawing cards for seniors. Many universities and colleges offer programs tailor made for senior citizens who retire to their communities.

Evaluate your health needs. Be sure your home is agreeable with the state of your health. At the least, be sure it will allow you to grow old there. "First floor living is primary," says Gilbert. "There may be a second floor with guest rooms, but one-floor living is primary." And don't overlook things like lever door handles, rails in the bathrooms, and wider doorways.

Another key factor is availability of medical services. "If someone is on a health plan such as Kaiser, they have to be careful that the plan is in existence where they're going to move." Be aware that doctors in some communities with large retirement populations are turning away folks who use Medicare. "They just can't handle any more, and it's not profitable for them," says Gilbert.

Seek an expert's help. You have retirement and a second home on your mind. Now it's time to find a real estate agent to help you through the process of finding a home that will suit you for years to come. That's where an SRES agent comes into the picture. SRES stands for Seniors Real Estate Specialist. "SRES agents are trained to understand the issues seniors have, problems they have to deal with, and how to help them in their quest for their real estate purchases," says Gilbert. Check out the SRES Web site, *www.seniorsrealestate.com*, or call their toll-free number (800-500-4564) to locate member agents in the United States and Canada.

Guide to mastering real estate red tape

Buying or selling a home these days involves a lot more hassle than it used to. The dizzying array of contracts, disclosures, exams, and reports can make you wish you had just stayed put.

Don't lose your head. Use this simple guide to master the maze with advice from expert Richard Gaylord, a Realtor with RE/MAX Real Estate Specialists in Long Beach, Calif.

Seller's disclosure statement. Sellers fill out this form when they put their home on the market. It gives potential buyers a heads up on serious damage to the home, health hazards like lead paint, and the age of its major systems, along with other information.

"It prevents surprises for the buyer," Gaylord explains. Be honest about problems if you are the seller, he adds. "You can't go wrong disclosing anything that affects the value or desirability of your property."

Purchase contract. Once you find a property, you and your agent will fill out an offer, or purchase contract. "It outlines what the buyer is willing to pay, the financing terms, the down payment, and when ownership changes hands." Other crucial details are mentioned as well.

Prequalification letter. If you are buying a home, chances are you have asked a lender what you can afford. Before you make an offer, request a prequalification letter from your lender.

Good letters impress the seller. "Anybody can call a lender and get a prequalification letter," says Gaylord. "I want one that tells me the lender has done some homework on you." Talk to a loan officer before you make an offer. "Giving him permission to run your credit report and verify your employment makes the process move much more quickly."

Earnest deposit. The buyer puts up cash along with the offer, usually 1 percent of the purchase price. Bigger deposits really get the seller's attention and can give you the edge in a hot real estate market. Earnest money goes toward the buyer's closing and down payment costs, so it's not money lost.

Counteroffer. The seller may accept the offer as is, or reply with a counteroffer. "The seller may say to the buyer — everything in your offer is acceptable except I want $10,000 more on the purchase price." It's possible to negotiate other things, too.

"Sometimes counteroffers go back and forth two and three times," says Gaylord. When one party accepts the other's offer, the two finally have a contract.

Inspection report. Now it's time to inspect the house. Typically, the buyer hires an inspector and pays for the report, but occasionally a seller gets an inspection in advance. "They don't want any surprises for themselves or for prospective buyers," Gaylord explains.

A general inspection sometimes reveals a serious problem, such as a cracked foundation or roof damage. When that happens, the buyer should call in a special inspector or contractor to evaluate the problem. Big repairs can be used as leverage to renegotiate the purchase price.

Either way, hire a professional. "Some people insist on doing it themselves, but a professional inspector has a list of things to look for, and he's sure not to miss anything."

Preliminary title report. At this point, the lender, closing attorney, or escrow agent orders a title report, which reveals easements, liens, or other title issues. "It's a very important document to review," according to Gaylord. Look it over before the closing if you are the buyer, and make sure it mentions all the property. For instance, each parking space you buy with a condo should appear there, too.

Preliminary closing statement. A week before your closing, ask the attorney or escrow officer for a copy of the closing statement. It lists the closing costs, purchase price, and other charges, plus how much each party owes or receives from the sale. "Look to see if anything seems absolutely outrageous," warns Gaylord. When he refinanced his own home recently, his prepaid deposit did not appear. He caught the mistake early and saved himself hundreds of dollars.

You may sign more papers and pay for more services aside from these. Different states have different requirements. Gaylord's final advice — "Read everything. Read it twice." Then call your agent with questions. "The more understanding, the fewer problems you're going to have."

Also, save all the papers you receive. "You want to keep them in the safest place possible," he adds. Your tax preparer or accountant may need them.

Best way to raise your home's value

Picture your home brightly lit, sparkling clean, and fabulously free of clutter. According to the experts at HomeGain, real estate information providers, a recent survey revealed that brightening, cleaning, and "de-cluttering" may be the absolute best way to raise the value of your home. What's more, the survey suggests these easy changes can give you the most bang for bucks spent.

Turn a showing into a sale. Kathy Braddock of Braddock and Purcell real estate consultancy in New York agrees. Not only does she recommend de-cluttering and clean up, she also suggests a process called "depersonalizing" to entice buyers.

"If the house has too many of your possessions or too much of your mark on it, you're going to narrow down the field of potential buyers," says Braddock. "You're trying to make the buyers want to see themselves in the home." To invite them to do that, make family pictures, unusual decorating, and other personal touches disappear from your home. After all, if you can inspire a buyer to make a sweet offer, you'll soon move those pictures and personal touches to a new place.

Aim for move-in condition. Braddock also suggests turning your home into a "finished product" — a house that no longer needs any repairs or other changes before the buyer can move in. When you do this, you've increased the value of your home because the purchaser won't have to spend any more money.

Rev up key rooms. Kitchens and bathrooms are also very important to potential buyers. Can remodeling or updating these rooms pump up your home's value? "That's where it has to be a cost/benefit analysis," says Braddock. "You really have to say to yourself, I'm willing to spend X because I think I can get Y. And you're not going to know what X and Y are until you price out how much it will cost to do and you know what your home is worth."

"You can get a pretty good valuation on your home by bringing in three different real estate agents from three different firms and getting them to tell you what homes are going for," says Braddock. Those agents can tell you the selling prices of other local homes similar to yours. Armed with estimates of home value and remodeling costs, you'll probably come to one of the following conclusions.

"If you've already kind of gilded the lily and you already have a ton of money in your home for various reasons, it may not be worth it to sink any more into it, because you're just not going to get it out," Braddock says. On the other hand, you could find that updating such items as countertops, sinks, or appliances could help. "Those things are going to be relatively inexpensive — depending upon where you are — and can greatly increase the sellability of your home and the price you can get," says Braddock.

Don't forget landscaping. Both the HomeGain survey and other studies suggest that landscaping increases the selling value of your home. Start by keeping your yard neat, trimmed, and healthy so potential buyers can get a good first impression when they pull in your driveway.

Learn more. To get more information about how various improvements can affect home values, examine the Prepare-to-sell survey results available from the newsroom section at *www.homegain.com*.

Sell your home fast

Top real estate agents say a few simple steps can really bring in the buyers.

- Keep the grass cut, the shrubs trimmed, and the yard neat.
- Clear the cobwebs from around doors and windows.
- Wash windows inside and out.
- Repaint doors and touch up trim inside and outside your house.
- Wash away visible mold and mildew around windows, doors, and walls.
- Remove clutter from counter tops, shelves, and other surfaces around your home.
- Clean the carpets, even if you have to hire a professional.
- Buy new appliances to replace badly outdated ones.

Make more $$$ on your home sale

When it's time to sell your house, you can hand it over to a real estate agent and put thousands of dollars into her pocket. Or you can sell it yourself, save the 6 or 7 percent fee she charges, and put those thousands into your own bank account.

Selling your own house is hard work, though, so it's not something to take on lightly. Here are just some of the things you'll have to do to manage a successful sale.

- File paperwork. Federal and state forms can be complicated and time-consuming.

- Research. Make sure you price your house fairly compared to similar homes in your area that recently sold. Consult the local classifieds and county clerk's office.

- Advertise. Place ads in newspapers and on the Internet. For a fee, you can even list with the multiple-listing service (MLS) available to brokers.

- Schedule appointments. You'll need to arrange times for showing your house to potential buyers. And be prepared to weed out the browsers and deadbeats from the serious, qualified buyers.

- Negotiate. Whether you deal directly with buyers or their representatives, you'll need to know when to make a counteroffer, or simply refuse or accept their offers. You'll probably want to hire a real estate lawyer to look over any contracts.

Before you put your house on the market, you may want to have a professional inspect your home to uncover any problems that may jeopardize the deal. Then you won't have any last-minute surprises.

If you're unsure about tackling the job yourself, you can contact a company that specializes in helping owners sell their own homes. They will assist you with the sales process, from providing signs to listing you in online directories. Their fees are based on the services you use.

Check out the Web sites on the following page for valuable information, advice, and assistance in selling your home without an agent.

Domania	www.domania.com
FiSBO Registry	www.fisbos.com
ForSaleByOwner.com	www.forsalebyowner.com

Save your home from foreclosure

Missing a few house payments doesn't have to mean losing your home. You can successfully fight foreclosure.

Odette Williamson, a staff attorney with the National Consumer Law Center and co-author of *Surviving Debt*, has helped many people do just that. Here she offers her insider knowledge on your rights and choices.

Understand your options. Whatever you do, don't ignore the notices from your mortgage company. They don't enjoy foreclosure any more than you do — it's expensive. Often, they will negotiate your payments, restructure your loan, or otherwise help you stay in the home. Williamson calls these "workout options." Here are just a few your lender might offer.

- pay the mortgage plus a little extra each month to cover the overdue amount

- reduce your payments for a short time, up to 18 months

- skip several mortgage payments over the course of a year or two

- modify the loan to make it more affordable, such as lower the interest rate or extend the length of the mortgage

- repay the past due amount over several years, or add it in to the mortgage balance and spread it out over the life of the loan

Leave without getting fleeced. Leaving your home might be the best way to avoid foreclosure in some cases, but you can still choose how to go.

- The lender may temporarily halt the foreclosure to give you time to sell your house. Selling may be a tough choice, but it's better than the bank seizing it.

- "If the property is worth less than the amount due on the mortgage," says Williamson, "the lender may agree to accept whatever a market sale brings, called a short sale, and forgive the rest."

- The deed-in-lieu is a last resort. "This allows the homeowner to essentially hand the property over to the lender," she says. By doing this, you skip both the sale and the foreclosure process. Unfortunately, you lose any equity you have in the house, as well as any legal arguments against the lender.

Contact your lender as soon as possible to work out a plan. Follow up every phone call you make to them with a letter on what you discussed, and keep a copy for yourself. Don't sit back and wait for their answer. Stay in contact with them until you work out a deal.

Seek expert help. You aren't alone in this fight. "If someone has missed one or two mortgage payments, a reputable housing counseling agency may be able to assist them," says Williamson. "Later in the process they may need an attorney." Start with these resources.

- The U.S. Department of Housing and Urban Development (HUD) offers a list of HUD-approved counselors on their Web site at *www.hud.gov.*

- Your neighborhood or city may have a legal services office, bar association panel of pro bono attorneys, or a legal assistance program for older adults.

These experts can also help you apply for financial assistance, like utility programs, emergency home repair, tax abatements, and even Supplemental Security Income, which could cover your other bills while you make mortgage payments.

Beware of people who contact you offering to get you out of foreclosure, buy the property from you, or help you file for bankruptcy. "Foreclosure is a public process in most states, and anyone in foreclosure will get offers for help from scam artists." Get trustworthy advice from a housing counselor or reputable attorney before you agree to any offer.

Prioritize debts. Pay your monthly mortgage first. Skip a few payments on low-priority debts, like credit cards and doctors' bills if you need to. It might not sound like a good idea, but the National Consumer Law Center says paying these bills late isn't as bad as missing a house payment.

Guard your goods from shady movers

You're finally making the move of your dreams. The movers load everything you own on a truck — and that's the last time you see your belongings.

Con artists have found a new way to steal dreams and rip off consumers. First, dishonest movers snag your business with a low-ball bid. "They get everything on a moving truck and then they tell you the real price of your move, which is normally thousands of dollars more than what you had expected to pay," explains Tim Walker, founder of the Web site MovingScam.com. Often, they demand you pay the difference in cash to get your belongings back.

Walker calls this trick "hostage freight." Schemes like this are illegal, but in most cases, the police can't stop them. Your best bet — avoid fraudulent movers in the first place.

Plan ahead. "Moving is one of the most stressful events people go through in their lives, right up there with marriage and divorce," says Walker. "So don't wait until the last minute to do it. If you start planning far enough ahead of time, you will end up with a good move."

Look locally. Start searching for good movers near you. Good real estate agents can often recommend reputable local movers. "Find someone locally and go to their office and meet their salespeople and their staff and check out their warehouses and see their trucks," Walker says.

Mom-and-pop outfits aren't your only choice. National companies have local branches, too. Look for evidence that they are who they claim to be — professional movers.

Beware of online moving scams

The World Wide Web can help you research companies, but it's also an easy way to find movers who will rob you blind. "The number one way consumers get matched up with a scam company is through the Internet," warns Tim Walker, founder of the Web site MovingScam.com.

Unlicensed, uninsured, and untrustworthy movers can make themselves look like top-notch professionals online. If you do find a moving company via the Internet, or if one contacts you this way, take time to check them out before signing an agreement.

Get estimates. "Get at least three in-home estimates," advises Walker. "Don't settle for someone who is in a hurry and wants to do an estimate over the phone." The real pros will want to see your belongings to give you an accurate price. Compare the three you receive and question any major differences between them.

Negotiate the terms. Movers issue three kinds of estimates — binding, binding-not-to-exceed, and non-binding. Non-binding gives you little protection. Walker recommends you ask for a binding-not-to-exceed estimate. This means the movers may lower the price if your goods weigh less than they anticipated, but they cannot charge more than their estimate. If they do, it's illegal. If they won't give you a binding-not-to-exceed estimate, negotiate for the regular binding variety.

Do your homework. Once you have found a few companies you like, do a little sleuthing on the Internet. Walker's Web site *www.movingscam.com* offers articles that lead you step-by-step through the process of researching a mover's license, insurance, and complaint history.

Still stumped? The volunteers at MovingScam.com will help you dig up information. Just type in a question on their message board. You can even ask for information about a specific moving company, and a volunteer will have answers within a couple of hours.

Fight back. Don't let a con artist have the last laugh. If you get scammed, take your story to these organizations.

- Tell it to the Federal Motor Carrier Safety Administration (FMCSA), which regulates the moving industry. Call in your complaint toll-free at 888-368-7238.

- File a complaint with the Department of Transportation's Office of the Inspector General by sending an e-mail to *hotline@oig.dot.gov*.

- Find out if your mover is a member of the American Moving and Storage Association (AMSA). If so, file for arbitration. Call AMSA at 703-683-7410 or visit their Web site at *www.moving.org*.

- Notify the Better Business Bureau in the state where the mover is located.

- Post a complaint to both MovingScam.com through their Web site at *www.movingscam.com* and to the Moving Advocate Team at *www.movingadvocateteam.com*.

Make money investing in real estate

It's one of the most popular and profitable ways to invest in real estate these days — buy a house cheaply, renovate it, and resell it for an immediate profit. Sound simple? It is, but only if the property is very cheap. If not, look for a better bargain.

Jody Kell, an Atlanta Realtor and partner in the Jody and Joan Team, specializes in real estate investing. Here's his advice to make this method work for you.

Make contacts. You can't do it alone. You need help from experts who know their craft. "Build your dream team of competent professionals — accountant, attorney, banker, lender, Realtor, contractor, and management company," says Kell. Start by finding a real estate agent you trust who has experience working with investors. Your agent will also have business contacts and can set you up with reliable professionals.

Pick the right property. "Identify a property in poor or outdated condition," Kell advises. A savvy real estate professional can locate a house ripe for renovation in an appreciating neighborhood.

Remodel carefully. End buyers, the people who purchase these fixed-up homes, are catching on to bad renovations, he warns. Do the job right, and you'll come out ahead of your competition. "Make sure you use high-quality materials and your contractor does excellent craftsmanship." Keep in mind you may need to renovate the kitchen, bathrooms, and bedrooms, and even replace the roof to update an older home.

Find good financing. All this work can wind up costing a lot of money. Never fear. "Short-term, private loan products, dubbed hard-money loans, can provide for 100 percent of the purchase and rehab costs, with little money out of pocket," Kell says. This is good news if you don't want to empty your life's savings.

But here's the catch. "These loans have very strict standards on the property, and all work must be done by a qualified contractor." Talk with your Realtor and loan officer about your financing options before you take the plunge.

Spot the scams. Don't fall for phony promises of instant wealth. "Let's face it — getting rich in real estate doesn't happen fast," Kell says. "It happens slowly." Be suspicious of get-rich-quick schemes and anyone asking for money upfront. "Remember, anything worth having doesn't come easy. You've got to get out there, work hard, and make it come to you."

Live for free on rental property income

Become a landlord and you could cover your full mortgage payment. This smart homeowner's secret works whether you buy several houses or simply turn spare space in your own home into an apartment.

The sooner you start, the more time you'll have to build equity, make back your money, and start living on your rental income. Try this step-by-step guide to realize your investing dreams.

Step 1: Get a good agent. "You vitally need a good Realtor for their knowledge of your local market," stresses Jody Kell, a successful Atlanta Realtor who specializes in investment properties.

An experienced real estate agent can locate houses with the characteristics you want and scout out the best neighborhoods to invest in. They're also an asset when it comes to negotiating the purchase and preparing the contract. "I see so many people fail, and the few who succeed always, always have a good, investor-friendly Realtor by their side," he says.

Step 2: Shop good neighborhoods. "I always advise my clients to purchase nice homes in nice neighborhoods," says Kell, "where the area is on the rise and future appreciation is imminent." Pass up homes in:

- declining neighborhoods
- areas with lots of public-assisted housing
- neighborhoods where people loiter in the middle of the day

Step 3: Choose the right house. Kell prefers nice, modest homes in middle-class or upper-middle-class neighborhoods. Stay away from overly large houses in run down areas. Greg Perry, a long-time

Enhance your retirement income

Sam, 55, and his wife Cathy, 52, wanted to supplement their future retirement income. A friend suggested they invest in real estate and become landlords.

The couple hired Dale, an experienced Realtor who specialized in investment properties. He helped them snag a great deal on a house that needed a few repairs, but nothing extensive.

Sam knew little about home renovations. He hired handymen, worked alongside them, and gradually learned how to do it himself.

Occasionally, Dale called them about other homes for sale. Sam and Cathy bought a few more. About 15 years and 15 rental houses later, they have paid off the first properties. Now, the rent they collect is almost pure profit, and they truly live off their investments.

landlord and author of *Managing Rental Properties for Maximum Profit*, advises against multi-family homes, like duplexes. "Your expenses will be higher, but single-family homes still attract the best tenants."

Fenced backyards and garages also help, he says, because good families often look for those traits in a home. Kell avoids those with picket fences in the front yard and swimming pools. The fence will need maintenance, and the pool creates a liability concern.

Step 4: Hire an inspector. "Once you find a good property, have a qualified inspector perform a detailed inspection." Failing to do so is one of the biggest mistakes new investors make, says Kell. An inspection can uncover hidden problems before you buy the house, which could save you lots of grief and money. Your agent can recommend a licensed inspector.

Remember, no house is perfect. You need an inspection to uncover the big problems. "Do not let the inspector scare you from becoming an investor unless the house has major problems," he warns.

Step 5: Renovate the home. Perry buys the worst-looking home in the best neighborhood, then fixes it up, a formula that has brought him much success. He suggests doing the work yourself, if possible, so you can pocket more profit. Kell, on the other hand, believes you should leave the remodeling to professional contractors. Either way, be sure to use quality materials. "Never, never be penny wise and pound stupid in this business," Kell advises.

Step 6: Start living off your investments. Even if you aren't ready to own other rental houses, Kell believes you can turn part of your home into an apartment just by finishing a basement or splitting your house into a duplex. He offers this advice.

• Make sure zoning allows these changes.

• Get the proper work permits.

• Install a separate utility meter for the new apartment.

• Hire a qualified, licensed contractor to do the work.

Perry still prefers separate homes. Adding an apartment to your own house can get expensive, and there's another concern. "You will not attract the same quality of tenant that you will with a separate home," he says.

He also suggests slowly building your base of rental properties, one house at a time. Soon, they'll be paying for themselves — and for you.

4 ways to attract good tenants

Tenants can make or break your landlord experience. When you get good ones, leasing is a breeze. But one bad apple could make you regret buying rental property.

Greg Perry, landlord and author of the book *Managing Rental Properties for Maximum Profit*, agrees. "Your greatest hassles are tenants, not the house. Your headaches won't be pipes breaking in the middle of winter. It'll be tenants leaving in the middle of the night without paying."

So what do you do? Learn how to attract good tenants and rent only to the best. Here's how.

Screen for financial stability. "They have to qualify," says Perry. "You can't discriminate against many factors, but you can discriminate against some, such as income and job security."

Check out their home. "Drive by where they are living now to see how they take care of their current place," he advises. If you don't like what you see, turn them down.

Keep them coming back. "When you get a good tenant, lower their rent unexpectedly after they've been there a few months or a year.

No other landlord will ever do that." They may thank you by renewing their lease.

Give them a gift. Let your good tenants know how much you appreciate them. "For Christmas, we send them a discount coupon for $50 or $100 off their January rent. This helps ensure they stay through January at least, which is a really bad time to find new tenants." Plus, it builds goodwill better than a Christmas turkey. Not a bad deal for keeping quality renters.

Things to consider before renovating

Remodeling your home can bring big returns — a more comfortable lifestyle and a more valuable home when you decide to sell.

Unfortunately, not all home improvements pay off at resale. Knowing which ones do may help you choose wisely so you won't lose money.

Each year, Remodeling magazine, a division of Hanley-Wood, LLC, compares the cost of certain remodeling projects with how much value they typically add to a home. See the table on the following page on how 10 common projects measure up.

Choosing one of these remodeling projects still doesn't guarantee a good return. Your neighborhood, climate, and current housing trends also affect what makes a house hot, or not, on the real estate market.

Dennis Gehman, president of Gehman Custom Builders in Harleysville, Pa., has been remodeling homes for over 15 years. He suggests considering these points before you undertake a major home remodel.

Your future plans. Planning on moving in the next few years? Think twice before you take on an expensive remodeling project.

Project costs and resale values

Project	Job cost ($)	Resale value ($)	Cost recouped (%)
Deck addition	6,304	6,661	104.2
Siding replacement (vinyl)	7,329	7,247	98.1
Bathroom addition (mid-range)	15,519	15,418	95.0
Finished attic bedroom with bath	32,863	30,500	92.8
Bathroom remodel (mid-range)	10,088	9,890	89.3
Window replacement (mid-range)	9,568	8,673	84.8
Family room addition	53,983	43,931	80.6
Finished basement	43,865	34,801	79.3
Master suite addition with bath (mid-range)	70,760	54,376	76.4
Major kitchen remodel (mid-range)	43,804	33,101	74.9

From the 2003 Cost vs. Value Report in Remodeling magazine, November 2003

These numbers are national averages and may not reflect exact remodeling costs or home values in your area.

Unless you live in a hot market area, you might not make all your money back when you sell.

Instead, improve your home with short-term cosmetic fixes, advises Gehman. "Spruce up the outside with some painting, landscaping. On the interior, a fresh coat of paint and new floor coverings make a world of difference." Instead of gutting an old bathroom, for instance, simply repaint, add shower doors, and replace the sink and vanity. These repairs are cheap, and they'll satisfy your need for change and help make your home ready for sale.

The neighborhood. "What's going on in the neighborhood?" asks Gehman. "Are you going to be overbuilding?" This question matters the most if you plan to sell your house within a few years of remodeling. If your renovated home far outshines your neighbors', you may not make your money back at resale.

Quality of life. On the other hand, overbuilding may not hurt if you plan to stay put for a while. Gehman sees many of his clients do this by taking on extensive renovations. "They like the neighborhood, the schools, the churches. They make a commitment to stay for as far as they can see in the future. With that in mind, they decide it's worth it."

If you think you will stick around, adding another room or putting in a high-end kitchen could pay off in other ways, such as dramatically improving your quality of life. Weigh the price tag with your future plans and think about how much happier you would be in your remodeled home.

Time commitment. "The biggest thing people don't realize is the amount of time and effort remodeling takes on their part," says Gehman. "Even when hiring a professional, there are just so many decisions people want to be involved in." You'll want to pick colors, choose materials, and approve the floor plan.

Living with a big remodel can be tough, too. Dust, debris, and gaping holes can make your home look like a war zone. Some projects last longer than others and involve more renovations. Think about how much time you have, whether you can live with the destruction, and for how long.

So in all Gehman's years of experience, which remodeling projects have brought the best financial return? Kitchens, bathrooms, master suites with a bedroom and bath, and large family rooms, especially those where the kitchen opens onto a great room, he says. Just remember — increasing your home's value can be worthwhile, but in the end, your happiness matters more than the money you make.

6 tips for choosing a contractor

The most important step in any renovation is finding the right contractor. "Choosing the contractor is key to the success of the project, no matter what that project is," says Dennis Gehman, president of Gehman Custom Builders in Pennsylvania.

Getting someone who is reliable, honest, and skilled can spare you from remodeling nightmares. Here's how you can choose the best expert for your job.

Ask questions. Take Gehman's advice — "Don't be afraid to interview the contractor." On the first visit, don't even discuss the project, he suggests. Instead, focus on getting to know them and decide whether you can trust them.

A good contractor will want to interview you, too. In that initial meeting, Gehman tries to learn about the client, their family, and their needs. "We're interviewing you, believe it or not, because not everybody is a fit for us, either." An honest contractor should tell you up front if they can't meet your needs or your budget.

Get references. Ask for a list of recent customers, then call them and find out if they were satisfied with the work. Gehman is adamant on this point. "Ask for references and check the references out."

Check licenses and insurance. While you're at it, ask the contractor for proof of his insurance coverage. Most states require them to carry personal liability insurance, workers compensation, and property damage insurance. Also, make sure the contractor has any licenses he needs to perform the work. Your state's local licensing agency can tell you if a contractor meets their requirements.

Window shopping?

Here are a few things you should know about energy-efficient windows to help you make a smart choice.

- Double-glazed windows consist of two panes of glass with a sealed pocket of air or gas in between. They lose half the heat of single-pane windows.

- Plain air between the panes works fine, but argon gas provides added insulation.

- Low-emissivity (low-E) coatings boost a window's insulating ability even more. You can buy windows with coatings fine-tuned for each climate.

- An R-value measures a window's insulating power, while the U-value measures how much heat passes through. Windows with high R-values and low U-values are the most efficient.

Don't go by price alone. "To me, one of the big mistakes people make is selecting the contractor simply by price," he says. "People would do best to find a contractor they feel they can trust."

Get at least three estimates in writing. These should include all the labor, materials, and verbal promises people made. Be suspicious if someone offers to do the job for much less than the other estimates.

Get second opinions. The building inspectors at your city's building department can recommend quality contractors. They try to stay impartial, but if you have narrowed your list to several names, says Gehman, an inspector may point out one above the others.

You should also call your local Better Business Bureau or Home Builders Association to find out if a contractor has complaints against him.

Learn the signs of fraud. Beware of contractors who:

- go door-to-door looking for customers, drive an unmarked van, or have out-of-state license plates.

- ask you to pay the entire cost of a job up front.

- encourage you to spend a lot of money on temporary repairs.

- ask you to obtain the permit for any work. It could mean the contractor does not have a license.

- you can only reach through an answering service.

- quote you a price that's vastly different from other contractors' estimates.

- make outrageous promises and pressure you for a quick decision.

When you are ready to sign a contract, make sure it includes all work details, warranties, time schedule, the quality of building materials, and cost. Fill in all the blanks in the contract. Never leave empty spaces for someone else to fill out later.

How to deal with shoddy contractors

Bad contractors can spell big trouble, especially if you have already paid them. Getting your money back may seem impossible — but it's not.

Most states have an agency to handle problems with contractors. In California, for instance, the Contractors State License Board investigates people's complaints. While a board like this can revoke a contractor's license, they may not help you get your money back.

Small claims court can. It's made for everyday people like you who want to represent themselves. The amount of money you can sue for varies by state, but it's generally small, $5,000 or less. Check with your state, then follow this advice to win your case in small claims court.

- Get the contractor's legal or business name and license number. The contractor licensing board for your state should have this information on file.

- Name the defendants properly. How you name the contractor in the court paperwork may depend on the kind of license they hold. For instance, a sole owner is different from a corporation. Ask your small claims court advisor for help naming the defendant and preparing your case.

- Go to the courthouse and watch a few small claims hearings to learn how the system works.

- Consider seeking an attorney's advice before a hearing, even though in most cases you cannot bring a lawyer to small claims court.

- Talk to potential witnesses before the hearing. Get all the facts straight and make sure their testimony supports your case.

- Ask your witnesses or experts to come to court with you to testify. The judge may not accept their testimony unless they give it in person.

- Rehearse what you want to say in front of friends or a mirror. Be clear and unemotional, and state the most important facts of your case in two or three sentences.

- Write down the main points you want to tell the judge if you think you might forget them.

- Give yourself plenty of time to arrive on the day of your hearing so you can relax and think about your case.

- Bring all the evidence you need to support your case — sales receipts, letters, contracts, leases, deeds, estimates, canceled checks, advertisements, photographs, or other documents. You need two copies of each original document, one for the judge and one for your opponent.

- Be prepared to explain why you are asking for this amount of money and be able to back it up. You may even want to itemize the costs for the judge.

- Don't speak to your opponent during the hearing. Talk directly to the judge.

- Listen to the judge, and answer his questions carefully and honestly. They may not seem relevant to your case, but he could be applying a law you aren't familiar with.

- Do not interrupt when the defendant tells his side of the story, even if you think he is lying. The judge should give you time to reply later.

- Never trade insults or argue with your opponent in the court-room. Stay calm.

The judge may issue a decision at the end of the hearing, or he may want time to think it over. In that case, you will get his decision in writing later.

Pros and cons of doing it yourself

Hiring a handyman to work around your home is a luxury many people can't afford. But before you decide to tackle a job yourself, ask yourself these questions to determine if you can handle things on your own.

How long will it take? Carefully consider how much time and sanity you're willing to give up. "If a contractor could take care of it in a month, it may easily take a do-it-yourself person a half year," points out Dennis Gehman, a Certified Remodeler (C.R.) and President of Gehman Custom Builders in Harleysville, Pennsylvania.

Are you familiar with the tools? Safety should be a priority. If you don't know how to use certain tools, you could cause more problems. "Saws and drills can certainly save time and make the job go smoother," Gehman says, "but they can also take a large chunk out of one's body if not used properly."

How complicated is it? Some jobs are fine for the do-it-yourselfer because any mistakes you make can be repaired. Other jobs should be left to the professionals. For example:

- Electrical work. Improper wiring creates a fire hazard. Saving a few bucks isn't worth losing your home.

- Plumbing. Never underestimate the importance of good plumbing. "If the drains aren't done right, you could have sewer gases backing up into the home," warns Gehman.

- Structural renovations. Projects that affect a home's support system — such as putting a window or door in a solid wall — can cause expensive damage if done wrong, from sagging doors to a collapsing roof.

Still hooked on doing it yourself? Your next step is to find out how and where to get the best deals on building materials. Check out these resources for cheap and free how-to help.

- Major hardware stores often offer classes where experts teach you how to use tools safely, lay tile yourself, apply special paint techniques, and other tricks of the trade.

- Look for how-to books with good photographs and illustrations in your local bookstores.

- Get help online through chat rooms and forums. Some, like *www.DiyNet.com* and *www.AskTheBuilder.com*, are set up for regular people doing their own home improvement. Type in your questions, look up projects, and get advice from experts.

For the best deals on building materials, Gehman has this advice.

- Watch the sale catalogs for local hardware stores. Certain projects tend to be seasonal. You may find just what you need on sale when you need it.

- Ask contractors for their scraps. Gehman's company, for instance, remodels a lot of kitchens. "A lot of the old cabinets that come out end up in the dumpsters simply because we don't have a source for getting rid of them and don't want to warehouse them." Offer to pick up the old materials yourself, and they may let you have them for free.

- Visit an overstock store. Some specialize in building materials — such as tubs, sinks, windows, doors, and other items — at deep discounts.

Uncover invisible energy leaks in your home

Professional home energy auditors can use blower doors to scout out air leaks and infrared cameras to spot heat loss, tune up your heating and cooling system, and teach you how to conserve hot water.

Many utility companies offer free basic energy audits, or you can hire your own auditor. Contact your utility company, cooperative extension service, or state energy office to learn more.

Older adults and low-income families may be eligible for the U.S. Department of Energy's (DOE) free Weatherization Assistance Program. Visit the DOE Web site at *www.eere.energy.gov/weatherization*, or call your state's department of energy.

Control skyrocketing utility bills

Utility costs can hold you hostage. You want to lower them, but you also need water, electricity, and gas to live. Never fear — you can cut your bills without cutting corners.

End water-bill woes. A few cheap, simple changes can slash your water bill. Test these tips from the Alliance to Save Energy.

- Get a gadget. Five dollars at the hardware store could cut your water use by thousands of gallons each year. Install a low-flow faucet aerator. It uses less water while increasing your water pressure.

- Fix leaks. A leaky toilet can waste up to 52,800 gallons a year. Deal with dripping or leaky faucets, and check for leaks in pipes, hoses, and couplings.

- Recycle water. Connect gutter downspouts to rain barrels or direct them to trees and plants.

- Add a hose nose. Use a hose with a shut-off nozzle while you water plants or wash your car. Better yet, use a bucket of water and a sponge.

- Wash full loads. Cleaning less than a full load of clothes or dishes wastes both water and energy. Wash your clothes in cold water for added savings.

Cut energy costs. You don't have to bake in summer or freeze in winter to enjoy energy savings. Try this advice from the American Council for an Energy-Efficient Economy (ACEEE).

- Wrap it up. Wrap an insulation blanket around your water heater. This thrifty device should pay for itself in less than a year.

- Drop the temp. Lower the temperature on your water heater's thermostat to 120 degrees, or the Warm setting.

- Change bulbs. Compact fluorescent lamps (CFLs) use a quarter of the electricity of regular incandescent light bulbs, and they fit most standard light fixtures. For the most savings, use CFLs to replace your 60- to 100-watt bulbs.

- Check filters. Remember to replace or clean old furnace, AC, and heat-pump filters regularly to keep these systems running efficiently.

- Insulate the attic. A foot of insulation in the attic floor adds up to energy savings in most parts of the country. Consider hanging it along unfinished attic walls as well.

- Seal off leaks. Weatherstrip doors and windows, or seal windows on the inside with plastic film. Installing storm windows over old single-glazed windows can save around a gallon of oil or one therm of gas per square foot of window each year.

- Pull the plug. You could save over $100 a year on your electric bill by unplugging the old, spare refrigerator in your garage. The ACEEE estimates that an old model costs between $50 and $150 a year to run. It's also cheaper to run one large refrigerator than two smaller ones. So instead of adding a spare for space, consider upgrading your main one.

Be prepared when disaster strikes

You never know when a disaster will strike. Don't wait until it's too late. Stock up your home in advance so you're always ready for an emergency. Create your own disaster kit with this advice from the Federal Emergency Management Agency (FEMA).

Water. Stocking water is a top priority, according to FEMA. Store enough to last three days — one gallon per person per day.

- Save water in sealable plastic, fiberglass, or enamel-lined metal containers. Don't use breakable containers or those that have held toxic chemicals.

- Thoroughly wash them out with a solution of one part bleach to 10 parts water.

- Fill the containers with water, write the date on them, and seal tightly.

- If you have untreated water, like well water, you will need to treat it before storing it. Contact your water supplier, state health department, or agricultural extension agent for instructions.

- Keep this supply in a dark, cool place, and change the water every six months.

Food. You don't need to buy special food for a disaster kit. Just check your cupboard.

- Canned foods are perfect since you can eat them without much preparation. Store them in a cool, dry place along with a manual can opener.

- Protect boxed and bagged food from bugs by putting it in sealed plastic or metal containers.

- Replace the food in your emergency supply every six months. Throw out old food and cans that have become dented, swollen, or corroded.

- Store a few paper plates, plastic utensils, resealable bags, and an all-purpose knife in your kit, as well.

> ### Food for emergencies
>
> - canned fruits and vegetables
> - ready-to-eat meats
> - juice boxes
> - powdered milk
> - canned soup
> - peanut butter and jelly
> - crackers
> - granola bars
> - cereal
> - trail mix
> - instant coffee
> - hard candy

First aid. Injuries or illness can make a disaster deadly. Make sure you have a first aid manual and these supplies in your emergency kit.

- cotton balls, needles, tweezers, scissors, latex gloves, a thermometer, and petroleum jelly

227

- cleansers, such as rubbing alcohol, hydrogen peroxide, soap, antibiotic ointment, and moist towelettes

- sterile bandages, including several pieces of gauze, adhesive bandages, and rolled bandages

- nonprescription drugs, such as aspirin and nonaspirin pain relievers, anti-diarrhea medicine, laxative, and syrup of ipecac to induce vomiting if necessary

- an extra pair of prescription eyeglasses or contacts

If you take prescription drugs, ask your doctor which ones you should keep in your disaster kit. Store them according to the label, and watch their expiration dates.

Tools. The right tools can save your life in a tight spot. Try including these handy items with your emergency supplies.

- flashlight and extra batteries

- signal flare

- whistle

- duct tape and scissors

- waterproof matches, or regular matches in a waterproof container

- a shut-off wrench, pair of pliers, and other tools you think you might need

- small, battery-powered radio with extra batteries, and a weather radio if needed in your area

Round out your disaster kit with a few basic items like a change of clothes, toiletries, and a warm blanket. Slip a set of spare keys, some cash, a credit card, and copies of critical documents into a waterproof container.

Keep your emergency supplies together in a bag near an exit door in your home so you can grab it fast if you have to evacuate. You may also want to put a smaller version of this kit in your car.

Draft a family plan before an emergency

- Ask an out-of-state family member or friend to be your contact person. Give their phone number and e-mail address to every member of your family.

- Pick meeting places for your family to gather should you have to leave your house. Choose a spot near your home, and another outside your area.

- Make sure everyone in your home knows how to turn off the utilities.

- Plan emergency exit routes from every room in your house.

- Have a disaster plan for your pets. They are not allowed in emergency shelters.

Investments

Keys to building a successful portfolio

The secret to becoming a millionaire

"The secret of getting rich slowly, but surely, is the miracle of compound interest," says Princeton University Professor Burton Malkiel, author of *The Random Walk Guide to Investing*. If you start early and stick to it, you, too, can become a millionaire.

Compounding is really pretty simple — it's just the process of earning a return not only on your original investment, but also on the accumulated interest that you re-invest. Benjamin Franklin described it best when he said, "The money that money makes, makes money."

Double your money in 7 years. At 10-percent annual interest, $100 will become $110 after one year. That amount will earn $11 the next year, and the resulting $121 will give you a $12 return the third year.

The key is to leave your money in your account. That's the most important factor in getting your money to multiply. The first couple of years may not amount to much, but it's surprising how fast it will pile up. At 10 percent, your money doubles in a little over seven years. After 25 years, you'll earn more every year than you put in to begin with.

It's even better, though, when you add to your investment every week or month. If you put in $500 a month and get a 10-percent return, you'll have more than $7.5 million in 50 years.

Because of the compounding effect, even if you only contribute for 25 years, you'll still have $7 million after 50 years. By that time, you'll be making more than $600,000 every year — four times the entire $150,000 that you put in during the first 25 years!

Use the "rule of 72" to determine how long it will take to double your money at other interest rates, Malkiel says. Take the rate of return you will earn from an investment, and divide it into the number 72. The result is the number of years it will take for your money to double.

Grow your nest egg faster. When interest rates are low, you can expect to earn less than 3 percent from your bank. That means it will take you a lot longer to double your money. To get a 10-percent return, you'll have to go to riskier investments.

Learn a million-dollar lesson

According to economist Burton Malkiel, here's a good example of why you should start saving sooner rather than later.

William and James are 65-year-old twin brothers. William set up an Individual Retirement Account (IRA) when he was 20 and contributed $2,000 per year until he was 40. James didn't start his IRA until he was 40 but has continued to put in $2,000 per year. Both brothers earn 10 percent per year. Who do you think has more money today?

Do the math, and you'll find that William has almost $1.25 million, and James, who put in 25 percent more, has less than $200,000. That's the miracle of compounding.

Malkiel encourages investing in index mutual funds. He points out that it doesn't matter if you buy when the stock market is low or high, the sooner you start the better. Don't depend on get-rich-quick schemes that require investment at exactly the right time, he advises.

"Time is far more important than timing," he says. "You can only get poor quickly. To get rich, you have to do it slowly, and you have to start now."

Make the most from your savings

You've probaby kept money in a savings account at your local bank ever since you first learned the value of compound interest. And that's good because you need to have some cash available at a moment's notice.

But even though that's the traditional way to save, you can — and should — do better. Your banker would prefer you keep your money in a low-interest savings account, but if you're smart, you'll switch to an account where your hard-earned savings can grow more quickly.

Try a different savings plan. Most banks offer money-market deposit accounts, which are a step up from savings accounts. They require higher minimum balances, but pay higher interest and are still covered by the Federal Deposit Insurance Corporation (FDIC).

Outfox a fox with mutual funds. A way to try and beat the bank is to buy money-market mutual funds. They are not FDIC-insured but are available from brokers and usually return more than bank money-market accounts.

They get their name from the U.S. money market — a huge, fast-moving system used by banks, large corporations, and government organizations. It's a wholesale market for low-risk, highly liquid, short-term IOUs.

Money-market mutual funds are considered among the safest and most stable of mutual funds. Their goal is to protect principal and produce some income at the same time. You can get to your money whenever you like simply by writing a check on the account.

There's no guarantee money-market funds won't fail, but it's not likely, and you'll generally get rates as good or better than the bank.

Go with CDs for better returns. You can also get better interest rates with certificates of deposit (CDs). The FDIC covers them, but you need to commit for at least six months to beat the money-market rate. If you lock in for two or more years, you can usually boost your rate another percent or two.

The problem with long-term CDs is you can't withdraw your money, and you're stuck with the current interest rates. You can get around those shortcomings by staggering the maturity dates of several CDs — a technique sometimes called "laddering." Once you get it going, you'll have different long-term CDs coming due at regular intervals.

Find the best money-market fund

Ask these questions before deciding which money-market account you want to invest in.

- How big is the fund? A mutual fund with over $1 billion in assets offered by a major fund company or brokerage firm should be well-diversified and well-managed.

- What is the expense ratio? Expenses reduce your yield, so stick with funds that are below .6 percent.

- What kind of investments does it make? Most funds buy commercial paper and government debt, which works best for most investors.

The table below shows four $10,000 CDs written for six, 12, 18, and 24 months. When the shorter maturities come due, they are renewed for two years. That gives you the advantage of two-year rates, but with access to a fourth of your money every six months. The table shows the approximate interest you would receive during each six-month period and your total interest earnings after the first two years.

You can modify this plan by having eight $5,000 CDs every three months, or four-year CDs coming due every 12 months. You can choose different combinations depending on your particular situation.

Another great benefit of laddering is the amount of interest you earn compared to reinvesting or "rolling over" one large CD. The table on the next page shows the interest your $40,000 would earn

CD Laddering

Amount	Term	Rate	June	Dec	June	Dec
$10,000	6	0.75%	37.50			
$10,038	24	2.25%		112.92	114.19	115.48
$10,000	12	1.25%	62.50	62.89		
$10,125	24	2.25%			113.91	115.19
$10,000	18	1.75%	87.50	88.27	89.04	
$10,265	24	2.25%				115.48
$10,000	24	2.25%	112.50	113.77	115.05	116.34
		Totals	300.00	377.85	432.19	462.49

Total interest earned in two years: $1,572.53

after a two-year rollover — almost $1,000 less than your laddered CDs. Obviously, laddering is a system worth looking into.

CD Rollover

Amount	Term	Rate	June	Dec	June	Dec
$40,000	6	0.75%	150.00			
$40,150	6	0.75%		150.56		
$40,301	6	0.75%			151.13	
$40,452	6	0.75%				151.69

Total interest earned in two years: $603.38

Map out a plan to build wealth

The key to financial success is your investment plan. That's the part of your overall financial plan that helps you figure out exactly how to build the wealth you need for retirement, college expenses, or a new house or car.

In an investment plan, you decide how much you want to put into certain kinds of investments to reach your overall goals. A structured plan provides discipline and helps you stay on track, says John Grable, associate professor of personal financial planning at Kansas State University.

Write a policy statement. Grable recommends writing your plan like a policy statement. Start with a goal, and then decide what kind of securities you are comfortable with. Set minimum and maximum percentages for the particular stocks, industries, or market segments you want.

Everyone's plan — or policy statement — should be tailored to their particular situation. Here are the factors Grable suggests you use to write your plan.

- Risk tolerance. This should be the starting point. Consider both your attitude and capacity for risk. You may be willing to take chances you can't afford.

- Asset preference. What kind of investments do you like? If you know a lot about the retail business or health care, you may want to concentrate on those stocks. Maybe you have a social agenda and want to avoid companies that sell tobacco or alcohol.

- Time horizon. If you need your money in three years, your strategy will be much different than if your goal is 30 years away.

- Objective. What are you shooting for? A plan for retirement income won't be the same as one to buy a house in five years.

Rebalance wisely. From time to time, you'll need to adjust your mix of assets. As stock prices rise and fall, you may buy more or less of one type and end up not following your plan.

"People find it difficult to sell winners," Grable explains, giving the late 1990s as an example. Stock prices soared — especially in the technology sector. Then the bubble burst, and big profits became losses.

"If something is going up, up, up in value, it's hard to rebalance that portfolio until it's too late," Grable says. "If I have a plan that says I'm only going 25 percent

"Less is best" when trying to decide how often to rebalance your portfolio, says financial planning professor John Grable. "Every six months – or even yearly – would be reasonable."

max in tech stock and I'm at 40, then I'm obligated to do something about it. Anything you can do to make the decision process easier is very valuable."

Use the target ranges in your policy as triggers. If you set international stocks at 0 to 15 percent, for instance, and all of a sudden they're up to 30, you know it's time to look at it. It's also important to remember why you set the ranges you did.

"If you build it correctly, you should be able to withstand the bear markets, and you shouldn't lose your head in a raging bull market," Grable says. "Discipline is the key for success."

Review and stay flexible. You need to review your investment plan from time to time to see if you should make changes. Your tolerance for risk most likely will change as you gain investing experience. You may become either more confident or more cautious. Life

Sidestep these investment traps

Common mistakes plague investors over and over. Here are some pitfalls to avoid.

- "Hot tips" and supposed inside information often lead to impulsive decisions on risky investments.

- Chasing last year's top performer is too late. Others doing the same thing drive the price up so high that it soon comes crashing down.

- Keep gut feelings away from your investing. Emotional decisions breed faulty judgment, impulsive behavior, and financial losses.

- Watch for excessive fees and high commissions. These expenses will eat up your profits, especially when investment returns are low.

changes — like jobs, income, and retirement — will affect your plan. So will external events like the 9/11 attacks.

"Your plan is sort of a living document," Grable says. "It changes as you change. You have to have a degree of flexibility. The danger is being too flexible and just moving with the financial winds of the day."

Take the time to monitor your investments, and learn about managing your money, he says. Then use common sense and the discipline you get from your policy statement to maintain an effective financial plan.

Keep your broker honest

"Trust but verify" was a favorite motto of the late President Reagan when he was dealing with the Soviet Union. It's also a pretty good guideline when you're dealing with your broker or financial advisor.

After all, it's your hard-earned money in that investment account, and it's up to you to make sure it's safe. So monitor your monthly statements carefully to verify your stocks are being handled the way you trust they are.

Associate professor John Grable teaches personal and family financial planning at Kansas State University. He lists two important steps to take when examining your statement.

- Check for hidden fees.

- Make sure there aren't any unauthorized trades.

Keep expenses low. "Your number one factor to achieve success as an individual investor is keeping expenses low," says Grable. "So watching for hidden fees is very important."

A lot of consumers pay fees they don't even know are there. They don't show up as commissions but are likely labeled account fees or custodial fees. They'll be listed in the cash transactions section or somewhere else you may not typically look. If they're quarterly fees, they won't show up on every monthly statement.

"Fees on these accounts can be so excessive that you actually lose money even though you are going up in value," Grable warns.

What should you do when you find these fees? Call the company and ask for an explanation, Grable says. Then ask them to waive the charges. Sometimes they will, but in other cases you'll probably have to move your account to get rid of them.

Require authorization. You should routinely check your statement for unauthorized trades just to keep the honest people honest.

Hidden fees hide true earnings

Your broker says your investment account earned an 8 percent return this year. But did it really? Use some simple math to find out.

Subtract your beginning-year balance from your year-end balance, and divide the difference by the beginning amount. Say you start the year with $1,000 and haven't made any withdrawals. Your ending balance is $1,040.

- $1,040 - $1,000 = $40
- 40/1,000 = .04

Your true yield was 4 percent. Chances are, fees and commissions gobbled up the rest. If that's the case, you may want to look for an account with fewer fees.

Most brokerage contracts contain a standard clause giving the broker discretion to trade without getting your specific permission.

"The general rule is never give discretion," says Grable. "Even the most honest brokers at some point in their life might be tempted to make a trade that might not be suitable."

Look for items bought or sold that you don't recognize or remember giving permission for. Every trade earns a commission, so you want to make sure you're not paying for activity you didn't authorize.

"For the most part, the industry is honest and ethical," Grable says. "But there are some people out there who do take advantage of people, particularly older Americans. You just have to watch out for your own interests."

Critical protection for your portfolio

You've decided to stop playing it safe with your savings and invest in the stock market. You know if the market drops, you could lose it all, and you're willing to take the chance. But here's another risk — what happens if the brokerage firm holding your stocks suddenly goes under? Does your investment sink with it?

Fortunately, that's one worry you can safely set aside, according to Stephen Harbeck, president and CEO of the Securities Investor Protection Corporation (SIPC). Thanks to the SIPC, you're not left in the lurch.

Protects brokerage accounts. When a brokerage firm closes due to bankruptcy or other financial difficulty, SIPC steps in to make sure you get your securities back.

"Our job is to return the contents of the customer's account," Harbeck explains. "We protect the custody function that brokers perform. We protect you against anything being missing from your account."

Nearly all brokerage firms belong to the SIPC — they have to if they're registered with the U.S. Securities and Exchange Commission (SEC). Look for the SIPC logo, or check with the SIPC, SEC, or National Association of Securities Dealers (NASD) to see your broker's regulatory history and make sure he's registered.

Takes over failed firms. The SIPC works with a court-appointed trustee of the failed brokerage firm and either transfers customers' accounts to another firm or divides up the assets among the customers. If there is a shortfall, it uses SIPC reserve funds to make up the difference.

Since it was created by an act of Congress in 1970, the SIPC has recovered around $15 billion for more than 623,000 investors.

Limits its coverage. Because stocks are different than bank accounts, SIPC does not provide blanket coverage like the Federal Deposit Insurance Corporation (FDIC) does for banks. You're on your own with market risk.

"We don't give you protection against fluctuation in market price of your portfolio," Harbeck says. "The risk of market fluctuation never leaves you because the reward of market fluctuation never leaves you."

Other limits are:

- It only protects up to $500,000 per account.

- It doesn't cover commodities futures contracts, currency, or investment contracts not registered with the SEC.

- It relies on the broker's records to tell what is in each customer's account, so make sure your statements are correct and you have copies to prove what is yours.

Does not guard against fraud. The SIPC also does not cover misleading statements about a security's value or outright fraud in respect to what a security is worth. Investors should study a business before they buy its stock and understand the financial basis of what they invest in, Harbeck says. Every investor also should take some basic precautions.

"An investor shouldn't buy anything he doesn't understand," he cautions. "An investor should resist cold calls. An investor should make sure that the person they are dealing with isn't trying to say 'you must act immediately or else you'll lose an opportunity.' Reputable people don't do that sort of thing."

Harbeck urges investors to learn as much as they can about how investing works. "There is an absolute host of investor education material available," he says. He recommends the Web site *www.investoreducation.org,* run by the Alliance for Investor Education, as a good place to start.

The first step to wise investing

Are you stumped by stocks? Looking for the first step to take toward wise investing? It may surprise you that the first thing you need to do involves a lot more than just the stock market.

"The first step in investing is to understand how the different asset classes relate to one another," says Maria Scott, editor of the American Association of Individual Investors' *AAII Journal.* "Then do an asset allocation plan to determine which amounts of your total portfolio to invest in each of those categories."

Scott lists stocks, bonds, and cash as the major asset classes. Burton Malkiel, in his book *The Random Walk Guide to Investing*, adds real estate to those three. He also mentions three other categories — insurance, collectibles, and gold — that are not investments.

You should buy insurance for protection, rather than a way to make money, he explains. Collectibles and gold are nice things to have, but they don't pay interest or dividends, and it costs a lot to store and protect them.

Keep some cash. Everyone needs a cash reserve to meet life's various emergencies, Malkiel says. Investment cash isn't just the currency and coins in your pocket, but money that can be changed into that quickly.

You can keep your cash in checking and savings accounts, money market accounts, and short-term certificates of deposit and Treasury bills. The key is to make sure you can cash it in within 90 days without forfeiting principal.

Loan your money. Bonds are simply loans to governments and corporations. When you buy a bond, you get an IOU with a fixed interest rate and a promise to return your principal at the end of a certain time period, sometimes 20 years or longer. Interest is paid on a set schedule, so you know exactly when and how much income you'll get.

Own a piece of the company. With stocks, you have a chance to make more money, but there's more of a risk you'll lose it. Stockholders are actual owners of a company — each share of stock is a piece of equity. When a company makes money, it divides up the profits, and pays each owner a dividend. However, stockholders never know how much they're going to get.

You can make good money by selling a stock whose price is going up, but you can also lose a lot if it goes down. Malkiel warns about "bubble" situations, which begin when the price of a particular stock or group of stocks rises rapidly. Investors drive up the price as they rush to get on the bandwagon. Eventually, though, the bubble bursts. Those left holding the bag are big losers when the stock drops back to its true value.

Invest in your home. If you're a homeowner, you're a real estate investor. For many people, their home is the biggest part of their

Learn from 2 historic bubbles

The tulip-bulb craze – In the early 1600's, people in Holland became fascinated with certain tulip bulbs. They began to treat tulip bulbs as investments, buying eagerly at higher and higher prices. Eventually, people began to cash out, and the buying frenzy turned into a selling frenzy, bankrupting thousands of tulip speculators.

The Internet craze – The Internet's promise of both new technology and new business opportunity sent prices of any stock with ".com" in its name to astonishing heights. The bubble burst in early 2000, and more than $7 trillion of market value disappeared.

investment portfolio. You can also invest in real estate by buying rental properties or shares in real estate investment trusts (REITs).

Make your investment plan. Once you understand these categories, decide how much you want to invest in each one. You can balance your risk by putting some money into safer places, especially if you're investing in something volatile like the stock market.

"Put a certain amount in the stock market, and then temper your risk with investments in the other categories," Scott advises. "Once you figure out how much you want to devote to stocks, you can focus on the different categories of stock."

Stock market smarts

When you listen to people talk about their stocks, the variety can be dizzying. Income stocks, growth stocks, value stocks — what does it all mean and how can you find one that will make you rich?

Actually, these terms don't always refer to precise groupings. More often they refer to a style of investing rather than to a particular category of stock, says Maria Scott, editor of the American Association of Independent Investors' *AAII Journal*.

"You can have a value style of investing or a growth style of investing," Scott explains. " But if you want to have a more conservative portfolio, for instance, you would concentrate on the core section of the stock market, which is large-cap stocks."

Understand the 'caps.' The abbreviation "cap" stands for capitalization or market price of a company. It is figured by multiplying the number of shares outstanding by the price per share. Thus, a company with 500 million shares and a stock price of $50 would have a market cap of $25 billion.

Scott describes large-cap stocks as generally the top 70 percent of the stock market — "the major corporations, everybody knows their names." Mid-caps are somewhat smaller. Small-cap stocks are very small — usually less than $1 billion — and tend to be faster growing companies. Each group has different risk and

Who really owns your stock?

When you invest in common stock, you buy a piece of a company. Theoretically, the company issues a new certificate of ownership whenever a security changes hands. But it's an awkward and time-consuming process when literally millions of shares are traded each day.

To make things easier, brokerage houses usually buy shares in a "street name" and give "book entry" credit to their customer. That means the brokerage firm actually owns your stock. You need to check your statements carefully to make sure you get proper credit.

growth characteristics. You can use different styles of investing with each one.

Look at types of stock. It's important to be familiar with the different types of stock so you can understand how risky each one is.

- Income stocks typically pay a higher dividend than average. They are good for people looking for regular revenue to pay for things like retirement or college expenses. Dividends give incentive for investors to purchase stock in companies that no longer need to use their profits to fund growth. You won't get rich from trading income stock, because both the companies and their stock prices are generally pretty stable. The trade-off is an income you can count on.

- Growth stocks have prices that rise faster than normal. They tend to be up-and-coming companies and are more unpredictable, Scott says. Growth-stock investors are willing to take the chance they will continue to appreciate and not take a dive.

- Value stocks are those bought for less than the company is worth. "For some reason, the market doesn't like that particular stock, but you as an individual think the market has misjudged it," Scott explains. But be careful — many stocks sell at low prices for good reason. "They really are lousy stocks," she says. "You have to make up your own mind about the outlook on a particular stock. Learn how to analyze an individual company."

Learn the ins and outs. You also need to study investing styles and how they relate to each other. "Within each style, there are many different methods of stock selection you can use," Scott says. "For instance, you can have a growth approach that takes value into consideration."

"You need to really understand how the stock market and stocks in general behave," she advises. She recommends looking at the different market caps in terms of your own time frame and risk comfort.

"What kind of returns can you expect over various time periods? Know — and be prepared to live with — the kinds of volatility within the different market caps."

Investment secrets that work

How would you like to beat the S&P 500 by more than 100 percent three years in a row? Sounds impossible, but Purdue University boasts a student-managed investment fund team that has done just that.

Associate Professor Michael Cooper advises Purdue's Krannert School of Management investment team — the best collegiate team in the country — and helps his MBA candidates use advanced statistical analysis to make those amazing stock picks.

Cooper also has practical ideas for people who aren't studying to be professional investment managers. Here are some of his basic rules for sensible investing that work even in today's uncertain economy.

Diversify your portfolio. "The first big mistake I see is that people, regardless of age — even people getting close to retirement — tend to not be well diversified," Cooper says. "Most people I talk to have most of their assets in just a few stocks or bonds. Lots of times it's because they work for a company, and a lot of their wealth ends up in just that one stock. That's a critical mistake."

Cooper cites the Enron debacle as a good example of the catastrophe that can happen if you have all your eggs in one basket. He also points out that of all the companies on the New York Stock Exchange, about half of them will fail over a 10-year period. When you are well diversified, you own enough different stocks that the ones that succeed make up for the ones that don't.

Stay away from single stocks. Cooper suggests the average investor buy mutual funds instead of owning any individual stocks. He warns against trying to "profit from the prophets"— scoring big gains with frequent trades on the advice of stock analysts and other so-called experts.

"Trading is hazardous to your wealth," he says. Most studies show it is difficult to beat the general stock market by just buying individual stocks. He says to look for well-diversified passive index mutual funds that just try to follow an index like the S&P 500 or the Wilshire 5000. The manager is not trying to beat the market, so there are fewer transactions and fees.

"By the time you account for the fee difference, you see an amazing conclusion — passive funds strongly outperform the active ones," Cooper says. "So, for the average investor, it's much better to invest in the so-called passive index funds."

Pick a value fund. "There are some other tricks to find asset classes that beat others over the long run," Cooper confides. "One of the best things you can do is have some money in a value index fund."

Value is an investment style that chooses stocks that are under-valued when comparing their fundamental performance numbers. The Purdue student investment teams look for high book-to-market, cash flow-to-price, and earnings-to-price ratios to find value stocks. They tend to show good long-term prospects but poor recent performance.

Cooper says diversification is even more important when buying these stocks because their failure rate can jump up to 60 to 70 percent.

"But here is the kicker," he says. "As long as you invest in a big basket of them — like 100 or 200 of them — which you can do with the mutual funds, then you're OK."

Avoid complex investments. Another secret to investing success for the average person is to stay away from more complicated funds. These include commodities, futures, and options. Each has special

Investments

rules and characteristics, and only more advanced investors
should deal with them.

"The average person has no business being in those things,"
says Cooper.

Invest like 2 top market moguls

An "intelligent investor" should buy common stocks with a margin
of safety, a large discount to book value or "intrinsic value," and
sell when prices approach full value. This timeless advice comes
from the late Benjamin Graham who consistently beat the stock
market during a lifetime of investing in the 20th century.

Stock prices usually go up and down for rational reasons. But
occasionally they will drop or climb for reasons that have nothing
to do with the earning power or value of the company. As an intelligent investor, you should never forget that you are buying not
just a stock, but also a part ownership share in a business.

Buy when shares are low. In the long run, the success of investing
in any stock will be determined by the value of that company. In
the short run, you may have the opportunity to buy shares of a
good company at a bargain price when the market is depressed
after a crash or for other reasons that prove to be temporary.

It takes courage to buy at a time when everyone is rushing to sell
because the stock has dropped like a stone. But if you do your
homework and know the company is sound, you will eventually see
an end to the market's depressive phase as prices start to go up.

Watch out for irrational peaks. After stabilizing, the market can
later go into a "manic" phase, and your stock may soar. This was
the case with the tech market where irrational excitement caused
stocks to rise quickly. They then peaked in a bull market that

250

ended in another crash. You need to be careful you don't get swept up in that type of situation.

Know when to sell. Figuring out when to sell can be more difficult than deciding whether a bargain stock may be profitable. Graham analyzed price and value, then bought stocks of companies with little debt and lots of cash or marketable securities per price of each share. He then unloaded the stocks after they went up about 50 percent, even though many still sold for less than book value per share.

Another super-successful investor, Warren Buffett, follows a different method. Buffet studied under Graham and grew to appreciate the importance of buying not just "bargain" stocks, but attractively priced stocks of companies that had competitive advantages that made them more profitable than their competitors.

Buffett now buys only a handful of stocks of the best businesses with extraordinarily good management. They also have strong "moats" that prevent competitors from successfully attacking markets for their products. Buffett buys when the price is right and holds stocks, sometimes for decades, as long as they keep their competitive advantages. This avoids paying capital gains taxes that would be due if he followed Graham's methods.

Hold on to your shares. Buffett's technique is better for most investors. The decision to buy stock in a good company at a bargain price should be your main focus. By following Buffett's "holding" philosophy, you won't have to constantly wonder if you should sell the stock when it goes up.

The only time you should sell is if you see a fundamental change in the business that takes away its long-term competitive advantage. Or you may want to take advantage of a manic phase in the economy and sell when the stock price is inflated way beyond the value of its current and projected earnings.

As an ordinary investor, you can learn more about how to invest like Graham and Buffett by reading *The Intelligent Investor* by

Benjamin Graham and *The Warren Buffett Way* (2nd edition) by Robert Hagstrom. These books will give you key insights into using the methods of these market moguls to identify exceptional values in the stock market and profit from them.

Track the highs and lows of risky stocks

You must understand the concept of risk-reward when choosing which investments to get into, says Michael Cooper, Purdue University associate professor of finance.

"The basic law in finance is the risk-return trade-off," he says. "Higher return means higher risk. It's always there."

Before you invest, you need to know your own risk aversion — how much you can stand having the value of your portfolio bump up and down over time — and how long you have before you'll need your money.

Different asset classes have different risks and rewards over different time periods, Cooper explains. The riskier categories seem to work best over longer periods of time. If you only have a year or two before you need your money, go with more conservative choices, and you'll have less chance of big losses.

Cooper developed the chart on the following page to show how different investment classes have done in the past and to help investors decide the risks they want to take. It uses actual data from 1926 to 1998 for three groups of investments — small-cap stocks, large-cap stocks, and long-term bonds. The top figure is the average return for the time period involved, and the bottom number is the worst-case history for the same number of years.

The chart shows, based on 72 years of experience, that small-cap stocks posted an average one-year gain of 18 percent, which is a good return, Cooper says.

"But here is where the risk-aversion part of it comes in," he warns. "The worst-case scenario for one year over that period was minus 58 percent. There is a small possibility you could lose 58 percent of your money in just one year if you invest all your money in small stocks."

If you stay in small stocks for 20 years, though, the picture appears to improve. The chart shows the worst you might do is a 200-percent gain — an average of 10 percent a year. Plus, you're looking at an average appreciation of more than 1,700 percent.

That sounds like a phenomenal increase, but be careful about using that as a justification to invest solely in small-cap stocks. Some studies have questioned whether small stocks really have outperformed large stocks over the long run. The answer may change depending on the time frames examined.

Investment results from 1926 to 1998

		1 year	5 years	10 years	20 years
Small-Cap Stocks	Average	18%	124%	277%	1,752%
	Worst case	-58%	-80%	-44%	205%
Large-Cap Stocks	Average	13%	74%	211%	834%
	Worst case	-43%	-49%	-9%	84%
Long-Term Bonds	Average	6%	35%	82%	191%
	Worst case	-8%	-11%	10%	30%

Cooper's chart reflects the highs and lows of different investments over a 72-year span. Although small-cap stocks appear to outperform all others by a large margin, some studies question whether they truly outperform large-caps even over a long period. Smart investors will weigh the risk of losing 58 percent of investment money in just one year if they purchase only small stocks.

Your safest investment is long-term bonds, which, according to the chart, never lost more than 8 percent in any one-year period. However, bonds gain less on average over 20 years than either type of stock.

3 ways to deal with investment risk

Risk is a fact of life in the investment world. And now that more people are switching from savings to investment accounts, they're experiencing the perils of risk first-hand.

Investment risk goes with the game, says Frank Armstrong III, a certified financial planner and president of Investor Solutions, Inc. "You get paid extra returns for subjecting yourself to additional risks. There's no way to avoid risk unless you are content with the zero-risk rate of return — which we mostly think of as the Treasury bill."

Experts say it's important to strike a balance between saving and investing and the amount of risk you're willing to accept.

Diversify to avoid business risk. Every business has the chance to fail, whether it's because of mismanagement, economic conditions, bad luck, or outright fraud. It's impossible to know which company will make it and which one won't.

But Armstrong has a solution. "I think business risk can be almost completely diversified away by index funds," he says. "Anyone who gets caught in an Enron or Global Crossing disaster generates their own misery because it's completely avoidable."

Single companies often go broke, but entire markets don't, he says. "If an investor owns a single stock and that company goes broke, the investor has lost his entire portfolio. If the company that went broke is only one-tenth of one percent of the investor's portfolio, the investor will hardly notice."

Accept market risk. "Market risk is the risk that's left after we've diversified as fully as we can. And it can't be diminished," Armstrong says. No matter how good a company is, its stock price may be affected by broad market trends.

"You have to live with and accept market risk," he continues. "Be prepared for what I call the good, the bad, and the ugly in short-term returns. The longer you hold a risky asset, the closer to the expected rate of return you should get."

Because short-term risk is more unpredictable, Armstrong recommends not using stocks or long-term bonds for obligations coming due in the next five to seven years.

"Let's suppose your daughter is about to enter Harvard," he explains. "The chance that the market may go down 20 to 30 percent is always there. That minus 30 percent may be the difference

---

The dangers of day trading

Day trading may seem like an easy path to riches, but high-risk schemes like this are almost sure disasters, says investment advisor Frank Armstrong.

Day traders buy and sell stocks rapidly throughout the day in the hopes of making money as prices rise and fall. A government report concluded that only about 11 percent of day traders had the basic skills to make a profit, and 70 percent lost their entire investment.

The U.S. Securities and Exchange Commission (SEC) warns that day trading is extremely stressful, generates huge commission expenses, and can bring severe financial losses.

---

between Harvard and night school some place. You ought not to take that risk because the risk is simply too high."

Watch out for interest-rate risk. Bonds are the chief target of interest-rate risk. Rising interest rates push bond prices down, so you take the chance of losing money when you buy bonds during times of low interest rates. This is something you should be concerned about, Armstrong says, even if you're happy with the rate the bond pays.

"If rates go up, you are sitting on a bond with greatly diminished value," he explains. "If you had that money in cash, you could buy a bond for a higher yield.

Armstrong says to stick with shorter-term bonds — from one to five years — because longer time periods don't pay off as well. "Risk goes up a lot, yield goes up a little," he says.

Can you make a fortune with mutual funds?

If Johnny Carson's Carnac the Magnificent gave the answer "buy mutual funds," what would the question be?

- How can you gain access to a world of money?

- What is an easy way to make a fortune?

- How do you buy hundreds of stocks with just a small investment?

If you chose all of the above, you'd be right. Mutual funds give you millions of dollars of buying power for a huge assortment of investments. They open the door to a simple, uncomplicated path to increased wealth. They're also the best way to diversify your holdings and spread your risk, even when you only put in a few dollars a week.

So what exactly is a mutual fund? It's a company that gathers a large pool of money and invests it in a broad range of stocks according to a specific set of rules. Each investor owns shares according to how much cash they put in. As the portfolio gains or loses value, so does the value of each individual share.

The beauty of mutual funds is that they have enough money to invest in a wide range of stocks, bonds, or whatever else their prospectus allows them to. And instead of owning a few shares of just a few companies, you can have equity in lots of companies.

Choose according to your taste. Thousands of mutual funds exist, and each has its own specialty. A fund may concentrate on large-company stocks, government bonds, a business sector like communications or energy, or an investing strategy like growth or value. Within that specialty, it will buy as many different assets as it can.

Mutual funds have managers and staffs of analysts who save you the time and effort of studying and tracking individual investments. Choose a fund that fits your particular taste, and you'll watch your wealth grow as that entire segment of the economy grows. It's a slower, but surer, path to making your fortune than betting the farm on individual stocks.

> When you find a mutual fund that interests you, take the time to check it out thoroughly. Just because it's a mutual fund doesn't mean you'll automatically make money on it.

Of course, nothing in the stock market is guaranteed to make money, including mutual funds. But when a fund owns hundreds of stocks, the failure of one or two of them has little effect. That diversification protects you from losing your shirt if one or two stocks take a dive.

Consider management style. The biggest difference in funds is whether they are actively or passively managed. An active mutual fund is one where the manager tries to beat the market by picking out the winners. He or she will actively evaluate and trade stocks, generally on a daily basis. These funds will have management fees to pay for the extra effort needed to try and score higher gains.

On the other hand, passive funds such as index funds or exchange traded funds only try to copy a certain index, such as the Standard and Poor (S&P) 500 or the Dow Jones Industrial Average (DJIA). It contains just the stocks — or bonds — in a particular index, so its value follows that index.

Because there is little trading, you pay minimal fees and commissions. Many experts believe these funds, which cover all the bases, actually outperform actively managed funds that depend on hitting the right buy at the right time.

Compare types of funds. Most mutual funds are open-end funds, which means they have no limit to the number of shares they can issue. At the end of every trading day, the fund determines its net asset value (NAV), which is its total assets minus total liabilities divided by the number of shares outstanding. This NAV is the price a fund will charge you to buy new shares or pay you if you sell.

Closed-end funds have a fixed number of shares. Once those shares are issued, they are traded just like any other stock. You deal with a broker instead of going directly to the fund. Prices depend on the mood of the market and can change minute-to-minute instead of just once a day. Shares may sell at a discount (less) or at a premium (more) compared to the actual NAV. It's better to have some investing experience before you deal in closed-end funds.

Watch out for charges. Loads are sales commissions charged by mutual fund companies and can range from 1 to 8.5 percent of your investment. If you put $1,000 into a fund with a 5-percent front-end load, only $950 is invested, and $50 goes to the fund. If you cash in $10,000 from a 5-percent back-end load, you only get $9,500.

In addition to loads, funds — especially active funds — may charge management, custodial, or maintenance fees. When evaluating a mutual fund, it's important to subtract the extra fees from the gains it makes when figuring your overall yield. Index funds and exchange traded funds are a good choice because they have ultra-low charges, often a fraction of 1 percent per year. See *Invest in index funds for a sure bet* on page 260.

Proven path to investing success

Experts recommend you buy shares of mutual funds every month whether the market is up or down. They call this investment technique "dollar-cost averaging." Princeton University Economics Professor Burton Malkiel says this can help you lower — but not avoid — risk by making sure your entire portfolio is not bought at temporarily high prices.

"You'll buy fewer shares when prices are high and more shares when prices are low," he explains. "The average cost per share is actually lower than the average of the share prices during the period when the investments are made." The table below shows what you would earn if you invested $150 for three months at various share prices.

Period	Investment	Price of Shares	Shares Purchased
1	$150	$75	2
2	150	25	6
3	150	50	3
Total cost:	$450		
Average price:		$50	
Total shares owned:			11
Value of shares earned: $550 ($50 x 11)			
Average cost: approximately $41 ($450/11)			

When the stock market takes a dive, the market value of your portfolio will still lose value, too. But don't be tempted to sell out, Malkiel cautions. He points out that the market as a whole always goes back up, even though individual stocks may not.

"A critical feature of the plan is that you have both the cash and the courage to continue to invest during bear markets as regularly as you do in better periods," he says. "Indeed, if you can buy a few extra shares whenever the market declines, your dollar-cost averaging will work even better."

Invest in index funds for a sure bet

Active traders try to time the market by figuring out the trends and then picking the best time to buy or sell. These experts are eager to show you how you, too, can beat the market.

But before you jump into the trading frenzy, listen to what Dr. Burton G. Malkiel has to say. Malkiel, a Princeton University economics professor, has studied and practiced investing for more than 50 years. He has written many articles and books, including *A Random Walk Down Wall Street*, and *The Random Walk Guide to Investing*.

Be a smart investor. "I think timing is a fool's game," Malkiel says. "In all my years, I have never met anyone who was able to time the market with any degree of regularity. I don't even know anyone who knows anyone who has been able to do it consistently."

The former chairman of Princeton's economics department and dean of the Yale School of Management admits that sometimes people do get it right. But, he adds, today's winners are usually tomorrow's losers, and you never know ahead of time who the winners will be.

Stay in all the time. If you're going to invest, you need to stick with the market through its ups and downs, Malkiel says. If you decide to get out of the market and happen to miss a few good times when it goes up, it will destroy your return.

For example, one dollar invested in the stock market in 1928 would have grown to $1,600 by the year 2000. But staying out during 1933, 1954, and 1985 — years when all the experts were pessimistic — would have reduced your take to just $463.

Getting in and out of the market also means paying transaction fees and capital gains taxes, which cut into your profits, Malkiel says

Buy index funds. So what to do if you don't trade stocks? "My view — from the time I first wrote *A Random Walk Down Wall Street* 30 years ago — is to buy index funds," Malkiel says. "They are low cost. They themselves don't trade. They are tax efficient. Over the long haul they beat three-fourths or more of the active managers. I say you buy and hold an index fund, which itself is a buy-and-hold strategy."

Index funds are passively managed. They hold all the stocks in whatever index they follow, so buy-and-sell decisions are automatic and don't require a professional manager. The mix only changes when the index changes. Fees are few and the fund's value creeps up with the market. You may miss the chance of making a killing on a super performer, but you won't be wiped out when one goes bad.

Own some of everything. "The best index fund to own is something called the total stock market index," Malkiel suggests. "It's usually approximated by the Russell 5000, which actually contains about 7,000 stocks. You basically hold everything."

Malkiel also recommends investors use index funds to diversify among asset classes. Simply buy into bond indexes or money-market indexes as well as the stock indexes.

Use ETFs for lump-sum investment

Exchange traded funds (ETFs) are index funds that are traded on major stock exchanges. You don't have to wait until the end of the day to buy, sell, or lock in a price.

Known by nicknames like Spiders and Vipers, ETFs are a quick, easy way to buy into index funds. They're tax efficient and have low expenses.

ETFs are not recommended for savers who contribute a little at a time because you pay a brokerage fee for each transaction. But they're ideal if you have a large amount to invest since there's only one commission.

Four funds that were among the most stable, broad, liquid, and low-fee in 2004 were SPDR Trust (SPY), iShares S&P 500 Index Fund (IVV), DOW Diamond Series Trust I (DIA), and iShares Dow Jones U.S. Select Dividend Index Fund (DVY).

You can even buy real estate index funds that own shares of real estate investment trusts (REITs), which own portfolios of commercial real estate. REITs work a little like mutual funds, except they are traded just like common stocks, and they own office and apartment buildings, warehouses, and shopping malls instead of stocks and bonds.

Keep retirement funds safe. Even though he believes strongly in index funds, Malkiel doesn't rule out trading individual stocks.

"Investing is fun," he says. "I understand people will want to do it. What I say to them is this — for your serious retirement money, index it. Then, you want to play around — sure. I don't think you're going to beat the market, but you'll have fun doing it. Just make sure that the core of your retirement portfolio is in safe index funds."

The truth about bonds

Bonds are an important mix in a good investment portfolio and a smart way to offset the ups and downs of the stock market. Bonds are considered safer than stocks, although historically their return is lower. But don't buy bonds just because you think they're the safest thing to invest in.

Although some kinds of bonds are extremely safe, some are almost sure to cost you money. Treat bonds just like any other investment — look at them objectively, measure their risks against their rewards, and consider who stands behind them.

Learn what to expect. When you buy stock, you buy a piece of a company. A bond is more like an IOU. You lend your money to a government, corporation, or other issuer, who then promises to pay you interest until the bond comes due. At that point, you get your money back.

Some good reasons to buy bonds include:

- they diversify your portfolio and provide a hedge for your stock holdings.
- they give you predictable income in the form of interest payments.
- some offer valuable tax advantages.

Because a bond comes with an interest rate and payment dates, you know exactly when and how much you will get from your investment. That's why bonds are often used to fund retirement and college education.

Evaluate the downside. So what's not to like about an investment where you get back your principal plus a guaranteed interest rate?

- The interest rate is locked in for up to 30 or more years. You get the same return later as you get now, no matter what happens in the financial world. That's fine when rates drop, but you're left behind when they go up.

- Bonds are only as good as the company or governmental unit that issues them. Some bonds are backed up by specific assets that can be sold to pay off bondholders before anyone else gets their money. Unsecured bonds are backed only by the ability of the issuer to pay its bills. If it gets in trouble and defaults, you're left with nothing.

Consider when to sell. Changing conditions may prompt you to sell your bonds before they mature. However, you probably won't trade them for their face amount. A bond may sell for a premium — more than its value — or at a discount, depending on several factors.

A bond's credit worthiness and time remaining until maturity both affect its price. If the credit rating drops, you may want to sell for less rather than risk losing it all if the company goes belly up. Or you may want your money right away and give a discount in order to cash out the bond before maturity.

But the biggest factor in bond pricing is interest rates. When over-all interest rates rise, bond prices fall. When rates are down, bonds are up. Consider:

- A $10,000 bond at a 7-percent rate will pay $700 per year.

- A $10,000 bond at 10 percent will pay $1,000 per year.

- At 10 percent, it only takes $7,000 to get $700 per year.

In over-simplified terms, you lose $3,000 when rates go from 7 percent to 10 percent, because a buyer can get a higher return on $10,000 with a new bond. If you want to sell yours, you have to discount it to $7,000 so that it earns at the same rate as a new one. Of course, falling interest rates will work in reverse. Your bond will be worth more, since it will pay better than a new one.

Despite the relative safety of bonds, the risk of losing money is just as real as with the stock market. As with all investments, you need to review your bond holdings each year to be sure they're keeping pace with your goals.

Minimize your bond risk

You have many types of bonds to choose from, so where do you start? Think of the different types of bonds as climbing a ladder. The closer you are to the ground, the more stable and safe you are. As you climb higher, there's more risk, but the payoff — interest yield — gets bigger. And each rung has its own rules and procedures.

Breathe easy with government bonds. Bonds from the United States Treasury are at the bottom where it's almost impossible to fall off. Backed by the full faith and credit of the federal government, they're as close as you can get to a sure thing. But the interest rate is also lower.

The next step up is U.S. agency bonds, issued by groups like the federal Farm Credit System and major mortgage-related agencies — almost as safe as treasuries, but a little higher yield.

Municipal bonds — nicknamed "munis" — are issued by state and local governments and related organizations like highway commissions, airport authorities, and sewer districts. General obligation bonds are backed by the full taxing authority of a jurisdiction. Revenue bonds — a notch riskier — are supported only by a specific project.

The big attraction of munis is they are exempt from federal income tax and, in some cases, from state taxes, too. Their advantages depend on your particular tax situation. You also need to look closer at their risk potential — especially with revenue bonds.

Check corporate bonds carefully. Corporate bonds are on the top rungs, and there are a lot of them. They can range from practically a sure thing to a serious risk, depending on the financial shape of the company issuing them.

Professional agencies like Standard & Poor's Corp. and Moody's Investors Service evaluate the credit worthiness of companies and governments and rate their bonds accordingly. The best-rated bonds are investment grade. Then the ratings range from speculative to a warning of real danger of default.

Beware of junk bonds. If someone tempts you to buy "high-yield" bonds, remember that their other name is junk bonds. The higher interest rates are a trade-off for the likelihood they'll turn bad. Make sure you know what you're doing before you get into junk bonds.

Be careful with commodities

Why do some investors go crazy over pork bellies, crude oil, and soybeans? If you're a commodities trader, you know these products can bring you quick fortune — or financial ruin.

Experts usually warn inexperienced investors to stay away from commodity markets. You need sophisticated investment knowledge and enough money to accept a high amount of risk.

Commodities do not appreciate over long periods of time at rates comparable to other investments, although they may offer some protection during periods of high inflation.

If you're unfamiliar with the commodities market, you need to know that commodity traders don't buy and sell actual products. They deal in futures and options.

- Futures contracts are commitments to a certain price for a certain product on a specific future date.

- Options are the right to buy or sell something at a certain price.

"With a futures contract, I must deliver the contract as stated or buy my way out of it. My potential losses could be relatively large," says investment advisor Frank Armstrong, author of the *Informed Investor: A Hype-Free Guide to Constructing a Sound Financial Portfolio.* "With an option, I don't have the obligation to buy it. I can just walk away from the deal if it goes against me. The premium is the total extent of my loss."

Farmers use futures and options to guarantee a price for their grain and livestock — a hedge against the risk of lower prices at harvest time. Other producers also use hedging to guarantee a selling price for their own particular product. Airlines, meat packers, and public utilities use hedging to manage their purchase costs for jet fuel, live cattle, and electricity.

Watch out for slick deals

Don't be tempted by alternative investments that have risks you don't understand, warns investment advisor Frank Armstrong.

During financial downturns, unethical salesmen may call pitching "pie-in-the-sky" deals, he says. If you've lost money in the stock market, you may be tempted to try anything. But you'll most likely lose again if you don't understand what you're getting into.

Armstrong says an investment should be transparent — with all the costs, risks, and details revealed. Don't believe dealers that say, "Give me your money, I'll do something smart with it."

Armstrong warns that individual investors shouldn't try to compete with these big commodities players. They use options and futures as part of a high-level business strategy. But an individual investor tends to be a little more wild and crazy, he says.

"He's gambling, only gambling, and the expected return on that gamble is negative," he emphasizes. "The transaction costs for individual speculators are so high that it is very unlikely you're going to guess right often enough to cover your costs. You don't have a chance in that game."

Learn and earn in an investment club

Learn about investing in a fun, relaxing environment by joining an investment club. It's an ideal activity if you don't know a stock from a bond and can't seem to figure it out on your own.

"Investment clubs are about education. They are for people who want to learn," says Lynn Ostrem, who helped organize three investment clubs and is now president of the Crow River Investment Club in the Minneapolis suburbs.

"It's kind of like college," she explains. "You go to college to learn a trade, and then you go out and use that trade. With an investment club, you are educating yourself for your future."

By joining a group, you get the advantage of other investors' knowledge, time, and money as well.

Gain ideas and insight. The main benefit of an investment club, Ostrem says, is that you get ideas for your own personal investing. You also learn how to invest in the stock market and establish the habit of regular investing.

"Attending meetings every month keeps investing in the forefront of your psyche and keeps you investing personally," she says.

In a typical investment club, members study an assigned stock and then report on it to the entire group, which then decides what to buy for the club portfolio. As time goes on, members gain more and more investing expertise.

Monthly dues — usually $50 to $100 per month — are used to purchase stock. That won't be enough to make you rich, but you can use what you learn for your own portfolio. Your long-term retirement plan will still need diversification among stocks, bonds, mutual funds, etc. Investment clubs tend to focus on just stocks.

Choose club carefully. Investment clubs are usually easy to get into, but it's best to do some homework before you join. Find out about clubs in your area by contacting the National Association of Investors Corporation (NAIC), the American Association of Individual Investors (AAII), talking to people, or searching the Internet.

Many clubs use a unit-based accounting system to keep track of members' stock values. The total portfolio value is divided by the number of units purchased to get a cost per unit. That number fluctuates with the market, but it's a fair and easy way to determine what your shares are worth.

Once you've found a club, attend a couple of meetings before you join. Watch how they do their research and deliver information. Get a feel for the people and how they do business. See how well informed the members are and if they do more socializing than studying.

"You have to remember you are investing your money," Ostrem cautions. "This is a business, and it needs to be run like a business. I have money invested in this company because of your recommendation. I expect you to pull your weight."

Know how to get out. You may get into an investment club and later on realize it's not meant for you. So make sure you know how to leave if you want to.

"Look at a partnership agreement and see how much it costs to get out of the club and when you can get your money," Ostrem advises. "You should have your money a month after you tell them you are going to leave."

You'll have to pay the expenses of selling down the portfolio to get the cash to pay you off. You also may have to pay an exit fee, which Ostrem says shouldn't be more than $25.

Check to see if the club uses a unit-based accounting system. If so, buying into the club — as well as leaving it — should be relatively simple.

Head off frustration with compatible group

Your investment club should have the same ideas you have, advises Brenda. That includes both investment philosophy and members' willingness to participate.

Brenda joined a club sponsored by her alumni group to learn more about investing. She's discovered that some women like the social hour more than the business part of the meetings. It frustrates her that they don't take things as seriously as she does.

"I don't like it when they expect us to make buying decisions from their careless reports," Brenda says. "I've learned quite a bit, but I've had to do a lot of research on my own."

Taxes

Easy ways to soften Uncle Sam's sting

Cut taxes with charitable giving

The Bible says it is more blessed to give than to receive. But when it comes to taxes, the blessings you bestow on others benefit you as well. The IRS allows you to deduct charitable expenses, so you can feel good about helping your favorite organizations and get a tax break at the same time.

The IRS only allows you to take deductions on qualified nonprofit groups, though. Here's a short list of acceptable charities taken from IRS publication 526.

- religious, scientific, literary, and educational organizations

- nonprofit groups that help prevent cruelty to children or animals, and national or international amateur sports organizations

- governmental bodies, state organizations, and war veteran groups

Multiply your giving. Along with donating money, you can donate real or tangible property, which can actually increase your deduction. "From a tax perspective you get a deduction of the fair market value of what you contributed," says CPA and tax attorney Sandy Botkin, president of the Tax Reduction Institute and author of *Lower Your Taxes — Big Time*.

If you paid $100 for a share of stock that is now worth $1,000 and donated it to a charity, your charitable deduction becomes $1,000. Plus, you have no capital gains tax, and the charity benefits by getting $1,000 instead of $100.

Consider a lifetime gift. You can also receive a charitable deduction with a lifetime gift. "If you give a gift to a charity during your life, and they get to keep it when you die, or it goes to another charity — you get to take a deduction," says Botkin. And you take the deduction at the time you donate the gift. But if your gift is set to come back to your family when you die, it is called partial interest and is not deductible.

Create a remainder trust. A charitable remainder trust is specifically designed to avoid the deduction problem of partial interest gifts.

"A charitable remainder trust is where you donate property to a trust, such as stock or real estate, that has gone up in value

Watch out for scams

Take these steps to make sure your charity is legitimate:

- Check IRS Publication 78, available at *www.irs.gov* or by calling 1-800-829-1040. Or check *www.guidestar.org,* a national database for non-profit organizations.

- Have the organization fax you a copy of its exemption letter. Every tax-exempt organization has one unless it is part of the federal or state government.

- Ask to see an annual report of the organization's income and expenses. That way you can make sure the money is going to a legitimate charity and not into a con man's pocket.

tremendously. And you get a charitable deduction," says Botkin. "Then the trust gives you an income for life. At the time of your death, the trust receives the property."

Be sure to talk to a financial expert about this type of deduction, Botkin says. There are several types of charitable trusts as well as scam artists who may mislead you about their uses.

Watch out for limitations. When donating cash, you must subtract the fair market value of any gifts or meals given to you from your donation. For example, if you buy a $100 ticket to a fundraising dinner, and the meal costs $35, you can write off only $65 of your donation.

The IRS limits the amount of charitable deductions you can write off in a year.

- If you donate cash or non-capital-gains property, you can deduct the fair market value, up to 50 percent of your adjusted gross earnings.

- You can donate capital gains property you've held for over a year to a public charity. Because you're avoiding capital gains tax, your adjusted gross earnings limitation is 30 percent.

- You can also donate capital gains property you've held for over a year to a private foundation. But the adjusted gross earnings limitation is 20 percent.

In any of the above cases, your excess donations can be carried over for up to five years.

Keep your receipts. The IRS requires you to show proof of your donations, if asked. "Anytime you donate $250 or more in cash or property to any qualified charity at any one time, you must get a contemporaneous written acknowledgement from the charity," says Botkin. "If you donate property worth over $5,000, you must get a certified appraisal attached to your tax return."

Even if you just donate clothing or miscellaneous items, you must have an itemized list with the full market value for each item.

Beware of non-deductible donations

Not all donations are considered "charitable." Here are some you can't claim:

- donations made to an individual
- donations made to non-qualified organizations
- donations made to political candidates or organizations, such as Political Action Committees, lobbying groups, or the new political 527 groups
- the value of your time or services
- your personal expenses, or appraisal fees

If you have questions, see your accountant or IRS publication 526 for more information.

Tips to cut your tax bill — legally

You know you're obligated to pay taxes so you grudgingly contribute your share every year. But if you're not careful come tax time, you may end up paying more than you need to.

"Your objective should be to pay all of the taxes that are due, but not one penny more than the law requires," writes Jeff A. Schnepper in his book *How to Pay Zero Taxes*.

As a financial, tax, and legal advisor, Schnepper says if you don't know the rules, you can't win the game. That's why he offers these top tax-saving strategies. But tax laws and threshold amounts constantly change, so make sure you read your tax instruction booklet carefully or consult your tax professional every year.

Itemize deductions. By law, you can subtract certain expenses from your taxable income. These can be itemized on the form, or you can take a standard deduction. The standard deduction for married filing jointly in 2004 is $9,700 — up from $9,500 in 2003. You get more if you're over 65, blind, or both.

To figure out if it's worth itemizing, Schnepper says to first determine your medical expenses — less 7.5 percent of your adjusted gross income (AGI). Add to that what you spent for home mortgage interest, state and local taxes, charitable contributions, and other expenses allowed on Schedule A of the 1040 form. If the total is more than your standard deduction, then you can save by itemizing.

If your expenses are on the borderline with the standard deduction, Schnepper advises you to look for items you can pay early or late. Load up on expenses one year, he says, go light the next. That way you can alternate — take the standard deduction one year and itemize the next.

Use your home. Home ownership is one of the best tax breaks around — especially if you have a mortgage. Chances are, you can get paid simply for owning and living in your own home.

Besides claiming mortgage interest payments and real estate taxes, here are some ways you can use your home to cut your tax bill.

You may enjoy your large income-tax refund every year but, in effect, you're giving the IRS an interest-free loan. Adjust the number of allowances on your W-4 form, and you'll put more money in your own pocket throughout the year.

- Home equity. Interest on home equity loans counts against taxable income. These loans are based on the value of your home less the amount of your mortgage and other liens. You must use your home as collateral and can only deduct interest on the first $100,000.

- Home office. If you work at home, the portion of the house — office, workroom, storage — that you use for business is deductible. You can also add a percentage of utility bills, insurance, and depreciation to your business expenses. However, if you claim any depreciation on your home as a result of your business, when you sell, that portion of the gain will be taxable.

- Second home. Mortgage interest and real estate taxes on second or vacation homes get the same deduction as your main residence. If you rent it out for less than 15 days a year, all the income is tax-free. More than that is subject to formulas and computations.

Double your savings. Contribute to an individual retirement account (IRA) or a 401k plan, and cut your taxes while you build

---

Itemizing info you need to know

The more money you make, the less your itemized deductions may be worth thanks to the "itemized deduction phase-out." Tax attorney Sandy Botkin explains:

"If your adjusted gross earnings are over $142,700 for married filing jointly, or you're making more than $71,350 for married filing separately, for every $10,000 you make over those numbers, your itemized deductions are reduced by $300. What that means is you may actually have some of your itemized deductions, including charitable deductions, eliminated."

Talk to your accountant if you think this situation applies to you.

---

a nest egg. Those funds are deducted from the amount you pay tax on. If you're self-employed, use a simplified employee pension (SEP) or Keogh plan to save untaxed dollars.

Flex your medical spending. The IRS allows most employers to withhold pre-tax money from your paycheck, which you can then use to pay medical expenses. They're called medical savings accounts, cafeteria plans, Health Savings Accounts (HSAs), or flexible spending plans. According to Schnepper, it's a better deal than itemizing on your tax return, since you don't have to deduct 7.5 percent of your income from your expenses. Talk to your employer for details.

Get thousands of dollars tax-free

One of the best ways to put extra cash in your pocket is to take advantage of tax benefits that could save you thousands of dollars. Not all the cash you get is taxable, and knowing the difference will help you get the most out of the money you have and give you ways to find more when you need it.

According to Jeff A. Schnepper's *How to Pay Zero Taxes*, here are 14 payments the IRS can't touch:

- part of the profit from selling your home
- most social security payments
- a portion of annuities income
- interest on state and municipal bonds
- life insurance proceeds
- inheritances and other gifts
- many alimony and support payments
- court-awarded damages

- some scholarships and grants

- "cafeteria" or flexible benefit plans

- employer expense reimbursements

- workers' compensation

- employer-paid medical insurance premiums

- public assistance/welfare payments

By taking advantage of the tax-free status of these payments, you'll have more money in your pocket to spend. Most IRS rules have exceptions, though, so check with a tax professional for details.

Terrific tax breaks for seniors

Many Americans are unaware of the numerous tax breaks Uncle Sam has for them after they turn 55. If you've overlooked these federal tax loopholes in the past, now is the time to appreciate one more benefit of growing older.

Enjoy your lower income. When you retire you get built-in tax relief because your retirement income is usually less than when you worked. With less income, you pay less tax. Tax-deferred retirement plans, like an IRA or 401k and qualified annuities, are good deals because you don't pay taxes on them until you are in a lower tax bracket.

Social Security payments are usually part of retirement income. They are not taxable as long as half your Social Security plus the rest of your income is not more than $32,000 if you're married and filing a joint return. Even if it's more, only a portion of it is taxed, depending on your total income.

Itemize health expenses. It's a good idea for seniors to consider itemizing medical expenses instead of taking the standard deduction. The

7.5 percent of your income you have to subtract from medical deductions gets smaller as your income goes down. You're also likely to have more medical expenses as you get older.

- Most payroll deduction health insurance premiums are already tax-free, but when you start paying them yourself, you can deduct them on your tax return.

- Qualified long-term care insurance expense is deductible, and so is the cost of medical care in a nursing home or similar facility.

- If you drive yourself to doctors, you can deduct mileage, parking, and toll booth fees. The same goes for bus, taxi, train, or plane fares. You can also deduct ambulance service fees.

- Itemize the cost of weight-loss programs prescribed to treat a disease and stop-smoking plans.

- Frequently overlooked expenses include eyeglasses and hearing aids; special equipment like wheelchairs, braces, and crutches; and the cost of remodeling your home to accommodate a disability.

Cash in on your birthday. Once you hit 65, you can enjoy some automatic benefits on your tax return. First, you get an extra tax credit just for being that age. In addition, the minimum amount for filing a return increases at 65, as does the amount of the standard deduction.

You actually have a tax benefit you can take advantage of even earlier — when you're 59-1/2. That's the age you can withdraw from IRA and 401k plans without penalty. Before then, it costs you an extra 10 percent.

Look for personalized benefits. Pre-death life insurance payments to the chronically ill are not taxed. Neither are expense paybacks from volunteer organizations like the Retired Senior Volunteer Program, Foster Grandparent Program, and Service Corps of Retired Executives.

Learn more about these and other senior benefits by talking to your tax professional or reading the Internal Revenue Service Publication 554, *Older Americans' Tax Guide*.

8 ways to avoid a visit from Uncle Sam

Each year, the Internal Revenue Service (IRS) randomly chooses a few returns for audit. Most are picked because IRS employees and computers spot various red flags, says Scott Estill in his book *Tax This! An Insider's Guide to Standing Up to the IRS*.

Just because your return raises a flag doesn't mean you'll be audited, says Estill, a tax attorney and former IRS senior trial attorney. Someone has to review each return and decide who will get a letter from an auditor. If you don't want to be one of the chosen few, make sure you follow these steps when filling out your tax forms.

Be aware of being different. The IRS uses a computer-generated score called the Discriminant Index Formula (DIF) to compare your numbers with national statistics. The IRS uses the DIF to pick the majority of audited returns, so be aware that lopsided numbers attract attention.

For instance, if the average amount of charitable contributions for your income group is $1,000 and you claim $3,000, the computer will flag this entry. According to Estill, Schedule C (sole proprietorship business) losses are also known to boost the DIF score — and your chances of an audit.

Report everything. Unreported income is the main target of most audits. Since the IRS matches information it gets from other sources with your return, you're asking for trouble if you don't list the income from every W2 and 1099 you receive.

Use exact numbers. The IRS knows rounded numbers are probably estimates you can't support in an audit. Estill recommends using precise amounts — like $1,988 or $511 instead of $2,000 or $500.

Check your math. Computers screen your return and make automatic corrections if you add it up wrong, but errors give the IRS a reason to look closer. To slide through without calling undue attention, Estill advises you make sure your arithmetic is accurate.

Be neat and organized. Don't risk getting picked for an audit because the IRS has trouble reading or understanding your return. Inexpensive software is available to help you print it from your computer.

Document unusual deductions. If you have a casualty loss, theft, or other extraordinary deduction, attach police reports or similar explanations to the return. The IRS may look at it and decide you have enough proof, and an audit isn't necessary.

Save the right records

If the IRS finds a mistake on your tax return that warrants a look at previous returns, they can only look at three open tax years, with these exceptions:

- If you've omitted more than 25 percent of your gross income, they can go back six years.

- If they can show fraud, where you knew better, they can go back indefinitely.

- If you don't file a tax return, there is no statute of limitations, and you can be audited forever.

To be safe, tax attorney Sandy Botkin recommends saving your tax records for six years and your actual tax returns and attached documents forever.

On the other hand, Estill does not recommend attaching an explanation for any deduction you might question yourself.

File at the right time. Most tax experts believe you reduce your chances for an audit if you file as close to April 15 as possible. Estill says they believe variations in your DIF score will not stick out as much when so many returns are coming in.

Estill also says if you file late, the IRS will already have chosen most of the returns to audit. But he cautions that you must file an extension and pay at least 90 percent of the tax due before April 15 to avoid late payment penalties.

Be extra careful. Estill says the IRS targets specific occupations and professions like lawyers, nurses, ministers, construction workers, and mechanics. It also likes to schedule follow-up audits for taxpayers who were audited in the past and had to pay extra taxes. If you fall into these categories, it's best to have everything in order so the auditors won't find anything.

Come out on top in an audit

If you've been selected for an audit, don't panic. It's not the end of the world. It doesn't mean you're a bad person or you're on your way to jail. With a little preparation, you should come through the situation with a minimum of problems.

Despite what you may think, the IRS is not out to harass you. "The agent's goal is to get through your review and close the audit," says CPA/tax attorney Sandy Botkin, president of the Tax Reduction Institute and author of *Lower Your Taxes — Big Time*. "You can expect courtesy, and you can expect a reasonable amount of fairness from the IRS agent."

Preparation is key to easy tax filing

Gathering basic information beforehand simplifies your task tremendously. The IRS recommends you have:

- a copy of last year's tax return.

- social security numbers for you, your spouse, and any other dependents.

- all income statements, such as W-2 forms and 1099 forms for dividends, retirement, social security income, and unemployment.

- receipts for all itemized deductible expenses.

- bank account information for directly depositing your refund.

It's wise to hire an accountant to handle your audit, but if you decide to do it yourself, remember that anything you do to make the agent's life easier will benefit you.

Have a good attitude. "Your attitude toward the IRS agent should be, 'What can I do to help close this case? What do I need to give you?' In other words, cooperation, not 'I'm going to fight you tooth and nail,'" says Botkin. He also has this advice:

- Know your rights. Review the *Taxpayer Bill of Rights* found in IRS publication number 1. The two-page document should be sent to you with your audit notification.

- Call your assigned IRS agent ahead of time, and ask questions. Make sure you know exactly what the IRS is looking for.

- Arrive on time. If you're late, you give the agent more time to find other problems in your tax return.

- Ask to postpone your audit if you're having trouble coming up with your records.

Bring the right documents. Organize your paperwork, and provide only the documentation the IRS has asked for, Botkin says. If they're auditing your travel, for example, only bring your travel records.

In an IRS audit, you must justify your tax deductions with receipts or other adequate records. If receipts are missing, under the Cohan rule, tax courts allow you to make a reasonable estimate as long as you have a reasonable basis for that estimate. For example, if you don't have a mileage log to verify travel write-offs, but can show appointments in your date book that correspond to those miles, the IRS should allow that deduction.

However, you should try to reconstruct missing information as accurately as possible beforehand, based on your other documentation,

---

Watch what you say to your agent

After Ron's home office expenses were audited, the agent casually mentioned the sleep-away couch in Ron's office. "My mother likes to visit me, but I'd be afraid she'd get hurt sleeping on that."

"I've had plenty of people stay here, including my parents, and it never hurt them," Ron said.

A home office must be used exclusively for business. Ron just admitted he didn't meet the exclusivity test. The agent disallowed the entire home office deduction.

"There are only four things you need to say to an IRS agent," tax attorney Sandy Botkin says. "Yes, no, I don't know, and it's my accountant's fault."

Botkin advises. Don't exaggerate or mislead, and never try to tamper with or change any evidence.

Pay what's due. If it turns out you owe the IRS money, but can't afford to pay it in a lump sum, tell your agent. He should be willing to work out a payment plan. But consider that option carefully, Botkin warns.

"They don't accept payments without a lot of interest and penalties," he explains. "You're much better off borrowing the money, or charging it on your credit card than you are with a payment plan."

It's also possible to try and negotiate by an "offer in compromise." Basically, you tell the IRS you don't have the income or assets to pay off the debt, and you make an offer for something less than you owe. The IRS rarely accepts one, but it's worth a try.

Save time and trouble with e-file

Are you tired of running to the post office at the last minute with your tax return, or waiting forever for a refund? You can avoid such inconveniences by filing your taxes electronically.

Millions of taxpayers use this easy, convenient method, called e-file for short. Here's why you should be one of them.

- According to the IRS, e-filed returns show less than a 1-percent error rate, compared to a 17.5-percent error rate for paper-filed returns.

- The IRS sends you an acknowledgement that your return was received.

- You can get your refund in 10 days if you have it deposited directly into your bank account.

- You can file early if you owe taxes, but you don't have to pay until April 15. Plus, you can authorize an electronic funds withdrawal from your bank account, or use a credit card.

You can only e-file through authorized IRS providers, which you'll find on the IRS Web site at *www.irs.gov.* You can prepare your own return and have the provider e-file it to the IRS, or have a tax professional prepare and e-file it for you.

If you're computer savvy, you can do it all yourself with tax software like Intuit's *TurboTax* or H&R Block's *TaxCut.* These programs will verify your math and walk you step-by-step through the e-file procedures.

If you don't want to pay for software or use an accountant or tax service, you may be eligible for IRS Free File. Go online to *www.irs.gov*, click on Free File, and follow the easy directions.

You can also e-file by phone if you're qualified to file form 1040EZ. Just follow the instructions in your TeleFile booklet. If you were

Taxes in a snap

Doug and Lisa Sharpton no longer dread April 15. They have found the no-stress way to take care of their taxes — by e-filing.

"It's easy to do," Doug says. "When I'm filing electronically, if I make a mistake, it's easy to go back and correct it. Plus, you don't have the hassle of making sure it gets into the mail on time."

"I like the fact that there's a minimal amount of paperwork to make it happen," Lisa says. "And we get our refund deposited directly into our checking account in less than two weeks."

Easy to do, no snail mail, and quick refunds — what more can a taxpayer ask for?

not mailed a booklet, look for one at your local library or post office. Or order one by calling the IRS at 800-829-1040.

After you file your federal taxes, why not do the same with your state taxes? Thirty-seven states and the District of Columbia currently support e-file. Check with the IRS online, or call its toll-free number, to find out if your state participates in the e-file program.

Choose IRS-approved software

If you e-file your own return, choose a tax software program that has been tested and approved by the IRS. You'll find a list of IRS software partners at *www.irs.gov*. Look for the following features.

- Ease of use, good error checking, live tax advisors, and a drop-down program help menu.

- The ability to import data from your prior year's return and financial programs like *Quicken*.

- Tips on extra deductions and information on new tax law changes.

- All IRS forms and publications, including those that relate to home-based businesses.

Don't get caught in the AMT trap

Most people have never heard of the alternative minimum tax (AMT). That is, unless they're blindsided by it at tax time. The government created this second income tax system to prevent the wealthy from itemizing their way out of paying taxes.

Unfortunately, low-to-middle-income taxpayers are finding themselves caught by the AMT as well.

Watch these triggers. As the name suggests, the AMT is an alternative way to calculate the minimum amount of tax you need to pay. If you meet one or more of these conditions on your tax return, you may be surprised to find yourself facing a higher tax bill.

- large deductions for your state and local taxes, such as property tax and state income tax

- interest on your second mortgage if it's used for something other than to build and improve your home

- a large amount of miscellaneous itemized deductions, like unreimbursed employee expenses

- a large number of personal exemptions

- taking the standard deduction instead of itemizing deductions

- a large amount of medical expenses

- exercising large incentive stock options

- interest that is exempt from regular income tax

- large capital gains that can reduce or eliminate the AMT exemption amount

Defer deductions. The only way to ensure you won't have to pay this tax is to periodically check your income and deductions during the year. By knowing where you stand, you can defer certain deductions or incentives to keep you within the AMT limits.

Unfortunately, there's no general guide to tell you when your alternative tax will exceed your regular tax. The IRS says that point may come when your taxable income, after all deductions and credits are taken, exceeds the following amounts.

- Married filing jointly or qualifying widow(er) — $58,000

- Single or head of household — $40,250

- Married filing separately — $29,000

Calculate your tax. You'll have to fill out IRS form 6251 to find out if you owe additional taxes under the AMT. If you prefer, you can use a tax software program. Besides eliminating errors, it can save you time and money by choosing which tax system to use and calculating your taxes for you.

Tidy up your finances

Nothing is more frustrating than trying to find a misplaced record. Follow these tips to easily locate the records you need.

- Photocopy all receipts. Receipt ink has been shown to fade away over time.

- Ask your bank for your canceled checks so you won't have to search for proof of an expense.

- Store financial documents in a safe-deposit box.

Computer software is available to record your important information and keep it in one location. One to try is Kiplinger's *Your Family Records Organizer*. You'll find it at *www.kiplinger.com/software*.

Plan ahead to avoid tax woes

Proper planning can keep you from owing the government money at income tax time. It's wise to make sure you have enough withheld throughout the year to cover the taxes you'll owe.

But what if a tax bill catches you by surprise? Try to pay on or before April 15 so the IRS won't impose late payment charges. If you can't afford to pay on time, here are some options to consider.

Turn to family and friends. Ideally, you can borrow what you need in a no-interest loan from a family member or close friend. You'll save money by not having to pay the IRS's interest and penalty charges or the interest on a bank loan.

Try a payment plan. Ask the IRS if you can make payments to pay off your tax debt. Unfortunately, the IRS has recently become less friendly, says tax attorney Sandy Botkin, president of the Tax Reduction Institute, and author of *Lower Your Taxes — Big Time.* The government may allow you to make payments on a one-year installment plan, but it rarely goes for anything longer than a year, he says.

The IRS's payment plan includes a $43 setup fee, plus annual interest and a monthly penalty each month it's not paid off.

Weigh the credit option. If you keep a credit card for emergencies, this may be the time to use it. But experts have different opinions on whether it's a good idea. Some warn against using your credit card because it may cost more than you think.

Credit card companies charge vendors $25 for every $1,000 of charges. In this case, the vendor is the IRS, and by law, it is not allowed to pay these fees. So guess who has to pay them? That's right, you. They're automatically added to your credit card bill.

If you can't pay your credit card bill in full, you'll need to figure in monthly interest charges, too. Still, Botkin believes you're better off borrowing the money, even on a credit card, than you are paying the IRS with the added interest and penalties.

Your best bet is to compare the costs for both a credit card and IRS payment plan and go with the one that costs you less. You may want to consult a credit counselor for help in figuring your costs and deciding your best course of action.

Consider a loan. Another option is to get a home equity loan from your local bank or credit union. You will have to add the cost of a home appraisal, but the interest on an equity loan can be tax deductible. Check with your accountant to see if you can deduct the loan's interest on your next year's taxes. If you don't own a home, you may have to offer some other form of collateral like a used car.

Plan for next year. After you get your unexpected tax bill paid off, make sure you don't ever have to face the problem again. A simple way to plan ahead is to look at your total taxes on line 60 of last year's form 1040 tax return. Use that amount as a starting point for the taxes you need to have withheld this year. The federal government allows you to file a new W-4 to change your withholding allowance at any time and for any reason.

Don't drastically decrease your withholding to the point where you pay a penalty for under withholding. At the same time, you don't want to over withhold and give the government an interest-free loan. Make your best estimate, then monitor your withholdings closely throughout the year, and adjust them when necessary.

Save a fortune in estate taxes

Thanks to the U.S. Congress, your heirs may owe no federal taxes on your estate when it comes time to divvy up your inheritance. And that's true even if you have a million-dollar-plus estate.

Congress passed tax relief legislation in 2001 that gradually repeals the federal estate (death) tax. Over the span of nine years, the estate tax exemption goes from $675,000 to $3.5 million. Plus, the tax rate drops from 55 percent to 45 percent.

The estate tax disappears altogether in 2010. But it will be reinstated in 2011 with just a $1 million exemption unless Congress permanently repeals the tax before then. The table below shows the changes you can expect from 2004 to 2010.

Estate and gift tax exemptions

Year	Estate tax exemption	Gift tax exemption	Estate and gift tax rate
2004	$1.5 million	$1 million	48%
2005	$1.5 million	$1 million	47%
2006	$2 million	$1 million	46%
2007	$2 million	$1 million	45%
2008	$2 million	$1 million	45%
2009	$3.5 million	$1 million	45%
2010	Estate tax repealed	$1 million	35% (gift tax only)

Until the estate tax is eliminated, it's best to maximize your tax deductions to protect your kids' inheritance. "Federal and state taxes can consume one half of the estate above the property that is exempt," says Indiana tax attorney Jerry Cowan. So plan ahead to ensure your estate pays as little tax as possible.

Calculate your estate's net worth. Before doing any estate tax planning, determine the value of your estate. Use a copy of the *Estate Net Worth Balance Sheet* on page 295 to figure out your estate's net worth.

As you add more assets to your estate from retirement benefits, 401k plans, inheritance, or plain hard work, you'll need to recalculate your estate's balance sheet. Redo your estimates before making any large changes to your estate to see the effect on your overall financial situation.

Share your wealth. One of the best ways to reduce your estate taxes is to spread your wealth around while you're still alive. Here are some ways you can do it.

- Use the annual gift exclusion. You are allowed to give away $11,000 a year tax free to as many people as you want without filing a gift-tax return. Married couples can give $22,000.

  Cowan recommends the gifts be made as a trust to people under 21 years old. "You're putting a lot of money into a younger person's hands that they might not handle wisely," he says. You could also use part of the $11,000 as a contribution to a Roth IRA, which they can save for retirement, use to buy a new home, or pay for future qualified higher education tuition payments.

- Pay medical or school expenses. You also have an unlimited annual exclusion for payments of a person's medical expenses or tuition. The payments must be made directly to the educational institution or medical provider.

  This is useful when you've already gifted $11,000 to an adult child, grandchild, or friend and still want to help them without paying any gift taxes.

- Offer a gift of stock. If you give away stock in the amount of the annual exclusion, you

Congress did not repeal the federal gift tax but permanently raised the exemption rate to $1 million. You can give away that amount in taxable gifts over your lifetime before owing any federal tax. However, you are still required to file a gift-tax return each year if you exceed the $11,000 annual exclusion.

eliminate the value of its future growth from your estate. That helps your tax situation because $11,000 worth of stock may grow to several hundred thousand dollars in the future.

- Donate unwanted assets to charity. You may not only get a tax write-off, but you'll also lower your estate's net worth. By donating property, such as real estate or securities, you'll eliminate the future growth of the asset from your estate, too.

Consider moving to a tax-free state. It may be a drastic solution, but moving may solve a lot of your tax problems after you retire. Because of the way the tax relief law works, state governments are losing their estate-tax revenue. Many have retaliated by increasing their estate taxes or establishing inheritance taxes. If it looks like your estate will be hit hard, you may want to pursue this option. Check with a tax attorney to find out which states are estate tax-free.

Strike back at high property taxes

Americans have believed in their right to fight unfair taxes ever since their ancestors first tossed crates of tea into the Boston harbor. You may have no say in most of the taxes you pay, but you can voice your discontent in at least one area — property taxes.

Whether your annual tax has jumped dramatically, or you think it's too high on principal, you can take measures to get it changed.

Examine your assessment. All states allow residents to appeal their property taxes within 30 to 60 days of getting an assessment notice. So make sure you read it carefully as soon as you receive it.

Your taxes are based on the appraised value of your land, including any structures you have on it. If you meet any of these conditions, you should file an appeal.

- Errors on your property report, such as the wrong number of bedrooms or bathrooms.

Estate Net Worth Balance Sheet

Date: _____ Husband: _____ Wife: _____

DOB: _____ DOB: _____

	Husband	Wife	Joint	Total
Assets				
Cash				
Checking/Savings	____	____	____	____
Other	____	____	____	____
Real Estate (market value)				
Residence	____	____	____	____
Other properties	____	____	____	____
Life Insurance (face value)				
Personal	____	____	____	____
Group	____	____	____	____
Personal Property (autos, furniture, etc.)				
____	____	____	____	____
____	____	____	____	____
____	____	____	____	____
____	____	____	____	____
____	____	____	____	____
Investments (market value)				
Retirement plan	____	____	____	____
Mutual funds	____	____	____	____
Stocks	____	____	____	____
Bonds	____	____	____	____
Total Assets	____	____	____	____
Liabilities				
Credit cards	____	____	____	____
Mortgage	____	____	____	____
Auto loan	____	____	____	____
Other loans	____	____	____	____
Miscellaneous	____	____	____	____
Total Liabilities	____	____	____	____
Net Worth	____	____	____	____
(Assets minus liabilities)				

- Other homes in your neighborhood are paying less, and they fall into the same tax classification as yours.

- Your home isn't worth what the assessor thinks it's worth.

If you win the appeal, your future tax bills will be lower. This trick could save you thousands of dollars over the life of your home.

Fight it yourself. Filing an appeal is surprisingly simple. You can get information from the county assessor's office outlining what you should do and how to document your claim. They can also help you find information on the tax rolls, which show you taxes on similar properties in your neighborhood.

Hire an expert. If you can't handle the fight for lower property taxes yourself, hire a specialist, such as a real estate attorney. They usually charge a third to a half of the money they save you in the first year.

> Even if you plan to appeal your property taxes, you must pay them when they're due. If you don't, it could result in your losing your home.

Take the deduction. If you fail to win your appeal, take comfort in the fact that property tax is one of your best income tax write-offs. Make sure you include it on line 6 of Schedule A when you itemize deductions.

Also, some states charge a property tax for items considered personal property. These may include boats, cars, trucks, motorcycles, mobile and motor homes, trailers, aircraft, and even business personal property. You can deduct all or a portion of these taxes under IRS rules on line 7 of Schedule A.

Enjoy home-business tax perks

Would you like a job with no boss, no commute, and plenty of tax deductions? Then start a home-based business that makes you the boss, keeps you active, and may save you thousands in taxes.

Few people know the IRS has two sets of tax laws, says former IRS attorney Sandy Botkin, CPA and president of the Tax Reduction Institute. The first is for employees, and the second is for people who own a small business. And the business owners' tax laws are much more attractive, Botkin says in his book *Lower Your Taxes — Big Time: A guide to the powerful tax advantages of being a consultant, independent businessperson, or small business owner.*

"A home-based business will make you better off than a second income," he says. "You will probably save $2,000 to $10,000 per year by starting your own part-time business." That's because you can deduct many of the expenses you already incur on a daily basis.

If a home business is something you'd consider, do your homework first. Start-up costs are usually minor, and in most cases, you can operate your business with little or no overhead costs, Botkin says. Therefore, you need to focus on the type of business you want to start. See *Cure for the retirement blues* in the Retirement chapter for some ideas.

Once you get your home business off the ground, you can take advantage of its many tax benefits. You'll find you can write off almost anything you do as long as you conduct business at the same time. Here are just a few examples.

- The IRS defines associated entertainment as anything fun done with your client before or after a business discussion. You are allowed to deduct 50 percent of the cost of entertainment if it precedes or follows your meeting.

- Season tickets to sporting events and concerts are treated as individual events. If you have season tickets for 10 home games, and your client goes to eight, you can deduct a portion of the cost of eight games.

- If you invite a couple to your home for dinner and discuss business during the evening, you can deduct the cost of dinner. You can also deduct the costs of small parties if you discuss specific business with your guests at some point during the party.

- Drive to a business seminar, take your family along for some vacation time after, and deduct all your car costs, just as if you drove alone.

- Business-related meals, and in certain circumstances, your spouse's meals, are deductible.

- Dues to business clubs or civic organizations can be deducted under the right conditions.

Before you decide to take any of these deductions, check with your accountant for specific details. But make sure you take advantage of all the tax perks you can, Botkin advises.

"The choice between being rich and poor, for you and millions of others, is the opportunity that starting your own consulting or

---

Deduct a portion of your vacation

Bob manages his own rental properties in Florida. He decides to expand his business by managing other people's rental properties. Bob's son, Tom, a graphic artist, goes to Florida with his family for a prearranged business trip with his dad to discuss the new business's design needs.

Over the course of the week, they eat dinner, play golf, and go see a movie. In each case, they have an ongoing discussion about the type of design Bob wants for the business. A portion of Tom's trip and entertainment will be deductible, and he still got to vacation with his family.

small business offers. If you have one going already, then you need to make sure you're enjoying the many tax advantages your brilliance in so doing offers you."

Slash home-based business taxes

Would you like to keep some of the money your small or home-based business pays into Social Security and Medicare? Here's how — create the right circumstances to take advantage of a legal loophole in the tax system.

You can reap the rewards of this IRS sanctioned benefit by making your business an S corporation, thereby eliminating up to 40 percent of your Social Security and Medicare taxes.

Grasp the rules. If you want to operate as an S corporation, you must file Form 2553 with the IRS within the first 75 days of the tax year. Your accountant or tax attorney can provide the forms you'll need to get the process started. The cost to become an S corporation varies from state to state.

Once your business is converted from a regular corporation to an S corporation, it won't pay taxes on its earnings. Instead, the earnings are divided according to the percentage of shares owned by each shareholder of the corporation.

For example, if you're the only shareholder in the corporation, the earnings are all yours. But with two equal shareholders, the earnings are divided in half. If shareholder A owns 60 percent of the shares, he gets 60 percent of the earnings. Likewise, if Shareholder B owns 40 percent, he gets 40 percent of the earnings. In any case, you add your earnings to your individual tax return.

"The key to saving Social Security taxes is that with an S corporation you pay self-employment tax on wages, salaries, and bonuses but not on dividends," says Sandy Botkin, CPA, tax attorney, president of the Tax Reduction Institute, and author of *Lower Your Taxes — Big Time!* So pay yourself as little in salary as possible and as much in dividends as possible. Doing this will wipe out most of your Social Security tax.

Watch your salary. The IRS requires you to pay yourself a reasonable salary for your profession. Plus, according to IRS rules, you're not allowed to take all of your S corporation earnings as dividends. Don't even try because they could reclassify your entire dividend as wages, and Social Security taxes will be due on every dime.

What's a reasonable salary? The IRS defines it as what similar companies, under the same circumstances, would pay for the same services. Simply put, it's what you would pay someone else to do your job.

Before you decide on a salary, Botkin says consider these seven factors to help you determine what is reasonable.

- actual services performed
- responsibilities involved
- time spent
- size and complexity of the business
- prevailing economic conditions
- compensation paid by comparable firms for comparable services
- salary paid to company officers in prior years

In addition, Botkin advises that you check with a good accountant or tax attorney when setting any salaries and bonuses for yourself. He also recommends getting comparable salaries from government publications.

Protect your money with the right accountant

Legend has it the best tax accountants have figured out that two plus two equals three. Meaning, they know their way around the tax laws and will fight to legally get you all the deductions you are allowed.

But realistically, the best way to find a good accountant is to ask questions, says tax attorney Sandy Botkin, author of *Lower Your Taxes — Big Time*. Here are some questions Botkin recommends you ask during an interview.

- What credentials do you have? Look for certified public accountants, ex-IRS agents, and enrolled agents — those who have passed a special IRS exam. If you want an aggressive preparer, consider using a tax attorney.

- How many years of experience do you have in tax preparation? Rookies need not apply.

- Do you prepare all returns by computer? If they're up to date on technology, you can hope they're up to date on new tax laws.

- Do you teach any tax courses, or have you written any tax publications? More is always better.

- Do you specialize in taxes? If they say no, find someone else.

- What is your attitude toward tax audits? Some tax preparers will recommend not taking legitimate tax breaks so they won't trigger an audit. "These accountants are a hazard to your wealth," says Botkin.

- How do you treat gray areas? He should let you know what the gray areas are and give you your options. Botkin advises that you stay away from preparers who say, "The area is not clear, so don't take the deduction."

- What do you do after tax season? The person you're looking for should do other accounting work and be marketing for new clients.

- Have you ever been disciplined by the IRS or any accounting society? If an accountant refuses to answer this question or acts insulted, find someone else.

- How many other clients similar to me do you have? More than 10 are good.

This is only a sampling of the questions Botkin recommends in his book. Nevertheless, they should help you decide if the accountant you're interviewing is right for you.

Retirement

Living the good life in your golden years

9 retirement planning traps exposed

Don't make any of these nine common retirement mistakes!

Depend on the government. "The biggest faulty assumption is that Social Security, Medicare, and Medicaid will take care of all their financial and medical needs in retirement," says Cheri Meyer, American Savings Education Council program director and director of the Choose to Save media-based education program.

Fail to set a goal. "Many Americans have never done a calculation to see how much money they will really need to live in retirement," Meyer says. "People often overestimate how much annual income their nest egg will provide and what social programs, like Medicare and Social Security, will provide."

Expect a short retirement. "Typically, people underestimate their longevity, how much money they'll actually need in retirement, and at what age they are eligible for full Social Security benefits," Meyer explains.

Underestimate taxes. Taxes might take a bigger slice of income after retirement than before. Be prepared.

Overlook medical costs. "Many people feel that their employer or Medicare will take care of all of their retiree medical needs, including long-term care. The truth is that most of us will be responsible for our own medical care costs in retirement," says Meyer. "Unplanned-for medical bills can wipe out a retirement nest egg in a fairly short time."

Forget about inflation. Because of inflation, a dollar will buy less in the future. Plan saving and investments accordingly.

Carry too much debt. "Large amounts of debt can torpedo savings efforts," Meyer says. "You may earn 6 percent on your savings, and yet you may pay 18 percent on your debt."

Expect to keep working. "Many people assume they'll be able to work forever," Meyer points out. Yet many retire earlier than planned due to company downsizing or medical problems.

Wait to start saving. "The longer you wait to save the more you will need to save each year," says Meyer. "It's not impossible, but you may need to save a lot more money and retire later than you'd hoped."

Design a smarter retirement plan

Follow this expert advice to figure out how much money you'll need to enjoy the retirement of your dreams.

"Your calculation should include everything — taxes, inflation, housing, health care, etc.," says American Savings Education Council (ASEC) program director and director of the Choose to Save media-based education program Cheri Meyer.

Estimate expenses. Determine how much your per year retirement expenses might be. "I have yet to find a client who spends less in retirement than they did when they were working," says Cheryl Holland, Certified Financial Planner and president of Abacus

Planning Group in Columbia, S.C. "I think whatever you take home now in your paycheck is what you're going to need when you retire."

Expect a long retirement. "We always plan for clients to live to 100," says Holland. If you retire at 65, you may need to plan for 35 years of retirement expenses.

Include inflation. If inflation averages just 4 percent a year, the income needed to cover living expenses doubles every 18 years. So if $20,000 a year covers today's living expenses, you may need $40,000 a year if you retire 18 years from now.

Add extra for medical expenses. Meyer points out that longer life can mean more medical expenses.

Do the math. Once you know how much money you'll need for retirement, see how much retirement income you can expect. Check your latest statement from the Social Security Administration to get an update on your social security estimated benefits, suggests Stewart Welch III, Certified Financial Planner and founder of The Welch Group in Birmingham, Ala. Add that figure to other expected sources of retirement income, such as pensions, to see what you have.

"Do a retirement needs calculation," says American Savings Education Council (ASEC) program director Cheri Meyer. "Start with a simple form, like ASEC's Ballpark Estimate worksheet. And then move on to a comprehensive worksheet or talk to a financial professional." You can get the Ballpark Estimate worksheet free from *www.asec.org*.

Tally taxes, too. If you put money into a retirement plan without paying taxes on it, you will probably pay taxes on some or all of that money in retirement. Consider how that can shrink your retirement income and plan accordingly.

Try a retirement calculator. To estimate your retirement expenses, retirement income, and how much more you need to save, talk with a financial advisor. But you can try ready-made retirement calculators or worksheets as a starting point. Holland recommends an online calculator available at *www.vanguard.com*. To find it, click on the "Personal Investors" link. Then click on the "Planning & Advice" tab at the top. Next, on the far right, click on the "Planning tools" link.

For a rough estimate worksheet, order ASEC's Ballpark Estimate. For information, write American Savings Education Council (ASEC), Suite 600, 2121 K Street NW, Washington, DC 20037-1896.

Beef up your retirement savings

You retire in 10 years but haven't saved nearly enough. Where do you start?

Take charge. "Do a budget analysis to see where you are," says Stewart Welch III, Certified Financial Planner and founder of The Welch Group in Birmingham, Ala.

"Track every single penny you spend," advises Cheryl Holland, Certified Financial Planner and president of Abacus Planning Group in Columbia, S.C. "As boring and unfun as this is, it can make a big difference in understanding where your money goes."

"Look at places where you could cut expenses," says Welch. By cutting expenses, you free up cash to invest in retirement.

Set a goal. To help figure out how much you need to save, estimate how much money you think you'll need for retirement, Welch says.

Match up and catch up. Invest in your company's retirement plan. "If at all possible, contribute as much as the company will match," says Holland.

How much will today's bills cost when you retire?

Say you live on $20,000 a year and expect a 3-percent annual inflation rate from now on. If you retire 11 years from now, you'll need $27,600 to cover those same expenses. (By using the year 11 figure from the 3-percent column, you find that 20,000 x 1.38 = 27,600.)

Inflation Rate

Years	3 percent	4 percent
1	1.03	1.04
2	1.06	1.08
3	1.09	1.12
4	1.13	1.17
5	1.16	1.22
6	1.19	1.27
7	1.23	1.32
8	1.27	1.37
9	1.30	1.42
10	1.34	1.48
11	1.38	1.54
12	1.43	1.60
13	1.47	1.67
14	1.51	1.73
15	1.56	1.80
20	1.81	2.19
25	2.09	2.67
30	2.43	3.24

If you're over 50, ask your employer or financial advisor about possible catch-up contributions to a 401k or IRA. You might be able to add extra money — thousands to a 401k or hundreds to an IRA.

Save automatically. Make the most of your money and spend less with automatic payroll deductions that contribute to your employer's retirement plan.

If you can also qualify for a traditional or Roth IRA, open that IRA with an organization that can deduct from your checking account each month. "The more you can get your checking account set up to automatically pay items and automatically save for you, the better," says Holland.

Think about extra options. Consider these possibilities, too.

- pay extra on your mortgage now to limit that expense during your retirement
- think about investing more in stocks
- take a higher-paying job or a second job
- delay retirement or work part-time during retirement

Changing laws and economic conditions can make or break savings efforts. Talk with a financial advisor to help determine what you should do.

Keep tabs on your 'pot of gold'

You've been smart all along and saved for your future just as you were advised. But if you haven't checked on your retirement finances in years, you may be sabotaging your future "pot of gold." The plan you set up years ago may no longer fit your needs today.

"Things change in people's lives," explains Alan McKnight, a Certified Financial Planner (CFP) and Vice-President of Kays Financial Advisory Corporation. "We encourage clients to come in at least once a year for a financial physical."

When McKnight meets with his clients, he looks at four major issues. Use these as a guide for your own financial checkup — and make sure you discuss each area with your advisor.

Evaluate cash flow. Compare your monthly expenses to your monthly income. Find out if you are spending more than you receive each month.

Ask yourself, what are my monthly needs? Have they changed since we last met? It's important to evaluate your situation regularly, particularly during retirement, because you don't want to overspend and run out of money before the end of your life, explains McKnight.

Manage your risk. This includes all the insurance you carry — home, auto, life, personal liability, health, disability, and others. Your advisor will look at how much insurance you have and propose adjustments. He may also help you decide if you should purchase long-term care insurance, and whether you need and can afford to buy private health insurance.

Count your pennies. Ask yourself if you are meeting your goals for retirement, says McKnight. You and your advisor should look at how you've invested your money, then discuss any changes you need to make to stay on track. If you have a company 401k plan or other investments, discuss your choices and allocations to determine if they are still compatible with your goals and current market conditions.

Plan your estate. Make sure you have legal documents in place to protect your estate and your health. "We just want to make sure you have a simple will, a living will, and some type of power of attorney for health care and financial circumstances," McKnight says. Reexamine each document to see if anything needs to be changed to reflect your current situation.

Also, be sure to review your assets and the methods you've devised to pass them on to your heirs. Make sure you've chosen the most efficient — and tax-free — course. Ask your financial advisor about additional ways to protect your estate, such as setting up college funds for your new grandchildren.

By keeping tabs on your retirement finances each year, you'll spot problems and fix them before anything serious happens. You'll then have the security of knowing your retirement "pot of gold" will be there when you need it.

Size up early retirement offer wisely

You've just gotten an early retirement offer. Is it a rewarding bankroll or fool's gold? Before you make a decision, be sure you have all the facts.

Review retirement readiness. The offer's value may depend on your financial needs and future plans. Will you continue working? Do you have enough money to retire now?

"Review what your expenses are going to be until Social Security kicks in or you can begin to take retirement distributions penalty-free," says Ted Toal, a Certified Financial Planner in Annapolis, Md. "That's the amount of money you are going to have to make up — and then you have to factor in inflation."

If you can't retire, look for a severance amount that can cover your expenses during the three to 12 months needed to land a new job.

Check for a sweeter deal. "Pension formulas are based on time served — usually on the three years of highest salary or last three years' average salary," says Toal. So retiring early could mean a lower pension. But some employers bolster your payout by beefing up employment length or other pension ingredients.

Factor in health insurance. Many early retirement offers lack health insurance. Although you may be able to continue your employer's coverage under COBRA (Consolidated Omnibus Budget Reconciliation Act) for awhile, you'll probably pay higher premiums. After that, you're on your own until you qualify for Medicare.

"Unless your spouse is working or you get another job with group benefits, you are going to have to pay that expense yourself, and it's going to be extremely expensive," Toal says. So if you find health care in your package, it may be a winner.

For more information about COBRA, see *Preserve your group health insurance* in the Personal insurance chapter.

Watch for warning signs. If a company offers early retirement to salve its financial troubles, the offer may be poor. Sadly, that may mean you should accept. If you refuse early retirement, you could still lose your job later — and get no early retirement benefits.

This complex decision may have long-term financial effects, so talk with a financial planner to determine which option may work best for you.

Tips for picking the right payout

Which is better for your retirement — a monthly pension or a lump-sum payment? These tips can help you decide.

Consider a third option. Ask about a "direct trustee to trustee transfer" to roll your retirement payout into an IRA. Although you usually can't make penalty-free IRA withdrawals until age 59 1/2 you then control how you take withdrawals until at least age 70 1/2. Meanwhile, IRA money not withdrawn may continue to grow tax deferred.

If you choose an IRA transfer, be sure your employer makes the check out to the trustee of your IRA — not to you. Otherwise, that money can be taxed.

Pay Uncle Sam. "If you take it as a lump sum and don't roll it into an IRA, then all of that is going to be taxable as income to you right then and there," says Mark DiGiovanni, Certified Financial

Planner (CFP) and president of Marathon Financial Strategies in suburban Atlanta. You could even rise to a higher tax bracket. Yet, if you pick the IRA rollover or pension payments, you'll probably spread payments and taxes across multiple years.

Beat rising prices. Find out whether pension-style payments will be adjusted for inflation. If not, your payment will cover less of your living expenses with each passing year.

Provide for your family. "A pension can be structured for joint and survivor so payments continue after you die," says Clif McIntire, CFP. Payments continue as long as the surviving spouse lives, but other heirs get nothing.

Both spouses and children can inherit leftover IRA money or cash lump sums — if unfortunate spending or investing choices don't interfere.

Think about your odds. Here are a few more things to consider.

- If your family history and health favor a long life, pension payments could mean decades of guaranteed income.

- If you take a cash lump sum or IRA rollover, your future retirement income may depend on whether you invest profitably.

Changing laws and other issues may affect retirement payout options. Talk with a financial advisor before you choose.

Steps to take to protect your pension

Your pension could be in danger. "People need to be aware that they cannot make assumptions about their pensions," says Mary Browning, manager of the Minnesota branch of the Upper Midwest Pension Rights Project.

It's important to take these defensive steps against threats that could shrivel your pension.

Snare paperwork errors. Mistakes can cut a pension amount. Scour your pension benefit statement for correct birth date, years of service, and social security number. Correct any errors you find.

Also, double-check pension calculations. Use the pension formula from the pension's summary plan description. If your results differ from your employer's, ask your plan administrator for a breakdown of the pension calculation.

Know your stuff. Pension plans can be changed, converted to a different retirement plan, or even terminated. Be prepared.

For more information about protecting your pension, visit the Department of Labor's Employee Benefits Security Administration at *www.dol.gov/ebsa*. To seek help from the Pension Counseling Project, visit *www.aoa.gov* and type "pension counseling" into the site search box.

Read the summary annual report and summary plan description very carefully. "It's dangerous to assume that the plan is going to interpret any provision in your favor," Browning says. So be sure you understand how the plan works.

"If you have questions about a pension plan, call the plan administrator," Browning says. Employers and union staff may not understand all the plan's provisions.

File your defense. Store all pension statements, summary annual reports, W-2 forms, tax returns, and your summary plan description in a file. Refer to these if errors or problems occur.

Plan ahead. If your pension plan goes bankrupt, you'll have little time to make decisions. "Understand the terms of your plan and what will happen if the plan terminates," says Browning.

Confirm information. If you leave a company before retirement, get written confirmation of what your deferred vested pension will be or what you're eligible for, Browning says. Also, verify your address with the plan administrator every few years.

Locate a lost pension. If your employer goes bankrupt, you might get your lost pension from the Pension Benefit Guaranty Corporation. Contact them at *www.pbgc.gov* or Pension Benefit Guaranty Corporation, Pension Search Program, 1200 K Street NW, Washington, DC 20005.

Make the most of your social security

You've earned your social security benefits — but don't expect the government to tell you how to get them. It's up to you to make sure you get all you're entitled to.

Every year, your employer tells the Internal Revenue Service (IRS) and the Social Security Administration (SSA) how much money you made. The SSA records these numbers and uses them to estimate your social security benefits.

But what if your employer gets your name or social security number wrong, or doesn't report all of your earnings? If you don't catch the mistakes, chances are no one will.

The government sends out regular statements showing the earnings your employers reported along with your estimated social security benefits. This earnings record is your best tool for finding errors, says Mary Jane Yarrington, a Senior Policy Analyst at the National Committee to Preserve Social Security and Medicare. Here's her advice for getting the social security you're due.

Should you take Social Security early?

Start taking Social Security benefits at 62 and your individual payments will automatically be smaller. Yet, that might be worthwhile if you need the money or if your family tends toward a low life expectancy.

But remember, if total income soars above $25,000 – or $32,000 if filing jointly – at least 50 percent of your benefit may be taxed away. And if you still work, your benefits shrink $1 for every $2 of income over $11,640 (2004 limit) until you reach your designated full retirement age. For updates and details, visit *www.ssa.gov.* or call 800-772-1213.

Check the statement closely. Compare the amount the earnings record says you made to your W2 earnings statements. Make sure the numbers match up, especially if you worked more than one job in a given year. The SSA admits mistakes are more likely if you had more than one job or changed jobs often. Check this record every two years.

Report errors promptly. Visit your local Social Security office, or call the national office at 800-772-1213. Take copies of your W2 forms for the year in question. If you are self-employed, bring copies of your federal tax return, plus a certified copy of your cancelled check showing the amount of tax you paid.

Request a current statement. If you haven't checked your earnings record lately, call the SSA and have them send you an application for a statement. After mailing in your application, you should receive your current earnings statement in about a month.

If you have specific issues, Yarrington is a good one to ask. This expert answers questions about social security in her column "Ask

Mary Jane." Go to the Web site *www.ncpssm.org*, and click on the link Contact Us, then Ask Mary Jane. From here, you can e-mail her with your questions and read past answers.

Secrets to avoiding IRA tax penalties

By April of the year after you turn 70 1/2, you must start making withdrawals from your traditional IRA. Otherwise, a 50-percent tax penalty could poach your nest egg. Learn more about this required minimum distribution law and help keep your nest feathered.

Play by the rules. If you own a traditional IRA, not a Roth IRA, the IRS says you must start taking the required minimum distribution by April 1 of the year following the year in which you reach age 70 1/2.

Think strategically. Should you play it safe and just start taking those distributions sooner? Although you can start taking them at age 59 1/2 without penalty, you may prefer to wait.

Got more than one traditional IRA? You have two choices. Take the minimum withdrawal from each IRA. Or use the statements from your custodians to write down the minimum distribution for each IRA and total them up. The IRS says you can take the whole amount from just one IRA.

"The IRA distribution is taxed at ordinary tax rates. You get no capital gains treatment on that money," explains Alan McKnight, a Certified Financial Planner and vice president of Kays Financial Advisory Corporation. Yet, if retiring moves you to a lower tax bracket, you'll pay a lower tax rate on any IRA withdrawals you take during that time. In other words, you'll hang on to a bigger slice of that money than you would have during your higher tax bracket days.

Evaluate your retirement account

	Traditional non-deductible IRA	Traditional deductible IRA	Roth IRA	401k
Who funds it?	You	You	You	You, plus employer's match
When does money go in?	after taxes	before taxes	after taxes	before taxes
Are contributions tax deductible?	No	Yes	No	Yes
After age 50, how much can you contribute every year?	up to $3,500	up to $3,500	up to $3,500	10% of income, up to $16,000
How long can you contribute?	to age 70 1/2	to age 70 1/2	to any age	to any age, if working full-time
When do you have to start taking withdrawals?	after age 70 1/2	after age 70 1/2	never	after age 70 1/2
When do early withdrawal penalties apply?	before age 59 1/2	before age 59 1/2	before age 59 1/2	before age 59 1/2
When you withdraw after 59 1/2, what do you pay taxes on?	only the interest earned	the entire amount withdrawn	nothing, if the IRA is at least 5 years old	the entire amount withdrawn

You can only fund these retirement accounts with earned income. Check with your tax and financial advisors. These rules are accurate as of 2004 but have exceptions and may change.

Communicate with your custodian. Of course, you could still pay a 50-percent tax penalty if you don't take a high enough withdrawal amount. But you may not have to calculate the amount yourself. "Each individual custodian is supposed to send you the actual calculation each year based on the IRAs they have for you," explains McKnight. If you haven't received that information, contact your IRA custodian.

Ignore the exception. Although IRS law allows you to delay the first minimum required distribution for a short time, that can mean you must take two distributions the next year — and pay income tax on both. McKnight doesn't recommend this for his clients.

Tax laws governing IRAs can change. To make sure you're doing the right thing, check IRS Publication 590, *Individual Retirement Arrangements* available from *www.irs.gov*. You can also call the IRS at 800-829-1040 or speak with your financial planner or tax professional.

Cure for the retirement blues

Remember when your teen-age son couldn't wait for summer vacation? Then, after several days, he'd mope around the house with nothing to do? For some people, retirement is just like that.

After a few months of relaxing, you may have wondered why you ever wanted to retire. But there is a simple fix, and it's probably what you told your teen-age son — get a job.

Whether you retired early or at your full retirement age, you'll need to decide if the benefits of working outweigh the risks.

Take a look at some of the benefits:

• Going back to work gives you a sense of purpose, keeps you active, and might help you live longer.

- You can put more money in your retirement savings account.

- There are no limits or penalties on what you can earn after reaching your full retirement age. When you earn enough to support yourself with your new job, you could postpone taking your Social Security benefits. They will continue to build, so when you do retire you'll receive a larger amount.

Bear in mind a few risks:

- Earning more money means you'll pay more taxes if your extra cash puts you in a higher tax bracket.

- If you exceed yearly earning limits before reaching your full retirement age, it could reduce your annual benefits from Social Security.

- If you have any health problems, certain jobs could aggravate them.

If the benefits outweigh the risks for you, now may be the right time to pursue those dreams you had years ago.

Start your own business. Begin with a little soul searching. What are your motives and goals? Describe your values, interests, and

---

Work for fun during retirement

A retired doctor teaches part-time at a nearby medical school. Another retiree does storytelling in pre-school. A third works part-time at a local zoo. "There are a lot of ways to do what you love and sort of supplement, a little bit, your extra spending money," says Certified Financial Planner Cheryl Holland. "I think there are a hundred ways to do that that can bring joy to your life."

abilities. What kind of experience and knowledge can you bring to a business? What is your financial situation?

Choose a business that meets your goals and is consistent with your values, interests, and abilities. Keep your motives in check. A wrong motive can condemn you to hard work at a business you may hate. Don't exclude the idea of turning your hobby into a business.

Your business may also provide special tax advantages, see *Enjoy home-business tax perks* in the Taxes chapter.

Become a consultant. The easiest way to become a consultant is to use the contacts you have in your field of expertise. Ask them to spread the word that you've started a consulting business.

As a consultant, you can stay current, maintain your skills, earn extra money, and control the hours you work as you share your knowledge and experience with others.

Return to your previous job. If you really miss the job you retired from, go back as a part-time employee. It's like having the best of both worlds. You get to socialize with your former co-workers and have free time to pursue other interests. In addition, if you work less than 20 hours a week, you may get a paycheck and your pension.

Expand your horizons. Do you want to enhance your social life and stay active? Find a part-time, easygoing, service job in retail, like the perfume counter or hardware department of a major chain store.

Gain a sense of worth. Hospitals, retirement homes, political candidates, and churches are always looking for volunteers. Helping others can make you feel better about yourself and your life. You'll also get a great feeling that comes from giving without expecting anything in return.

5 tips for starting a second career

Going back to work after you've retired can be a challenge. You might run into a recruiter who is concerned about your age. Fortunately, they're usually more interested in your energy level, health, salary expectations, and ability to learn new skills.

Don't worry — just turn on a positive attitude and follow these five steps to make your transition into a new career easier and successful.

Seek out a career coach. If you're not sure how to get the career ball rolling, consider hiring an expert to guide you through the career maze.

Career coaches can help you identify your goals. They'll also assess your interests and abilities and help you choose a career path. Many career coaches know the specifics of different companies and can refer you to the right one.

You can also sign up with a temp agency that will sort out your skills. They'll send you to work at different companies on an as-needed basis. This could give you the flexibility you're looking for.

Update your image. Don't give a recruiter any reason to negatively judge you by your age. You may not be in your 20s, but you can still project a healthy, energetic, and enthusiastic image.

- Update your appearance with a flattering hairstyle and classically styled clothes.

- Don't peer over your bifocals. Remove them. You'll look much younger.

- Watch your posture and use a firm handshake.

- Make good eye contact. It's an indication of a confident, vibrant, high-energy person.

Invest in your education. Recruiters love to see that you've gone back to school to update your skills or gain new ones. It shows them you have a flexible attitude and are willing to learn.

Many junior colleges have day and evening classes on the latest versions of Windows and Microsoft Office programs. They also offer adult education classes in a variety of non-credit courses. Plus, many of them have off-campus sites in the surrounding communities.

Looking for a bigger challenge? Try one of the many certificate programs junior colleges offer. It's possible to be certified in a new profession in less than two years.

Research salaries. Show the recruiter you're familiar with the salary range for the position you're seeking. Do some research online at *www.salary.com*.

On top of that, make sure your recruiter understands that you don't expect an exorbitant salary because of your age or experience in other fields.

Unleash your network. This is where the rubber meets the road. You need to get out and talk with people. Networking with old friends, co-workers, family, and even college buddies can help you find the position you want.

Retire successfully on a shoestring

Many people must survive retirement on their Social Security benefits and perhaps a small pension. If you're living on a fixed income, here is some advice on easy ways to supplement your budget.

Retirees Jim and Georgia Goodridge of Arnold, Missouri believe flea marketing is a great way to bridge the financial gap during your retirement years. Founders of the Independent Dealers Association of America and authors of *The Flea Market Shopper's Companion*, they also operate the Web site *www.goodridgeguides.com*, which details the ins and outs of buying and selling at these popular markets.

Goodridge believes flea marketing is an easy business to get into because everyone has items in their attic or garage they no longer want that will appeal to someone else. If you're looking to make extra money, he says, flea markets are a great way to do it.

"You can spend Saturday and Sunday at the flea market and get a lot of cash, and it's a lot better than sitting at home watching TV and worrying about money," he says. "The only thing you're going to be out is the space rent, and that's usually just a few bucks."

Goodridge recommends browsing through a flea market first to learn how things operate. "You can go there and walk in two or three aisles, and you can sort of figure out what is selling, how things are being sold, what the pricing structure is, how dealers are operating," he explains. "A little knowledge makes you a lot more comfortable."

If you know your way around a computer, you can skip the flea market and do your selling online, using the popular Web site Ebay. Simply log in and register at *www.ebay.com,* and you'll find all the help you need to get started.

Knowledge and comfort will help you sell your possessions as well, he adds. If you're a fisherman, for example, you'll probably be highly successful selling your old equipment because you're comfortable talking about it and can hold an intelligent conversation with a prospective buyer.

If you need more ideas on beefing up your monthly retirement check, John Howells, author of *Retirement on a Shoestring*, offers these suggestions for cutting costs and adding to your income.

- Lower housing costs by either moving to a less expensive home or to a low-tax area.

- Get experts at the power company to help you "weatherize" your home. Contact the Department of Energy, Division of Weatherization Assistance, at 1000 Independence Avenue S.W., Washington, D.C. 20585 or call them at 202-586-2207.

- Share a home or apartment with a housemate or two if you're single. You'll save when you split rent, utilities, and other costs each month.

- Earn extra money with a part-time position, seasonal job, or temporary work. Just be sure your pay isn't high enough to cut your Social Security benefits.

- Use hobbies you enjoy — like woodworking, crafts, or painting — to add to your funds. Hire out or sell your creations at arts and crafts shows to boost your budget.

- Take advantage of senior services. Call the Eldercare Locator at 800-677-1116 to discover what's available near you.

Discover the secret program for free money

Supplemental Security Income (SSI) could give you as much as $5,000 to pay your bills. To qualify, you must be at least 65 years old or blind or disabled. Although you must also meet requirements for low income and limited belongings, you may be surprised at what won't count against you. You must own less than $2,000 worth of items if you're single – or $3,000 for couples – but your car and home don't count. For more information on eligibility requirements and how to apply, call 800-772-1213. If you qualify for SSI, you might be eligible for food stamps and Medicaid, too.

• Find out if your community has a senior citizen newspaper. It may help you uncover valuable discounts, opportunities, and benefits you never thought of.

Find the community of your dreams

Your idea of the perfect place to retire may not be the same as your best friend's or neighbor's. Or maybe you're still trying to figure out what that perfect place would be. Don't worry. By doing some well-planned research, you'll learn which areas are most compatible with your wants and needs. Before you know it, you'll be relaxing in the retirement community of your dreams.

Pinpoint the location. Whether you're looking for a college town, big city, rural neighborhood, or adult community, the first thing to do is explore the area you are considering.

Think of the local newspaper as your gateway to the community. Your own library may carry papers from larger cities, while the Internet offers an excellent resource for viewing small-town papers. Just check *www.NewspaperLinks.com* to see the online versions of newspapers around the country.

Once you select a community you like, the local Chamber of Commerce is a good place to get information on area activities.

Investigate housing costs. The same house that goes for $250,000 in one city may only cost $100,000 in another. Decide how much you want to spend, then check prices. Contact real estate agents in that area or do your own research online. The Web site *www.realtor.com* lists more than 2 million properties for sale around the country. You can search a city by price, or specify a number of bedrooms, acreage, and amenities. You will also find a wealth of information at *www.realtylocator.com*.

Look into taxes. State income tax, county property tax, local sales tax — how big a bite will your new home take out of your income? The Internet can quickly put you in touch with the tax division in each state. Go to *www.taxsites.com*, and click on State & Local Tax. Or call the state's tax division for their latest rates.

Check healthcare availability. Everyone needs a doctor at some point, but if you have a serious health condition, it's especially important to live near high-quality medical facilities. Start by visiting the American Medical Association's Web site at *www.ama-assn.org*. Here, you can search for doctors by location. Your current doctors may have advice, too, on where to go for good hospitals and specialty centers.

Consider the weather. Climate can have a huge impact on your health, quality of life, and the size of your utility bills. Track the weather trends through local newspapers, or watch a national news station like the Weather Channel. Weather Web sites like *www.weather.com* and *www.WeatherBase.com* offer a wealth of information on locales around the nation — or the world.

Know the crime rate. Everyone wants to feel safe. Find out ahead of time how your would-be retirement community stacks up. Read the headlines in its local newspaper. If a small crime makes big news, it may be a safe city. On the other hand, if a murder gets buried on page 15, it could be a sign of a high crime rate.

You can also check crime rates in the latest Federal Bureau of Investigation (FBI) Uniform Crime Report. Go to your library and ask for a copy, or view it online at *www.fbi.gov* under Reports & Publications.

These are just a few slices of life to think about before settling in a new place. You should also consider the convenience of local transportation and airports, theater and music offerings, local churches, outdoor activities, and even educational opportunities. The Web sites on the following page can lead you to more information about the best places to retire.

Sperling's Best Places	www.bestplaces.net
Retirement Living Info Center	www.retirementliving.com
MonsterMoving	www.monstermoving.com
MSN House & Home	www.homeadvisor.com
U.S. Recreation	www.recreation.gov

Clever ideas for budget travelers

You can experience the vacation of a lifetime, even on a fixed income. Be a wise consumer and take advantage of these incredible deals and unusual offers.

Forget hotels. Swapping homes is a great way to spend $0 on lodging and car rentals on your next vacation. Just participate in a home exchange program. While you and your family enjoy the comforts of another family's home, that family enjoys the comforts of yours. You'll have your own kitchen, TV, plenty of space, and even use of the family car.

Join one of several homeswapping services to browse the list of available homes and add yours to the list. See some online examples below. Find a match, and work out the details with the other homeowner. Make sure to check references before entrusting your

Home Exchange	www.homeexchange.com
Digsville Home Exchange	www.digsville.com
Seniors Home Exchange	www.seniorshomeexchange.com

home to a stranger. Not only will you have a wonderful, inexpensive vacation — you might make new friends for life.

Uncover cheap airfare. Checking for bargains online should be your first step. Most of the time, you can save more by booking through a Web site like Orbitz or Priceline than you would with a senior discount. But during peak travel times, or when the airlines aren't offering deals, senior discounts are the cheapest way to go. For example, if you're 65 or older, the most you'll pay for a one-way ticket on Southwest Airlines is $129.

Here are some good places to check for low fares.

Best Fares	www.bestfares.com
Expedia	www.expedia.com
Cheap Tickets	www.cheaptickets.com
Hotwire	www.hotwire.com
Orbitz	www.orbitz.com
Priceline	www.priceline.com
Travelocity	www.travelocity.com

Have fun for less. David Smidt, president and CEO of SeniorDiscounts.com, knows a thing or two about discounts for older adults. Here are some of his suggestions for entertainment deals.

- Movie theaters. "Almost every movie theater gives a senior discount. Those tend to be in the 40 percent range."

- Museums. "Almost all museums give free admission to seniors or a senior discount at least."

- Amusement parks, such as SeaWorld or Disneyland. "Most of them will give some sort of senior discount, and you definitely should ask."

- National parks. Residents of the United States who are 62 or older can get a Golden Age passport for $10. This serves as a lifetime pass to all national parks, monuments, and historic sites.

You can search for local senior discounts at *www.seniordiscounts.com*. In addition to entertainment deals, you'll find discounts for local restaurants, dry cleaners, moving companies — even car dealerships.

7 ways to save if you're over 50

These nifty senior discounts start as early as age 50.

- AARP membership discounts. Go to *www.aarp.org* to see what they offer.

- Restaurants and donut shops. Do some investigating to find out which ones have the best deals.

- Banking services. Ask about special offers for seniors at your bank.

- Hotels and motels. Phone ahead for details.

- Car rental. Call around for the best discount.

- Ski vacations. Contact the Over the Hill Gang International club (*www.othgi.com*).

- Golfing. Ask about senior discounts at your favorite course.

How to find excellent long-term care

You're determined to find the best nursing home or assisted living community. But how can you tell which places provide outstanding care and which ones spell trouble? Start with these pointers to help you make a smart choice.

Enlist Web assistance. The Web can help you begin or narrow down a list of possibilities. For information about nursing homes or assisted living in your area, visit the Eldercare Locator at *www.eldercare.gov*. You can also call 800-677-1116 on any weekday from 9 a.m. to 8 p.m. Eastern time.

Get nursing home quality ratings, staffing information, and inspection violations, if any, from Nursing Home Compare at *www.medicare.gov* or 800-MEDICARE (800-633-4227).

Ask voices of experience. Talk with people who are familiar with the long-term care facilities you are considering, advises Marilyn Rantz, co-author of *The New Nursing Homes*. Their impressions and opinions could be a big help.

Take a tour. Visit each of your top contenders. Schedule a tour and take a half hour to walk through the facility. While you're there, notice traits like these.

- How does it smell? You should never smell bad odors.

- Is it clean? While it doesn't have to be spick-and-span, it should never be dirty.

- Do you spot resident friendly features, such as helpful hall handrails or doors wide enough to accommodate wheelchairs and walkers?

- Do the residents seem comfortable, happy, and well cared for?

- How does the staff interact with residents? Rantz asks, "Do they talk to each other? Do they seem happy with each other? Do they smile at each other?"

Visit with visitors. Question family members or friends visiting a resident. Ask how long they have been coming to the facility, and what they think. "You'll get an earful real quick if it's good or if it's bad," says Rantz.

Interview employees. Introduce yourself to the staff. Ask how long they've worked there. Look for longevity. "If everybody you talk to was hired this year," warns Rantz, "you have to think there is something wrong." Also, ask questions that will help you get a sense of how much personal care residents receive.

In either informal chats or formal meetings with employees, cover topics like these.

- Find out if each resident has a written care plan.

- Ask plenty of questions about nursing and medical care, especially when you consider nursing homes.

- Ask the appropriate staff member for a list of fees, payment options, and related financial information.

Learn all you can. To learn more about choosing nursing homes, ask for Rantz's book *The New Nursing Homes* at your local bookstore, or order it directly from the publisher, Fairview Press, by calling 800-544-8207. You can also get Medicare's *Guide to Choosing a Nursing Home* from *www.medicare.gov* or 800-MEDICARE (800-633-4227).

Download free information about choosing an assisted living facility from the Assisted Living Federation of America at *www.alfa.org*.

Volunteer at local nursing homes ahead of time, recommends Marilyn Rantz, co-author of *The New Nursing Homes*. "You'll find the good ones before you need them," she says. Plus, you'll build a social support system with staff and residents.

Estate planning

Wise safeguards for your family and finances

Organize estate for peace of mind

You may have done everything you can think of to ease your loved ones' burdens after you're gone. But will they know where to find all those important documents you've created? Your carefully laid plans can fall apart if no one knows where you've filed your will, insurance policies, or financial information. Here are some easy ways to organize your estate and achieve a lasting peace of mind.

List important names. Get yourself a notebook, and on the first page, write your date of birth, social security number, and your legal state of residence. On the next page, write down the name and address of:

- your attorney.

- anyone you have given power of attorney.

- all the people who are dependent on you for care or financial support.

- anyone you want notified if something happens to you.

Record vital documents. Next, create a page to list your important documents. You'll add information to each entry as you go along. Include:

- will

- power of attorney

- medical records

- funeral arrangements

- insurance policies — life, accident, home, auto, medical, and any others you may have

- birth certificate or citizenship papers

- passport

- marriage certificates

- divorce information

- titles, deeds, and registrations for your home, your car, and any property you own

When appropriate, list next to each one a policy number, company, contact name, phone number, and beneficiary.

Itemize your accounts. Turn to a new page in your notebook, and list your financial accounts — loans, credit cards, checking, savings, investments, retirement, and mortgage.

- Write down the name on each account and the account number. Include any beneficiaries you have for these.

- List contact information for each. Give the name, phone number, and address for the institutions that manage these accounts, such as the bank or mortgage company, and an agent's name if you have one.

- If you have created any trusts, write the names, phone numbers, and addresses of the trustees.

- Tell where your tax records are located and the name of your tax accountant if you have one.

Store everything safely. Now it's time to put all this information in a secure place.

- Make copies of all the important documents you have listed, and place them in a binder along with your logbook.

- Store the originals in a fireproof safe or safe deposit box. Give an extra key to your spouse or someone else you absolutely trust. If you get a safe deposit box, you also need to give this person the authority to open it without you.

- Don't store the original copies of power of attorney documents. In general, the person you name as your agent should keep these. Also, don't place your final arrangement papers in a safe deposit box.

- Return to the list of important papers in your notebook, and write down where you put each document.

Reap the benefits of estate planning

Estate planning allows you to control your assets, both during your life and after your death. Its main objectives are to:

- ensure you can always provide for you and your family.

- make certain that your assets go to the people and/or organizations of your choosing.

- minimize the amount of taxes, fees, and court interference associated with settling your estate.

Most importantly, proper estate planning lessens the stress on your loved ones.

Inform your family. Make a last entry in the notebook, giving instructions on how to locate your safe deposit box or home safe and who is authorized to open it.

Tell your executor, attorney, adult children, or someone else you trust where you put the binder and notebook. If no one can find them, all your hard work will be for nothing.

Keep your valuables safe

Have you ever worried about losing important papers or keeping valuables around the house? If so, you should give some thought to storing your important items in a safe deposit box at your local bank. You can rest assured that your possessions are safe, secure, and organized. As an added benefit, you can deduct the annual cost of the box on your tax return.

That cost is determined by the box's size, says Bernadette Amis, a financial service representative for Sun Trust Bank. The smallest box (2x5 inches) will start at around $30 a year, and the largest box (10x10 inches) can be close to $150 a year.

The contents of your box are private — no one but you will know what it contains. The bank will give you a key and keep another that unlocks only one side of the box. "No one can get into their box without both keys," says Amis. "There is a room for the customer to go into to transact their business in privacy."

Here are a few suggestions on what you can store in your safe deposit box.

- important papers such as passports, birth certificates, and your mortgage

- gold and silver bullion, or expensive jewelry

- collectables like coins, stamps, or baseball cards

The following are not allowed:

- any liquid, especially alcohol or chemicals

- illegal substances such as drugs

- explosives, firearms, ammunition, or any other hazardous or harmful materials

- perishable goods

Top 5 estate docs you need

Experts say these are the most important documents you should have to protect your estate and ease your family's burden when you pass on.

- will

- living will, also known as a medical directive or healthcare directive

- revocable trust or living trust

- durable power of attorney for finances

- durable power of attorney for healthcare, also known as a medical or healthcare power of attorney or healthcare proxy

---

Secure your loved ones' futures with a will

Everyone knows they need a will, but not everyone makes the time or effort to put one together. Your family will be the ones to suffer, though, if you don't plan ahead.

If you die without a will, or "intestate," the state you live in decides how to divvy up your property. The court follows a formula to determine who gets your precious assets, and you won't have any say in the matter. That's a risk you don't want to take.

Besides letting you decide who gets your cherished possessions, a will allows you to:

- choose the person who will administer your estate.

- name the guardian of your minor children.

- create trusts to ensure your children are provided for without the court stepping in.

- plan your estate to ensure greater tax savings for your heirs.

Do it now. Draw up your will as soon as possible. Although sound health is not required, a sound mind is. "The minimum requirements for being mentally able to write a will are that you understand what property you own and who your family members are," says Georgia estate attorney Karen C. Gainey. A mentally incompetent person may have a clear moment where they write or change their will, and that will is legally valid, she says. But others may disagree and decide to contest it, setting the stage for a legal battle.

Plan ahead. Before drawing up a will, consider meeting with a financial planner. "You need to sit down and identify specific assets you want to go to specific people, and the means by which those assets should be distributed," says Bob Weigand, president and CEO of CIMA Wealth Management, a financial planning company.

A will is one way to give away your good china, baseball card collection, tools, or other personal property to the people you love. But a will also allows you to set up trusts for your spouse, your children, and even charities. That way Uncle Sam gets as little of your estate as possible. Meeting with a planner will help you organize your finances and determine the best way to distribute them in the will, Weigand says.

Review periodically. Any change in your lifestyle or economic status should prompt you to review your will. If you lose your job; get promoted, married, or divorced; have a child; or acquire additional properties or assets, you'll need to take a fresh look at your situation.

"It doesn't mean you'll make a change, but you should at least review it, so you can see how it puts it into perspective," Gainey says.

Weigh the cost. You can set up your own will (see the following story) or you can have an attorney put one together for you.

"To set up a basic will — truly basic with no trusts — the expense probably ranges from $100 to $300. This price often includes a financial power of attorney and healthcare power of attorney," says Gainey. The cost of a complex will can go as high as $1,000 or more.

Usually those with larger, more complex estates can afford the steeper fees. Still, at any price, a will is worth the peace of mind knowing the important people in your life will be cared for when you're gone.

Change your will carefully

If you need to modify your will, don't mark up your original by writing in the changes. It may not hold up in probate court.

A codicil is the legal document you should use to correct problems or make changes to your will, and it must be signed with the same formalities as a will.

A simple codicil will cover minor revisions, but if your changes are extensive, experts recommend you write a new will.

Prepare your will for under $30

Skip the lawyer, write your own will, and you can save yourself hundreds of dollars. Just make sure you do your homework so you don't make any costly mistakes.

"Making your own will isn't difficult if your needs are relatively simple, but it does require attention to detail," says Terri Rudy, program director for HALT, an organization of Americans for Legal Reform.

Make it legal. You need to follow certain standards to be sure the will is legal, Rudy says. Your document must state that it's your will, name an executor, and make at least one provision for your property or underaged children. And you must:

- be at least age 18 when you sign the will — 21 in some states.

- be of sound mind — meaning you know your beneficiaries and you know the nature and extent of your assets.

- meet state requirements for signing and dating the will and for required number of witnesses.

Use a will-writing guide. Although it may sound complicated, you can find software, Web sites, do-it-yourself kits, or books to help write a will. Many products sell for under $30, and most are pretty mistake-proof, says Rudy.

"They take you through the process step by step and tell you exactly what you need to do to produce a legally valid will," she says.

Look for software programs like Quicken's WillMaker Plus that wave red flags if you forget to include a particular clause — or if information in one part of the will doesn't jive with another part, she suggests.

Choose wisely. Not all self-help products are equal. HALT's book *Do-It-Yourself Law: HALT's Guide to Self-Help Books, Kits &*

Software evaluates products that promise to produce legally valid wills. "We warn people to steer away from some products because the information given, while accurate, is overly broad," says Rudy.

Choose a product that uses lots of details, prompting, and extra background help to guide you through the will-writing process. These may prevent trouble later on that could keep your will from accomplishing what you want.

Prevent disaster. After you have completed your document, make sure you proofread it to remove typing errors. "A typo could be a misspelled word or it could be an incorrect dollar amount in a bequest — for example, $11,000 instead of $1,000," Rudy says. The smallest mistake could cause legal complications.

Know when to seek help. "The best self-help products will alert potential do-it-yourselfers about when to seek legal help," Rudy says. For example, you need a lawyer to make gifts that depend on conditions you set or to arrange special trusts.

Your estate may end up being more complex than you imagined. If you have questions or you're not sure whether you need legal help, play it safe and see a lawyer.

Will-writing do's and don'ts

At one time, wills could get a bit nasty. There were no guidelines, so people could say whatever they wanted and get away with it. Today, wills use standard language, but you can still get your wishes across by inserting special provisions. Here are a few options to discuss with your attorney.

Prevent contesting of the will. If you're concerned your will may be contested, you can include an anticontest — also called noncontest — provision. It states that if an heir contests the will and loses, he automatically forfeits any bequest made to him.

Disinherit a child. You have no legal obligation to leave something to a child, even if the child is a minor. But you should word your wishes to show the omission is intentional. Make sure you name all your children in your will, whether you bequeath them anything or not. Some states will interpret your silence on a child as intent to give them an equal share.

On the other hand, be careful about omitting children unintentionally. For example, you may want to include a provision for future children if that's a possibility.

Make a conditional bequest. You can attach a condition to any bequest as long as it is legal, not against public policy, and possible to carry out. You should always name a backup beneficiary in case your heir refuses to meet the condition or the court disallows it.

Some of the more common bequest conditions include:

- discouraging heirs from getting married or encouraging them to get a divorce. The divorce provision is against public policy and not enforceable. The court may uphold the marriage restriction depending on whether it is a total or partial ban.

- prohibiting an heir from converting to another religion or from bringing up his children in another religion.

- insisting on character improvement. You can require your heir to stop a bad habit or addiction to obtain his inheritance.

- requiring an heir to dress a certain way, go into a designated profession, keep a surname, or avoid talking to a specific family member.

Conditional bequests need to be well-thought-out and explained in detail, or you risk having them overturned by the courts. Make sure you discuss your wishes thoroughly with an attorney and understand exactly what you can and cannot include.

Here are some things you should not try to do in your will.

Disinherit your spouse. No matter how much you may want to, you cannot write your spouse out of your will. Most states give spouses the right to a share of the estate regardless of what your will says.

Donate your entire estate to charity. Although most states allow you to do this, some states limit the amount. And if you're married, you need to consider where you live. Most states won't allow it if you have a spouse.

Bequeath possessions to pets. A beneficiary must be a person or legal entity who can appear in court and accept a bequest. Therefore, you cannot make a bequest to an animal. Instead, make a conditional request giving someone you trust a specified amount of money if they agree to take care of your beloved pet.

Think twice about leaving a few nasty last words in your will. "Such language can give rise to a lawsuit against the estate for libel," says trust and estate attorney Alexander Bove. You're better off writing a personal letter to the one you dislike. It will probably have a more lasting effect.

Sort out property to avoid slip-ups

You probably think of property as real estate, such as fields, farm-land, buildings, and homes. In reality, property is anything you own, including your tickets to the World Series and that ragged shirt you can't bear to part with.

When drawing up your estate plan, it's important to understand the difference between various types of property. That way you'll be less likely to make a mistake when you divide up property in your will.

Real property. Real property is real estate, in other words, land. If you hold any type of deed, lease, or mortgage, you own real property. The structures built on the land are part of the real estate and, therefore, real property.

Personal property. This encompasses everything else you own. It includes stock, furniture, cars, IOUs, copyrights, cameras, and those World Series tickets. Personal property is divided into two categories.

- Intangible personal property has no value in itself but represents a right to something else. A copyrighted song, an IOU, and a share of stock all qualify as intangible property.

- Tangible personal property is anything you can move or touch with inherent value. This would include your cars, boats, furniture, jewels, clothing, and paintings.

Collectable items fall into this category, and for estate purposes, are considered one item. So your collections of 5,000 baseball cards and 400 stamps count as two items. If your will

Joint tenancy — know when to use it

If you're married with no children and few assets, you probably don't need a will. But make sure any assets you have are titled "joint tenants with right of survivorship" so they go directly to your spouse. And designate each other as beneficiaries for your life insurance and investment plans.

But watch out! If you do have children and you've remarried, you might unwittingly disinherit them. A surviving joint tenant becomes sole owner of the property – owing your heirs nothing. If you want certain assets to go to your children, protect your wishes with a will. That way your loved ones will get what you intend.

allows an heir to choose two pieces of property, they have the right to pick your two valuable collections.

Many people have a blanket provision in their will leaving all tangible personal property to a spouse or children. They may not realize that covers expensive paintings and jewelry as well as furniture, clothing, and other items of nominal value. If you own valuable items, you would be wise to bequeath them separately to avoid questions or problems later on.

Two more categories of property you should be familiar with are probate and nonprobate. When you die, all your property — both real and personal — falls into one of these two groups.

Probate property. Any asset you own at the time of your death is considered probate property. If you're a partial owner of property, it must go through probate if the other person is not permitted to take your share. For example:

- If you own real estate under a tenancy in common, your share must pass through your probate estate.

- If you are involved in a lawsuit before your death, the proceeds become part of your estate. If your death is caused by negligence, the executor can file a wrongful death suit. Part of the proceeds may be subject to probate.

- If you have a share in a partnership, it must be listed as part of your estate.

- Life insurance payable to your estate becomes probate property. Plus, any policy you own covering another person (the policy itself, not the proceeds) becomes part of your estate.

Nonprobate property. Anything you own that passes outside your estate by some other means is considered nonprobate property. For example, the contents of a living trust would not be disposed of through the will.

Guard your assets with a trust

When setting up an estate plan with your financial planner, expect him to protect your assets by including one or more trusts. They can be worth their weight in gold.

"Few people clearly understand what trusts can do or just how they work," says Alexander A. Bove, Jr., estate attorney and author of *The Complete Book of Wills, Estates and Trusts*. A trust can provide for you and your family, allow easy access to property, and help you avoid probate. But there are many different types of trusts, and they won't all do what you want, he warns.

"You must be careful that your trust accomplishes your specific wishes, has all the necessary ingredients, and will do the job you chose it for," he says.

Grasp the basics. A trust in its simplest form transfers assets from one person to another. It can bypass estate taxes, avoid probate, and revamp your life insurance to benefit your estate plan. A trust is one of the most flexible estate tools available today. It can do just about anything that's legal and not contrary to public policy, says Bove.

All trusts, from simple to complex, contain the same four elements.

- The donor/grantor/settlor is the person who creates the trust.

- The property includes all assets put in the trust. It's sometimes called the corpus.

- The trustee is the person who promises to follow the donor's instructions as set forth in the trust.

- The beneficiaries are those who receive benefits from the trust.

Assign your assets. Any type of asset can be placed into a trust, from antiques and real estate to bank accounts, securities, or life insurance.

But before you fill your trust, you'll need to pick someone to be your trustee. You can choose whomever you want, including yourself, your spouse, or your children. In other words, John Doe can be the trustee of the John Doe trust, or Janet Doe can be the trustee of the John Doe trust.

Make sure you have a "pour over" provision in your will to put any excess property into your living trust. That way, any property not mentioned in your will automatically becomes part of your trust and avoids probate.

After you decide on a trustee, you need to re-title your assets into the trustee's name. "If you go through the trouble of having a trust, and you don't put your assets into it, it's useless," says Bove. As trustee of your own revocable trust, you can keep control over your assets.

Choose the right trust. Everyone's needs are different, so talk to your estate planner about the trusts that are right for your financial situation. Here are three types of trusts you may want to consider.

- A living trust allows you to sidestep the time-consuming and public process of probate court. And you don't have to be rich to have one. Even if your estate is small, you'll benefit because a living trust will keep your estate in your loved ones' hands — not the government's. It also avoids probate if you become incapacitated for any reason, allowing you to change control of your assets in an organized, private manner.

- A bypass trust allows your estate to bypass taxes. The trust is designed to kick in upon your death, allowing your spouse to have almost full use of all funds in the trust. Upon your spouse's death, those funds would bypass his or her estate and go directly to your children.

  Determine if you need a bypass trust by using this simple technique. Take the total value of your assets, including life insurance, and subtract any debt. If the remaining amount is greater than the federal estate tax exemption (see table in *Save a fortune in estate taxes* in the Taxes chapter) a bypass trust can keep the IRS from getting their hands on your hard-earned money.

- A life insurance trust takes your life insurance out of your estate, allowing it to bypass taxes. To get the tax benefits, you'll need to have someone else as the trustee. "The trust is set up outside your estate, and you have no control over it," Bove explains. "Upon your death, the proceeds go into the trust and are held for your spouse and children. It's very effective and a wonderful loophole."

Determine your level of control

Trusts can be revocable or irrevocable.

Revocable trusts allow you total control over the trust, giving you the ability to change terms, remove property, or cancel the trust at any time.

Irrevocable trusts are the opposite. You cannot change or cancel any part of the trust. But power to do so can be given to other individuals in certain cases.

Each type of trust has particular benefits. Talk to your estate planner about which is better for you.

Avoid surprises – talk to your kids

It's rare for parents and children to discuss money. Most parents don't take the opportunity to discuss their finances with their offspring. And children may hesitate to ask because they don't want to look like fortune hunters.

But it could be a mistake not to let your children in on your estate plans. "Why work all your life, why create all of this, and then have havoc because you failed to address the situation?" says attorney Harvey J. Platt, author of several books on estate planning.

Consider future needs. Discussing your estate plan with your children can be a smart move for two reasons.

- If your children are developing their own estate plans, their financial advisors need to coordinate their planning with information about your estate. Much of their plans may be based on what they inherit from you. Likewise, if there's a chance you may need financial assistance from your children, they need to figure that into their future plans as well.

- If something happens to your health, you want your children to be familiar with your wishes so they know what to do. You should at least give them copies of your durable power of attorney and healthcare directives in case they need to act immediately on your behalf, Platt says.

Choose how much to tell. Some parents like to give their children all the details of their net worth, while others prefer to withhold the finer points. You may want to consider your children's ages and maturity levels when making your decision.

The simplest arrangement, says Platt, is to tell your children you have developed an estate plan, then give them the contact information for your financial advisor or the attorney who holds your original estate documents.

If you decide to let your children know the details of your estate plan, make sure they understand it's not set in stone. Your assets could increase or decrease, and you may change your mind about who gets what and how much. By discussing this with them ahead of time, you may help avoid problems later on.

For more information on this and other estate topics, you can refer to Platt's books, *Your Will and Estate Plan* and *Your Living Trust and Estate Plan*. They are available at *www.allworth.com* or by calling 800-491-2808.

Compare costs of will vs. trust

Don't be misled by a lawyer who says you only need a will and not a trust. It may be more cost-effective to have both. Ask the following questions.

- How much would a basic trust cost to prepare?
- If I died now, what would be the cost to probate my will and transfer everything I own to my heirs?
- What would be the cost to my heirs if all my assets were in a trust?

Include any fees your beneficiaries would pay, then compare the costs. It should be clear if you would benefit from a trust.

Handle executor duties with ease

Some day you may be asked to be the executor of a friend or family member's estate. Will you know what to do?

"The first thing an executor needs to do is look at the will and the wishes of the deceased," says Bob Weigand, president and CEO of CIMA Wealth Management, a financial planning company in Fayetteville, Georgia. Then, take care of these initial details:

- Notify family, close friends, clergy, attorney, accountant, financial planner, broker, insurance agent, business contacts, and creditors.

- Make physical and financial arrangements for all dependents, such as children or elderly parents.

- Make the funeral arrangements. Take into account any special requests the deceased made in his will.

- Locate all the deceased's important documents. You can obtain certified copies of the death certificate from the county Office of Vital Statistics.

Probate the will. As executor, you need to file the will in probate court, where a judge will decide if the will is authentic. If it is, the court will issue you a "letter of testamentary" authorizing you to assume the legal duties of the executor. For more on probate, see the following story.

Evaluate assets. Make a list of the deceased's assets, and determine the value of the estate. Use professional appraisers for real estate, antiques, paintings, and collections.

When deciding on an executor for your own estate, ask them to secure an executor's bond, which protects your estate from financial damages due to executor ignorance or unlawful acts.

Make sure all assets are secure from theft, even from family members seeking a few "mementos." Change the locks if necessary. In addition, make sure property assets, like houses and vehicles, are protected by adequate insurance.

Settle accounts. Weigand suggests executors use the following checklist as a guide.

- Open a separate checking account as executor for the estate. Transfer all bank account funds to this account, and close the deceased's accounts. Also cancel all ATM, debit, and credit cards. You should pay all bills from this account, and save all receipts.

- Cancel subscriptions to magazines, online services, and memberships in all organizations.

- Pay utility bills, property taxes, and insurances until the property is sold or given to an heir.

- Find out if the deceased had any outstanding salary, life insurance, pension, profit sharing, or bonuses due him from his employer.

- File life and any outstanding health and disability claims with the deceased's various insurance companies. You'll need copies of the death certificate to do this. Cancel medical, dental, and disability insurance.

- Discontinue benefit payments, like Social Security and pensions. Also, apply for survivor benefits for the dependents.

- File the deceased's income tax for the present year. If the estate is worth close to $1.5 million or more, have an accountant file estate taxes, which are due nine months after the deceased's date of death.

As an executor, never sign your name to contracts for services you take out in the estate's name. You may become liable for payment of these expenses if there's not enough money in the estate.

Avoid common mistakes. Watch out for mistakes, particularly financial, that could make your own life difficult. One common mistake is believing you're responsible for the deceased's debts if the estate runs out of money.

The executor should never pay the debts of the deceased out of his own pocket, says Weigand. Plus, he should be careful to keep the estate's assets separate from his own. "That's one of the reasons they should have a separate account, so they can have a clean accounting of what's being paid out from the estate account to pay the estate bills," he explains.

If you're related to the deceased, you'll also need to consider the emotional impact of his death.

"The biggest mistake the executor has to guard against is making decisions from an emotional standpoint," says Weigand. "The executor needs to separate the stressful part, and deal with the financial part, because he is going to be held accountable to the court on his decisions."

7 simple steps to probating a will

Now that you know your duties as an executor, you'll need to learn the finer points of getting a will through the complex process of probate.

Here are the basic steps you'll need to take. If the estate is complicated, it may be wise to put an estate attorney on retainer to advise you at different points along the way.

Head to the courthouse. Place an original copy of the will on record with the probate court in the county where the deceased lived at the time of his death. Petition the court to approve the will by filling out the appropriate court-supplied forms. If no one objects to the petition, the court will formally appoint you the legal representative of the estate.

Re-title assets. Re-title all the deceased's probate assets in your name in order to settle the estate. For example, you'd list yourself as "John Doe, Executor, Estate of Donald Doe."

Report estate inventory. Within one to three months of your appointment as executor, file a complete estate inventory with the court. The estate inventory becomes a matter of public record and is available for anyone to view.

Identify creditors. Place an official notice in the local newspaper to notify creditors to send in their claims during a time period specified by the state. Also notify all known creditors, and make an effort to identify others, to give them a chance to file claims within this time period. If the estate lacks the money to settle its debts, notify creditors they will get a pro-rated amount or nothing at all.

Resolve disputes. Settle all valid debts when they come to your attention. However, a debt does not have to be paid, no matter how valid, if it comes in after the above-mentioned time period. Do not pay out money to heirs before this time is up. The estate's debts need to be paid first.

Distribute inheritance. Before giving any heirs their inheritance, you should give them a copy of your final account of the estate, which will show all the distributions made by the estate. Then,

---

Plan ahead to avoid probate

Pat was asked by his in-laws to be the executor of their estate. His father-in-law placed everything he owned into joint tenancy with the right of survivorship with his wife. When he died, all Pat had to do was transfer the accounts and apply for social security and pension benefits for his mother-in-law.

After her husband's death, Pat's mother-in-law put everything she owned in joint tenancy with her two daughters. When she passed away seven years later, the family again avoided probate.

"Knowing what they both wanted to do before they died made taking care of their estate a lot easier," says Pat.

have them sign a release saying they accept the distribution in full and they release you from any claims or personal liability.

Close the estate. After you've finished settling all debts, fees, and taxes, and have releases from all the heirs, submit your final account to the probate court, and ask that it be allowed.

If approved, it means the heirs and the court have accepted the report as a complete and accurate account of the settlement of the estate. Once that's done, the estate may be closed, and you are discharged of your duties and liabilities as executor.

Discover the power of a DPOA

A power of attorney is a "must have" in estate planning. If you've had one for years, it's time to upgrade to a new and improved durable power of attorney (DPOA).

What's the difference? A regular power of attorney automatically ceases if you become disabled or incapacitated by illness. A durable power of attorney survives your disability or catastrophic illness and continues to allow someone to act legally on your behalf.

If you become incapacitated without a power of attorney, your county probate court will have to appoint a guardian or conservator for you.

"Most people associate probate with death," says Alexander A. Bove, Jr., Boston trust and estate attorney and author of *The Complete Book of Wills, Estates and Trusts.* "Few, other than those who have had to deal with it, realize that probate may be necessary during a person's lifetime — specifically on the person's disability or incapacity."

Avoid probate court. With a durable power of attorney, you can cover your assets and avoid probate court altogether during your lifetime. It is recognized as a legal document in all 50 states. Just like a will, it allows you to appoint one or more persons to take care of your legal and personal matters — but while you're still alive. Here are some things they can do.

- Sign checks you receive, enter into contracts for needed services, and buy or sell property such as your house or car.

- Deposit or withdraw funds from your accounts, and enter safe-deposit boxes to remove or add to their contents.

- Run your business, and create trusts for you.

- Make financial health-care decisions, or make gifts and other transfers of property.

In other words, the person acting on your behalf can do almost everything you could. On top of that, they can do it without a court's permission.

Appoint someone you trust. Obviously, a DPOA places a lot of power in someone else's hands. Although it guarantees your privacy, and saves time and money, it can also allow that person to financially wipe you out.

If you're concerned about a potential loss while incapacitated, you can choose one of three ways to shield your finances.

- Appoint two people who must act together on your behalf. But this may slow transactions down because two signatures are required on everything.

- Employ a 'springing' power of attorney, which becomes effective only after a doctor certifies you can no longer care for yourself.

- Have your attorney hold your DPOA until notified that you can't care for yourself. At that point, he gives it to your appointee.

Bove believes you're better off making a careful choice than relying on these methods to protect your finances. "If you're going to wipe me out, it would probably be easier to do it when I become incompetent," he says. "So either I trust you or I don't."

But he strongly recommends everyone have a durable power of attorney as part of their estate planning. "Don't leave home without it," he advises. Just remember that it's not a replacement for a living trust or a will. It only helps you avoid probate during your lifetime, not after your death.

Take charge of final health decisions

You hope you will never be involved in a catastrophic accident or become gravely ill. But it happens. That's why you need to have a legal health care document that states your wishes as to treatment and lifesaving measures.

Each state has its own requirements for the type of document needed. Some require a health care proxy, others a living will, and a few want a combination of the two called an advance care directive. Talk to your doctor and your attorney to learn what's required for the state you live in.

Choose someone to care for you. If you can no longer make your own medical decisions, someone with your best interests at heart should make them for you. That's why you need a health care proxy. Sometimes called a durable or medical power of attorney, it allows you to appoint a health care agent to oversee your well-being if you are incapacitated.

In addition, if you're terminally ill and can't speak for yourself, it gives him the power to withhold lifesaving measures and allow you to die. So make sure you discuss this important topic beforehand.

State your last wishes. The best way to ensure your final wishes are followed is to draw up a living will. It states whether you'll accept or refuse life-sustaining treatments if you're severely incapacitated, face imminent death, or are in a vegetative state. Some things it covers are:

- cardiac resuscitation

- artificial breathing

- feeding tubes

- major surgery

- blood transfusions

- antibiotics to treat life-threatening infections

- pain medication even if it shortens your life

You need to decide which emergency measures you wish to include in your living will, and under what circumstances. For example, you may want the hospital to use all possible means to revive you as long as there is hope of survival. Or you may want them to try a given treatment for a specified period of time, then withdraw it if you show no improvement. Talk to your doctor about your options so you understand what each involves.

Be clear about resuscitation. Another health directive worth considering is a Do Not Resuscitate (DNR) order. It tells the hospital staff or paramedics not to use heroic methods like cardiac resuscitation to keep you alive. This directive makes your final wishes crystal clear.

It's never too early to talk to your family, close friends, doctor, and even your spiritual advisor about these important decisions. They can help you sort through your feelings and values to come up with a plan that's right for you.

Give the gift of life

The opportunity to save someone's life doesn't come about too often. Become an organ donor, and you may someday do just that.

If you think you're an unsuitable donor because you're older or in ill health, think again. People of all ages and medical histories can successfully donate their organs and give another person a second chance at life. The important thing is to make your wishes known so doctors won't spend precious time trying to find out.

Put it in writing. Every state has its own requirements for organ donation. Here are three ways to go about it.

- Sign up as an organ donor when you get or renew your driver's license or state ID. Call your local Department of Motor Vehicles to see if your state participates in this program.

- Register online to become a donor. More than half the states have online donor registries, and more states are creating their own registries every year.

- Make organ donation part of your estate plan. Specify what you want done in a letter, and give it to your executor and immediate family members. At the minimum, be sure to inform your spouse of your decision.

When you're listed as an organ donor on your driver's license, all your organs become available for donation. If you want to donate specific organs or tissue, don't fill in the donor block on your license. Instead, go online to *www.donatelife.net*, fill out a donor card, and carry it with you.

Discuss your choice. Many people support organ donation, but unfortunately, most forget to talk to family members about their decision.

"One of the most important things you can do is to discuss your decision to become an organ donor with your family. That will help to insure your wishes will be carried out," says Annie Moore, spokesperson for United Network for Organ Sharing.

Many hospitals require relatives to sign a consent form authorizing organ donation. Your family may feel differently about it than you do, and if you haven't made your wishes clear, they may ignore them.

The Coalition for Donation makes it easy for you to take care of this step with a notification form you can send or e-mail to your family members. See the contact information on the next page.

Protect your decision. Most states protect your wish to donate your organs through a law known as "first person consent."

"That means if you have indicated 'yes' on your driver's license or if you are registered on the state donor registry, your family cannot override your decision," Moore explains.

Check with the Coalition on Donation to see if your state is among those that grant first person consent. If not, it's even more critical to notify family members of your decision because they will have to authorize your donation.

Get your questions answered. If you don't care what happens to your remains or don't want to make that choice, your family can make the decision for you. But why let someone else choose what happens to your body?

You can get more information to help you decide from the Coalition on Donation, an alliance of national and local organizations dedicated to promoting organ and tissue donation. Call 804-782-4920, or go online to *www.shareyourlife.org* or *www.donatelife.net*. You can also write to the address on the following page.

Contact: Coalition on Donation
700 North 4th Street
Richmond VA 23219

Plan your own thrifty funeral

Preplanning your funeral can spare your family the stress of trying to manage your final arrangements at a very difficult time. Plus, by doing it in advance, you can seek the best deals and possibly save your loved ones a great deal of expense.

"People need to look at funeral purchases in the same way they do any other major purchase — with the same level of skepticism and basic shopper's savvy," says Joshua Slocum, Executive Director of the nonprofit Funeral Consumers Alliance (FCA). Here are some of his suggestions on ways to go about it.

Compare prices. "The prices for comparable goods and services can vary by thousands of dollars in the same city," Slocum says. He advises everyone to call several funeral homes or stop by and ask for itemized price lists. Look them over at home so you won't feel pressured into spending more than you planned.

Take advantage of groups. Make use of memorial or funeral societies and nonprofit groups like the Funeral Consumers Alliance. FCA chapters, for instance, offer educational pamphlets, do price surveys on local funeral homes, negotiate discounts for their members, and fight back against funeral scams. They also offer an end-of-life planning kit to help you organize papers and personal information. Order this kit and find your local FCA chapter by visiting its Web site at *www.funerals.org*, or calling the national office at 800-765-0107.

Try a trust. You have several options for putting aside funeral money, but Slocum favors a Totten Trust, which you can set up with your bank or credit union. The money stays in your control — you can cash it out if you change your mind — and it becomes available to a beneficiary for funeral expenses upon your death. "You don't have to wait for a probate judge," says Slocum, "and that is a real advantage."

Record your wishes. Detail any final arrangements you have made in a document separate from your will — and don't put it in your safe deposit box. "The will usually isn't discovered and read until after you're buried," explains Slocum. And if your family has to make plans over a weekend or holiday, they may not have access to a safe deposit box. Give copies to your lawyer and family members, and keep another in an easy-to-find place.

Review your arrangements. Look over your final arrangements every few years and each time you go through a major life

Know your rights

The Federal Trade Commission (FTC) regulates how funeral homes sell goods and services and what they charge, among other things. Their pamphlet *Funerals: A Consumer Guide* answers common questions about planning funerals, handling costs, and securing your legal rights. Order it from the Federal Citizen Information Center by calling 888-878-3256, or visiting them on the Internet at *www.pueblo.gsa.gov*.

If you feel a funeral home has taken advantage of you, contact the Funeral Service Consumer Assistance Program at 800-662-7666. Or file a complaint with the FTC by calling its Consumer Response Center at 877-FTC-HELP.

change — like moving to another city or state, entering a nursing home, or marrying.

Slocum's organization believes everyone is entitled to a meaningful, dignified, affordable funeral, and that preplanning is the best way to get exactly what you want.

"We think planning ahead is the most important thing you can do," he concludes.

Beware of prepaid funeral plans

Preplanning your funeral may be a wise thing to do, but prepaying is not, says Joshua Slocum, Executive Director of the nonprofit educational organization Funeral Consumers Alliance.

He cites two ways to pay a funeral company up front to handle the arrangements after your death. Buy burial insurance through the funeral home, or pay into a trust fund.

"At first blush, it sounds so sensible," he says. "Lock in today's prices. Take care of this now." But in Slocum's opinion, prepaying has four major drawbacks.

- Not all states make funeral homes guarantee their locked-in rates, and changing your plan later may void any price guarantees.

- With burial insurance, you could pay more in premiums than the actual cost of your services.

- In some states, the mortician may keep up to 30 percent of your money as a commission.

- Prepaid plans don't change with your needs. Many are irrevocable, meaning once you buy them you're stuck with them. You can't cash out if you change your mind, and you could lose money if you need to change your policy.

"Unless you know what to ask for," Slocum warns, "you could be getting into a lot of trouble." So, if you're still sold on prepaying your funeral, ask the funeral home these questions before signing on the dotted line.

- Is the contract revocable or irrevocable? "Medicare only allows you to shelter money in irrevocable prepaid funerals," says Slocum.

- Is the plan transferable? "Large chains tell you since they have funeral homes all over the country, your plan will move with you wherever you go," Slocum says. But what if you move to a state or city where they don't have a branch nearby? Slocum says to make sure it's legally transferable.

- How much of your money will the funeral home refund if you cancel or transfer your policy? They may only have to return a fraction of what you paid.

- What if the goods you choose and pay for now aren't available when you die? Will your family have to buy more expensive versions?

- What goods and services are not covered by the plan? "No prepaid contract can include everything," warns Slocum. Flowers, monuments, and opening and closing the grave, for instance, generally come out-of-pocket. "Your family could face hundreds if not thousands of dollars in extra charges."

- Does the funeral company let the interest grow in your account to offset inflation, or do they skim it every year to pay their operating costs?

According to Slocum, states regulate prepaid contracts. "But," he says, "each state regulates them differently." Try contacting your state's attorney general's office to learn more about how their prepaid — also called pre-need — funeral laws protect you.

Index

401k plans 276-277, 317

A

AARP 329
Accidents, car 153
Accountants, tax 301-302
Advance care directives 357-358
Agents
  insurance 159
  real estate 191-193, 211-212
    Seniors Real Estate
    Specialist (SRES) 198
Air travel insurance 189
Airfare, discounts 328
Alternative Minimum Tax
  (AMT) 287-289
American Council for an
  Energy-Efficient Economy
  (ACEEE) 225
American Moving and Storage
  Association (AMSA) 209
Appliance, discounts 37-38
Assisted living 330-331
Auctions, online 39-40, 128
Audits
  energy 224
  tax 280-285
Automatic bill paying 64, 185
Automatic teller machines
  (ATMs) 67-68

B

Bank accounts
  automatic withdrawals 64,
  71-73, 185
  balancing 69
  checking 68-70
  fees 64-65
  money-market deposit
    accounts 233
  savings 233
Bankruptcy 57-60
Banks
  detecting errors 61-63
  selecting 60-61
Better Business Bureau (BBB)
  52, 210, 219
Bills, fraud 19, 22-23
Bonds 244, 256, 263-265
  types 265-266
Brokers 239-241
Budgets 1-9
  for retirement 309, 322-325

C

Call for Action 109
Cancer insurance 189
Car insurance 149-151
  filing claims 151-154
  for international travel 155
  rental 154-156, 190
Cars
  accidents and 153
  buying new 126-129
  buying online 128
  cost-savings on fuel 132
  donating 135-136
  fraud 133-134
  loans 129-130
  refinancing 127